The Ordeal of Mercy

The Ordeal of Mercy

Dante's Purgatorio
in Light of the Spiritual Path

by
Jennifer Doane Upton

edited by
Charles S. Upton

ANGELICO PRESS
SOPHIA PERENNIS

First published in the USA
By Angelico Press / Sophia Perennis
© Jennifer Doane Upton 2015

All rights reserved

Series editor: James R. Wetmore

No part of this book may be reproduced or transmitted,
in any form or by any means, without permission

For information, address:
Angelico Press, Ltd.
4709 Briar Knoll Dr. Kettering, OH 45429
www.angelicopress.com

Printed in the United States of America

978-1-62138-160-0 pbk
978-1-62138-161-7 ebook

Cover Design: Michael Schrauzer

*Once I stood at the foot of a great high mountain
That I wanted so much to climb,
And on top of this mountain was a beautiful fountain
That flows with the water of life.*

Traditional ballad as sung
by Dr. Ralph Stanley

Each one of our souls contains a well of living water. It has in it . . . a buried image of God. It is this well . . . that the hostile powers have blocked up with earth. But now that our Isaac [Christ] has come, let us welcome His coming and dig out our wells, clearing the earth from them, cleansing them from all defilement. . . . We shall find living water in them, the water of which the Lord says: "He who believes in Me, out of his heart shall flow rivers of living water" [John 7:38]. . . .

For He is present there, the Word of God, and His work is to remove the earth from the soul of each one of you, to let your spring flow freely. The spring is in you and does not come from outside because "the kingdom of God is within you" [Luke 17:21]. *It was not outside but in her house that the woman who lost her silver coin found it again* [Luke 15:8]. *She had lighted the lamp and swept out her house, and there it was that she found her silver coin. For your part, if you light your "lamp," if you make use of the illumination of the Holy Spirit, if you "see light in His light," you will find the silver coin in you. For the image of the Heavenly King is in you. When God made human beings in the beginning He made them "in his own image and likeness"* [Genesis 1:26]. *And He does not imprint this image on the outside but within them. It could not be seen in you as long as your house was dirty, full of refuse and rubbish . . . but, rid by the Word of God of that great pile of earth that was weighing you down, let "the image of the heavenly" shine out in you now. . . . The maker of this image is the Son of God. He is a craftsman of such surpassing skill that His image may indeed be obscured by neglect, but never destroyed by evil. The image of God remains in you always.* [Origen: *Homily on Genesis* I, 4]

CONTENTS

PREFACE
INTRODUCTION:
*The Eastern Orthodox Toll-Houses
and the Catholic Purgatory*

Canto I	7	*Canto XVIII*	145
Canto II	18	*Canto XIX*	157
Canto III	25	*Canto XX*	162
Canto IV	29	*Canto XXI*	173
Canto V	36	*Canto XXII*	180
Canto VI	46	*Canto XXIII*	190
Canto VII	51	*Canto XXIV*	194
Canto VIII	57	*Canto XXV*	199
Canto IX	66	*Canto XXVI*	209
Canto X	74	*Canto XXVII*	215
Canto XI	84	*Entre'acte*	223
Canto XII	92	*Canto XXVIII*	229
Canto XIII	100	*Canto XXIX*	242
Canto XIV	110	*Canto XXX*	255
Canto XV	115	*Canto XXXI*	267
Canto XVI	124	*Canto XXXII*	273
Canto XVII	135	*Canto XXXIII*	291

EPILOGUE:
The Meeting with God

THIS BOOK IS DEDICATED TO
Dr. Rama P. Coomaraswamy, 1926–2006
Requiescat in Pace

Preface

It has been my goal in writing this book to integrate a cultural presentation of Dante's *Divine Comedy*, which is so often treated exclusively as an artistic artifact, with an understanding of its spiritual dimension, and in so doing bring forward the teachings of the Universal Church, East and West, regarding both the afterlife and the spiritual Path, many of which are no longer taken seriously, or even taught. In order to further this goal I have brought together the teachings of a number of the Greek Fathers, notably St. Maximos the Confessor and St. John Climacus, with the writings of the Traditionalist or Perennialist School, including Frithjof Schuon, René Guénon, Titus Burckhardt, Rama Coomaraswamy, Leo Schaya, Martin Lings and Ananda Kentish Coomaraswamy. I have also drawn upon the works of several spiritual or metaphysical poets from the literature of the world, as well as the sort of comparative religion and mythology that the encyclopedic knowledge of our time has made available to us." In order to present the Church's teaching on eschatology I found it useful to explore Dante's understanding of the spiritual pilgrimage, of purgation in this life—an aspect the author definitely had in mind, since he presents himself in the *Purgatorio* as a living man engaged in a pilgrimage through the postmortem states. These states, since they pertain to eternity (though Purgatory itself is transitional and thus not one of the Last Things) are intimately related to all facets of our lives in this world. Going about our day to day lives we believe we are far from Heaven or Hell, whereas in reality these postmortem states are even closer to us than the impressions brought to us by our five senses. We must *learn* to see Eternity, however, even though it is the greater reality—a truth repeatedly demonstrated in the *Purgatorio*, where the figure of Dante must continually adjust his vision to discern and understand the realities he encounters.

To throw greater light on the spiritual dimension of the *Purgato-*

rio I felt it was also important to deal with the psychology of the spiritual life; that is, in my analysis of various emotions, I have tried to bring out their spiritual aspect. A spiritual understanding of the emotions takes us beyond the simple phenomenology of them, since it necessarily also deals with their moral and metaphysical qualities—qualities that modern psychology has largely neglected. All these dimensions are fully explored by Dante Aligheri himself in the *Divine Comedy*, which leads us to wonder why this glaringly obvious fact has been ignored by so many of Dante's critics.

My husband Charles has been indispensable in the writing of this book; as he "interviewed" me, canto by canto, he drew this commentary out of me by his questions. The version of the *Purgatorio* we have started out with is that of Longfellow (certainly not the best, but one that has the virtue of being in public domain) largely rewritten by Charles, with reference to the versions of Alan Mandelbaum and Lawrence Binyon. He has also provided the thirteen *Editorial Commentaries* following various chapters, and the footnotes. My husband's contributions have been largely in the area of detailed symbolic interpretation with reference to many different traditions; I have concentrated more on the use of the *Purgatorio* for spiritual direction—as a way of discerning and understanding the changing states of the soul in the course of the Spiritual Path. But there are certain passages in this book where neither of us can now remember whose words predominate, since the insights they express came to both of us in the same moment of question and answer. Charles acted as editor throughout, but the final executive decisions as to what would be included and what rejected were entirely my own.

Introduction

The Eastern Orthodox Toll-houses and the Catholic Purgatory

The Mountain of Purgatory, with its seven terraces and its ascending spiral path, looms before the souls that encounter it, as if it were a great work standing ready to be accomplished. It is not, however, so much a work as it is an endurance. The soul endures each of the stages of Purgatory until it is changed in its very being. In the case of an external work, we can see the end because it is outside of us. But the soul has no clear idea of when its task of purgation will be finished, because only at the end of that task will it have received the capacity to know that the end is at hand.

The suffering of Purgatory is very different from that of Hell, because hope is woven into its very fabric. The vehicle for the soul's purgatory is love—a love strong enough to allow it to repent of its failures, its betrayals of love in earthly life. The souls in Purgatory are capable of this kind of love because they can now receive the Mercy of God which falls upon the Mount of Purgatory like rain. Were these souls paradisical souls, they would not experience the Mercy of God as anything other than the greatest joy. However, these souls have yet to be perfected; therefore, when this Mercy touches their inadequacies and failures, it burns them until these dark places are completely released. For the purgatorial soul, "love is like the lion's tooth."

In the Eastern Orthodox Church there is a tradition regarding the "aerial toll-houses" which the soul encounters after death. Though it does not have the force of dogma, it is recounted by such Church Fathers as St. John Chrysostom, St. Athanasius the Great and St. Ephraim the Syrian. (The Orthodox Church maintains a certain dogmatic silence on matters such as eschatology, since these realities cannot be fully expressed in human language.)

According to the tradition of the toll-houses, the soul after death encounters realms in the "air"—the psychic or imaginal plane—ruled by the demons, who tempt it according to various sins, particularly those it had a special affinity for during life. If it passes through those realms without yielding to temptation, it ascends to Paradise. If not, it may reside in Hell for a period. The damned do not encounter the toll-houses, but go to Hell directly.

The reality which the Orthodox tradition of the toll-houses unveils is not fundamentally other than the Catholic doctrine of Purgatory, despite certain formal differences. According to a lecture given by Eastern Orthodox Bishop Kallistos Ware in San Francisco in 1996, we aren't changed ontologically by the mere fact of death, and so if our love still needs to be perfected, this happens in the afterlife. This is the truth behind both Purgatory and the toll-houses.

It is only believing Christians who encounter the toll-houses after death. The unbeliever gave up his soul long before his death. He saw no value in his spirit, therefore when the Evil One offered him worldly gain in return for his giving evil something like a spiritual valuation, he accepted the bargain without hesitation. And so, at the moment of his death, this man has nothing in his soul which can ascend even as far as the psychic realm—the only place where choice can be made, the only realm in which evil could possibly tempt him. Consequently he falls below the "earth," below the human state, into the infra-psychic realm where he finally witnesses all those demonic worlds which he was mercifully forbidden to see during his terrestrial life.

The believing Christian, however, has kept the spirit alive in his soul to a greater or a lesser degree, and that spirit longs to ascend homeward to Paradise. The spirit flies away toward Paradise, its only true love, with seeming unconcern for the soul it carries in its wake. The soul which had the single life task of conforming itself to that spirit, has nonetheless spent a lifetime trying to hold on to its worldly attachments and to the passions which seemed to give the world such richness.

Introduction

At the moment of death, however, this world is gone. If the soul is pure, the spirit enfolds the soul within itself, and becomes like a golden arrow which delivers the soul in a instant to its true home.

The soul with worldly attachments, however, is left hanging in the air as it were. It can't follow with simplicity the spirit in its ascent. The soul's passions keep reaching for a world that is no longer there. And the demons who can move about with greater suppleness in the psychic realm (which the soul has just now entered) than they could in this material world, offer themselves to the soul in lieu of the world it has lost. Here, if the soul does not listen to the angels which have been sent to it as helpers, it will not see that the demons are in fact offering it nothing, but instead are trying to take away its eternal life. Now more than ever the soul needs to understand the ways of the spirit. In life it far too often followed the ways of this world because that is all it could see through its passional vision. Had it only raised its vision higher it would have seen the comings and goings of the spirit creating a multitude of paths which fell like a golden web upon everything which the soul had taken to be merely this world. It is here, in a world of higher vision, that the soul wishes it had followed the spirit long ago.

According to the Roman Catholic doctrine, however—which forms the theological basis for the *Purgatorio*—no fall from Purgatory is possible. As envisioned by Dante, the terraces of purgation, unlike the toll-houses, have no demons in them. The souls in Purgatory are certainly saved, and therefore (if it is possible for us to imagine this) they embrace their suffering joyfully. And yet each terrace in the *Purgatorio*, like each toll-house, is related to a certain passion, a particular class of sin. Those Eastern Orthodox theologians who reject the doctrine of the toll-houses usually do so because they see the possibility that the soul after death might fail to pass a particular toll-house, and consequently fall into Hell, as a denial of the Atonement: if a soul is saved at the point of death, this salvation cannot be reversed by some "mistake" in the afterlife. And yet the Orthodox faithful are encouraged to pray for the souls in Hell, just as Catholics are traditionally taught to offer up their own earthly sufferings for the sake of "the good souls in Purgatory"—though not for the damned. This is because Eastern Orthodox speculation allows for *temporary* sojourns in Hell for the purgation of certain sins. And so we may see in the Orthodox toll-houses a doctrine similar to the Catholic Purgatory; those who yield to temptation at a certain toll-house, and so fall to the lower regions, are undergoing temporary purgation, not eternal damnation. And in the *Purgatorio* we see how Dante himself must suffer purgation at certain terraces—the terrace of lust, for example, in Canto XXVII.

Death itself carries with it its own spiritual dangers. The reality of after-death purgation implies that death is never simply a retirement to either a place or torment or one of blessedness. Rather, death is a challenge to the soul to become everything it was meant to be from its inception; resurrection is inherent within it.

Canto I

Dante and Virgil, having emerged from the Inferno on the shores of the Mountain of Purgatory, pause to prepare for their rigorous ascent. They encounter the guardian of the gates of Purgatory, Marcus Porcius Cato Uticensis, Cato the Younger, whose suicide upon Julius Caesar's victory in the Roman Civil War became the emblem of noble self-sacrifice in the cause of moral principle—in this case, the virtues of Republican Rome which were being submerged by the imperialism Caesar represented.

Dante finds himself on the shore of Purgatory, a mountainous island in the southern sea. He bathes in the new sense of freshness he feels, having just taken a grueling journey through the nine circles of Hell. In Hell, nothing presented itself to his senses that was not both gross and distorted. But now, when he lifts his eyes, he sees not only Purgatory but the starry sky above. This is deeply renewing to him; through the physical forms perceived by his senses the celestial archetypes are beginning to shine. The foot of the Mountain of Purgatory is in the southern ocean; from its slopes the travelers will be able to view the south pole. But its summit is in the north; the constellations of the north pole appear above it. This indicates that the Mountain is not a geographical feature (unless we take it as the axis of the turning earth itself, which is not justified by Dante's description) but a representation of the *axis mundi*, the path leading from material manifestation to its unseen spiritual Source.

The virtue that pervades this Canto is humility; Dante speaks of "my talent's little vessel," and when they encounter Cato, the travelers kneel. Humility is the kind of objectivity that allows each soul to accept its actual condition, and willingly submit to the cleansing that is required. St. John Climacus says of the virtue of humility:

The Ordeal of Mercy

The man who comes to know himself with the full awareness of his soul has sown in good ground ... this treasure is of a quality that eludes adequate description. It carries an inscription of heavenly origin which is therefore incomprehensible so that anyone seeking words for it is faced with a great and endless task.... Humility is a grace in the soul and with a name known only to those who have had experience of it. It is indescribable wealth, a name and a gift from God. "Learn from Me," He said ... "I am gentle and meek of heart." ... The appearance of this sacred vine is one thing during the winter of passions, another in the springtime of flowering, and still another in the harvest time of all the virtues. Yet all these appearances have one thing in common, namely, joy and the bearing of fruit, and they all give sure signs and evidence of the harvest to come.

St. Maximos the Confessor alludes to the intellective aspect of the virtue of humility when he tells us that "He who concentrates on the inner life becomes restrained, long-suffering, kind and humble. He will also be able to contemplate, theologize and pray. That is what St. Paul meant when he said 'Walk in the Spirit' [Galatians 5:16] ... humility frees the intellect from conceit and self-esteem...." [*Philokalia*, Volume Two, *First Century on Love*, 80]

> *And here let the Muse Calliope somewhat rise,*
> *To accompany my singing with that music*
> *Which left those wretched magpies so confounded*
> *They despaired of any pardon for their boast.* [9–12]

Here Dante invokes the power of the Muses, but only "somewhat." Because Dante could see Hell and not despair, his poetic gift was purified to the point where the power of Calliope, the Muse of epic poetry, could not crush him. The magpies are the Pierides, the daughters of King Pierus of Macedonia who challenged the Muses to a singing contest; they lost, and in punishment Calliope changed them into magpies. The Pierides' contact with poetry inflated them, and so they were lost. But Dante, as poet, used his dark vision of Hell to purify his gift, so that he was able to express it with humility.

> *Sweetest color of oriental sapphire,*
> *Bourne on the face of that serenity which stretched*
> *Pure from mid-sky to the far horizon*
> *Brought back all the happiness to my eyes*
> *As soon as I stepped free from that deadly air*
> *Which had filled with sadness both my eyes and breast.* [13–18]

Here we see the purity and freshness that underlies even the greatest rigors of Purgatory. This is the good all its denizens are moving toward, the love of which is the driving force behind all their sufferings. The sky's sapphire blue is the heraldic "tincture" of the Virgin Mary as Queen of Heaven.

> *The lovely planet that incites to love,*
> *Was making all the eastern heavens glad,*
> *Veiling the Fishes that followed in her wake.*
> *I turned then to the right and fixed my mind*
> *Upon the other pole—and beheld four stars*
> *Never before seen except by the primal men.*
> *The whole of heaven seemed rejoicing in those flames!*
> *O northern hemisphere, you are a widower*
> *Because you are denied the right to gaze on these!* [19–27]

The appearance in the sky of the planet Venus is the dawning of love; that it appears in the sign of Pices, the sign of Christ the Fish, shows it to be Christian love. At the foot of Purgatory—that is, at the beginning of the spiritual Path—love awakens; in the words of Maximos the Confessor, "Love is a holy state of the soul, disposing it to value knowledge of God above all created things." [*Philokalia*, Volume Two, *First Century on Love*, 1]

The Southern Cross (which as far as we know *had not yet been discovered* when Dante wrote of it) is the sign of the primordial, of "the Lamb slain before the foundation of the world" [Apocalypse 13:8]; it indicates that the Earthly Paradise is near. The four principle stars of the Southern Cross make up the archetype of this Paradise, four being the number of the Earth. (The southern hemisphere symbolizes the Substantial Pole, the receptive or feminine principle; the northern hemisphere is the emblem of the masculine principle, the Pole of Essence.) This constellation also represents the four cardinal virtues—Prudence, Justice, Fortitude and Temperance—which are the necessary "grounding" for the spiritual Path. Four indicates a strong "four-square" foundation, which means that Dante can now ascend without invoking a Promethean *hubris*. If the Northern Hemisphere, which cannot see this constellation, is "widowed," it is because it has departed so far from the primordial Earth that she is remembered only as a legend of far distant times. Nonetheless, the Eastern Orthodox doctrine that Mary restored Eve to her original beauty indicates that the Redemption includes not only man in isolation, but the *human earth* as well; this is the Terrestrial Paradise.

> *I saw beside me a solitary old man*
> *Who bore so venerable a countenance*
>   *That no son owes his own father more respect.*
>   *He had a long beard mingled with strands of white*
> *And the hair upon his head was also grizzled,*
>   *Two locks of which flowed down upon his breast.*
>   *The rays of those four consecrated stars*
> *So framed his face with light that to my vision*
>   *It seemed he was illumined by the sun.* [31–39]

The four stars frame Cato's face and illuminate it, in order to distinguish him from those in Hell. He is not *haloed*—his illumination does not proceed directly from within—but at least he can reflect the celestial light. Cato is the first soul encountered by Virgil and Dante who can act as a spiritual guide. Here is where *courtesy* and *deference* first make their appearance—virtues which are impossible in Hell.

For Pagan antiquity, Cato was the type of honorable suicide. Having opposed Julius Caesar in the Roman civil war, in defeat he ended his life so as not to lose his liberty. Cato's suicide is the outer form of a voluntary spiritual death that does not, as with the suicides in Hell, seal him into an eternal flight from himself.

Canto I

> *Swaying those august plumes, he spoke to us:*
>   *"Travelers against the blind river, who are you?*
>   *How did you escape from that eternal prison?*
> *Who guided you? Or who has been the lamp*
>   *That led you out from that profoundest night*
>   *That makes the infernal valley forever black?*
> *The laws of the abyss, have they been broken?*
>   *Or has Heaven somehow altered its decree,*
>   *That, being damned, you still approach my crags?"*
> *At this my Leader laid his hand upon me,*
>   *And then with hand and speech and sign together*
>   *He made me bend my knees and head in reverence.* [40–51]

No-one can find the approach to the shores of Purgatory—that is, the spiritual Path—without guidance from heaven. The heavenly decree has not been changed, but implicit in this question is the sense that it *might* be changed—and if it were, the nature of both Hell and Purgatory would be transformed. This possibility, however, is beyond the scope of the narrative; it lies within the realm of a more mysterious and universal eschatology. Nonetheless, had Virgil not been able to establish that they were acting under such guidance—which would have meant that the laws of the abyss had been broken—in all probability Cato would have blocked their entry and sent them back to Hell.

When Virgil forces Dante to show respect to Cato by grabbing hold of him, pushing him to his knees and making him bow his head, we know that even though Dante has in a sense been coerced, no law has been broken. Here respect for cosmic and spiritual law appears for the first time. In Hell, everyone is bound to the law, but no-one respects it.

The souls of the damned, who are always oppressing each other, would have never done what Virgil did, nor would they have submitted to it; there is no humility in Hell. Here the mystery of spiritual authority appears: that to surrender one's will to a spiritual guide can engender true humility. Abasement before the ego of another only locks oneself into one's own egotism, leading to the vices of flattery and sycophancy, but if one can take even a single step in true humility—which is impossible without faith and hope—then one has stepped out of Hell definitively. By the power of humility, a breakthrough has occurred. A man who has achieved this breakthrough has gone all the way through Hell, both alive and with the faith that his soul can be saved.

Virgil answers Cato:

> ... *I came not of myself.*
> *A Lady from Heaven descended, at whose prayers*
> *I aided this one with my company.* [52–54]
>
> *But since it's your will that I explain more fully*
> *Our condition, and the real truth behind it*
> *My own will cannot deny you that request.* [55–57]

In Purgatory, unlike Hell, the more *magnanimous* will prevails; thus Virgil defers to Cato. Virgil, here, is yielding his own self-identity, as guide, to the call of a higher Spirit, as every true guide must do.

> ... *The road I took*
> *Was the only one I could possibly have taken.* [62–63]

Because Virgil's soul is in Limbo— "highest" region of Hell—he had to pass through the totality of Hell in order to reach the shores of Purgatory.[1]

Virgil, speaking of Dante, now tells Cato:

---

1. The metaphysical necessity of evil, which is the origin of the moral necessity of Hell, is elucidated by Frithjof Schuon in the following terms in *Survey of Metaphysics and Esoterism*, 18:
   > ... it is in the nature of the Good to wish to communicate itself: to say Good is to say radiation, projection, unfolding, gift of self. But at the same time, to say radiation is to say distance, hence alienation or impoverishment; the solar rays dim and become lost in the night of space. From this arises, at the end of the trajectory, the paradoxical phenomenon of evil, which nonetheless has the positive function of highlighting the good *a contrario*, and of contributing in its fashion to the equilibrium of the phenomenal order.

Canto I

> *He seeks for Liberty—and just how dear she is*
> >   *The one who sacrifices his life for her knows well.*
> *You know it yourself; your own death for her*
> >   *Was not bitter in Utica, where you left behind*
> >   *The robe that will shine for you on that great day.*
> *By us the eternal edicts are not broken;*
> >   *This man's alive, and Minos does not bind me.* [71–77]

Minos is the warden of Hell in the *Inferno*, who determines which circle each damned soul is to occupy. Liberty, and obedience to spiritual and cosmic law, are here shown as one—unlike the condition of Hell, where the souls seek a liberty opposed to law, but find only bondage.

> *"But I am from that circle where the chaste*
> *Eyes of your Marcia are—visibly praying*
> >   *O holy breast, that you hold her as your own.*
> >   *For the sake of her love, incline yourself to us*
> *Grant us passage through your seven realms*
> >   *And I'll thank her for the kindness you bestow*
> >   *If you'll let your name be mentioned there below."*
> *"Marcia was so delightful to my eyes*
> >   *While I was still on the other side," he answered*
> >   *"That every gift she asked of me I gave her.*
> *But now that she dwells beyond the evil river*
> >   *She can no longer move me—by that law*
> >   *Which was invoked as soon as I left that place.*
> *But if, as you have told me, a Lady of Heaven*
> >   *Has sent you on a mission, you need not flatter;*
> >   *Only ask in her name, and that will be enough."* [78–93]

Chivalry has its place, but it cannot be valid when placed in relation to a wrong object. It is not simply personal feeling, but rather something objective.

Marcia is everything the world can give a noble man like Cato in the realm of love. She brought him a love that was in its own way genuine. Her love had a hook in it, however. It made worldly life

The Ordeal of Mercy

seem complete, and therefore trapped him inside this world and all its values. To the degree that Cato accepted the love of Marcia he could not see the spiritual dimension of things. Every soul in Purgatory sees the sky—that is, the spiritual realm—and knows that this, not the shores the two travelers presently stand upon, is its true home. Cato has to turn cold to Marcia and her old way of love. He calls Virgil's evocation of his famous attachment to her "flattery." And such a love *is* flattery, because in spite of the reality of the feelings involved, it is horizontal and worldly rather than vertical; it lacks spiritual hope. Therefore it can only be given, and received, by the ego. (Here not only Dante undergoes purgation; Virgil himself is beginning to break with the "mores" of Limbo, the vestibule of the Inferno where he is lodged, with its whole aesthetic of romantic despair.) Had Cato not turned his back on that love he would not have been able to acknowledge the heavenly lady guiding Virgil and Dante, and fulfill her request. He would not have been able to see a higher love than the one Marcia represented, nor recognize the lady who presides over it; consequently, he would have prevented Dante and Virgil from proceeding farther into that bright realm of which he is the guardian. Their journey would have ended there, at the foot of the Mountain. Nonetheless, Cato's understanding of Love as such is necessary at this point, in order to allow them to embark upon the path toward Heaven. This is Purgatory's first lesson: the purgatorial path, initiated by humility, is also a deepening of love.

> "Go, then [Cato tells Virgil]; *but first off, take a smooth rush,*
>   *Tie it around his waist, then wash his face*
>   *To clear away the lingering stains of Hell;*
> *It isn't fitting that eyes still dimmed with mists*
>   *Should approach the first of the angelic guardians,*
>   *Since he is of the company of Paradise.*
> *This little island, all about its base*
>   *Down there below, where the breakers crash*
>   *Bears rushes in the tidelands that surround it.*
> *No leaf-bearing plant, nor any plant that hardens*
>   *In growing can survive under these conditions;*
>   *They cannot bend to the pounding of the surf."* [94–105]

Canto I

The rush is like a symbolic sash, with which Dante is invested to symbolize his role as a penitent. Cato's command that Virgil wash the obscurity of Hell off Dante's face is a recognition that if he doesn't first pass through the necessary purgation, when he is finally required to face the Guardian Angel of Paradise he would feel an overwhelming shame. There is a holy shame that leads to repentance; there is also a toxic shame that results in despair. More specifically, Cato requires that Virgil wash the infernal darkness from Dante's *eyes*, thus allowing him to *see* the reality of Purgatory, and understand that he is no longer in Hell. This indicates that the essence of purgation is to achieve a fullness of vision, an enlightenment of the Intellect; it is not simply a *lex talionis*, a punishment for sin. We must never forget this when reading the *Purgatorio*, given that the *Divine Comedy* itself is all vision.

The only plant that can grow on the shores of Purgatory is the reed, both leafless and pliant. Leafy plants and plants that become hard as they develop cannot survive the blows of the waves. The leaf-bearing plant represents a soul harboring an unnecessary psychic complexity which obscures its true nature; the plant that becomes hard and brittle is a soul filled with fixed ideas, assumptions and prejudices which block its motion. Conversely a leafless plant is an emblem of simplicity of soul, while a pliant one represents a soul obedient to God.

> *". . . Let's turn back now, for here is where the plain*
>   *Slopes down to meet the banks of its lower boundary."*
>   *As dawn was conquering the final hour of night*
> *Which fled before it, so that in the distance*
>   *I could recognize the trembling of the sea,*
>   *Together along the lonely plain we went*
> *Like one returning to a path he'd lost*
>   *Who, till he finds it, seems to search in vain.*
>   *As soon as we had come to where the dew*
> *Fights with the sun, under sea winds, in the shade*
>   *Where very little rises into mist*
>   *My Master gently placed upon the grass*
> *His two outstretched hands; as for myself*

The Ordeal of Mercy

As soon as I saw the meaning of that gesture
I offered him my cheeks now wet with tears;
That was the very moment in which—completely—
He unveiled in me the color Hell had hid. [113–129]

Before continuing their ascent, the travelers must now descend a short distance; but this is not a regression. Such a descent is necessary in order to gather up the whole of the psyche, without which no true ascent is possible; this descent demonstrates that to be clear about one's spiritual *base* is necessary for the spiritual Path. If Dante had tried to ascend without first descending—that is, without embracing humility—he would have fallen into the sin of pride.

Cato asks Dante to wash the color of Hell off his face before he continues. The color of Hell is a sadness so deep that it turns into despair. Jean-Claude Larchet, in his book *Mental Disorders and Spiritual Healing* (page 98, paragraph 4), says: "The passion of sadness can take an extreme form, namely despair (apognosis). This is one of its most serious manifestations. 'An excessive sadness is dangerous,' remarks St. John Chrysostom, 'so dangerous that it can even cause death.'" According to Larchet, the ancient church fathers believed that all the passions were masks which hid the true face, the true personhood of the one they overwhelmed. And the truth is, all the passions are artificial. They burden the soul by attempting to transform it into something it can't really be. When Dante washes the color of Hell off his face, he returns to himself. All of Purgatory is the method by which souls, little by little, are restored to who they really are, to their original forms.

The cleansing dew does not win out by *conquering* the sun; rather, it is as if the sun courteously recedes because it knows that the fullness of the psyche needs to emerge in its own terms. If the sun had simply shone on Dante's face without this initial cleansing, the stains on it would have "set" and become indelible. The cleansing indicates that the psyche must humble itself in order to become receptive in a healing way to the rays of the sun—that is, the Spirit. (Dante, in the *Convivio*, declares that "No object of sense in the whole world is more worthy to be made a type of God than the sun.") Dew represents the gentleness and subtlety that allow the

Canto I

birth of the spiritual Path. It has the power to return Dante to himself, to return to him his real face. By contrast, this demonstrates the essential *unnaturalness* of Hell.

> *He bound me in cincture there, as another wished—*
> *O wonder! For as soon as he had taken*
> *The humble plant, it sprouted up again*
> *Immediately, at the very spot he'd picked it.* [133–136]

The reed (humility) grows back because Purgatory is a place of rejuvenation and refreshment [cf. Matthew 16:25, "For whosoever will save his life shall lose it: and whosoever will lose his life for my sake shall find it," and John 12:24, "Verily, verily I say unto you, unless a grain of wheat fall into the ground and die, it abideth alone; but if it die, it bringeth forth much fruit"]. The very ability to see the sky at daybreak refreshes—as do the washing with dew and the binding with a fresh reed. That the reed immediately grows back after being plucked demonstrates that Purgatory, unlike Hell, is not the home of death.

Dante has now reached the point from which spiritual regress is no longer possible.[2]

---

2. Cf. the Theravadin Buddhist doctrine of the *sotapanna* or "streamwinner," a spiritual station from which regression is no longer possible, even though *sambodhi* or Perfect Total Enlightenment has not yet been attained.

Canto II

The travelers enter Ante-Purgatory, the vestibule of Purgatory proper. A boat filled with souls arrives, piloted by an angelic helmsman. Dante meets the shade of his friend, the poet Casella, and learns the limits of the aesthetic approach to spiritual truth.

As many have pointed out, the *Divine Comedy* is a complete map of the spiritual life. In the *Inferno*, sin—both moral and intellectual—is discovered; in the *Purgatorio*, it is expiated; in the *Paradiso*, Divine Love leads on to Spiritual Knowledge.

Of these three, the *Purgatorio* symbolizes the spiritual Path per se. This truth becomes clear in Canto II, where Virgil and Dante arrive in Ante-Purgatory at dawn, at the foot of the Mountain which is Purgatory itself. As the sun rises, a boat full of souls, steered by an angel, glides swiftly across the waters. Among the souls Dante recognizes his friend Casella, the musician, who had set some of Dante's own poems to music. Casella is persuaded to sing, and all the souls gather around to listen—but then Cato appears and rebukes them for wasting time:

> *"What is this I see, you lazy spirits?*
> *What negligence, what paralysis is this?*
> *Hurry to the Mountain, throw off the sloth*
> *That stands in the way of your ever seeing God."* [120–123]

The souls, like frightened doves, begin their ascent.

✠

Dawn on the shores of Purgatory is initiation, the real beginning of the spiritual Path. As Venus rising in the first Canto is love, here "Mars . . . overcome" [line 13] indicates love overcoming hate:

Canto II

Just as the planet Mars, when it is conquered
   By invading mists of dawn, glows fiery red
   Down in the west, above the plain of waters
So there appeared to me—may I see it again!
   A light that shot across the sea—so swift
   No flight of bird could ever equal it.
And when I'd turned my eyes away for a moment
   So I could ask a question of my Guide,
   And then looked back, I saw it larger, brighter
Till I made out, on each side of it, a whiteness,
   Though not yet sure of what that whiteness was;
   Beneath it another whiteness slowly gathered. [13–24]

"See how he holds his wings, pointing to Heaven" says Virgil of the angelic boatman [line 34]. Both heavenly and fallen angels are "birds" [line 37], but the wings of the boatman are pointed up: he moves by virtue of his relation to the vertical dimension. Dante initially has a hard time making out the angel's shape [lines 16–28]. His vision must *rise to meet* the angel; it must train itself to perceive the angelic realm. First he sees a light; then two "whitenesses" on either side of it which he can't recognize; then another "whiteness" below (possibly the angel's reflection, as in the engraving of this scene by Gustave Doré). It is only then that he recognizes the first light as the angel's wings. Dante must discriminate between substance and accident here—between the angel and his reflection—placing substance "first"; this is all that is required for the accidental, the secondary reflection, to take its proper place, so it need not be explained or mentioned again.

As the boat crosses the water, the within it souls are singing the psalm *"In exitu Israël de Aegypto"* [line 46]. The Exodus is traditionally a symbol of the spiritual Path, and Purgatory is the realm of the spiritual traveler *par excellence;* anyone seeking initiation is asking to go through Purgatory in this life.

   He came to shore with a boat so swift and light
   That the water swallowed not one inch of it. [41–42]

The Ordeal of Mercy

Water here is heaviness and instability of soul, the weight of unredeemed material nature; the boat is like the "Spirit of God" that "moved on the face of the waters" in Genesis. Redemption is implicitly identified with creation, as in the Catholic prayer (based in part on Psalm 104), "Come, Holy Spirit, fill the hearts of Thy faithful, and enkindle in them the fire of Thy love. Send forth Thy Spirit and they shall be created, and Thou shalt renew the face of the earth." The Spirit in Purgatory moves up through all levels of the soul until the entire soul is purified.

According to Frithjof Schuon, Christianity, unlike Judaism or Islam, is an esoterism preached openly to the whole community—an "eso-exoterism." It is an initiatory Path, and the rite of initiation is Baptism, or Baptism plus Confirmation and the Eucharist. Dionysius the Areopagite, in *The Ecclesiastical Hierarchy* likewise presented Baptism, Confirmation and the Eucharist as in some ways similar to the three classical stages of the mystical Path: purgation, illumination and Union. If a Christian is more or less passive to the initiatory import of his Baptism, but is nonetheless faithful, he will not experience the fullness of purgation until the next life.

Dante, having passed "alive" (i.e. consciously) through Hell, and Virgil who is always at his side and so participates in this living consciousness, are the gnostics—not in the sectarian sense of the word, but rather those whose path to God is through knowledge. The knowers arrive "a little" [line 64] before the pious faithful, but they too are "strangers" at the foot of Mt. Purgatory [line 63], because the spiritual Path is the one Path for all—something the heretical sectarian Gnostics denied. Yet the "knowers," having had to do more conscious work earlier on, find their later path easier; having "taken up their cross," they finally discover that their "yoke is easy" and their "burden light."

After the angel blesses the souls and they disembark,

> *On every side the Sun shot forth the day;*
> *From high mid-heaven with its shining arrows*
> *It had already driven Capricorn away....* [55–57]

Canto II

Capricorn the Goat is like Lucifer expelled from Heaven; as the spiritual light dispels the heaviness of materiality, the residues are carried away by Lucifer, the scapegoat. According to René Guénon in *The Reign of Quantity and the Signs of the Times*, and Charles Upton in *The System of Antichrist*, it will be the function of the Antichrist to collect all the dead residues of the present age, and be destroyed along with them.

✠

This is Dante's initial encounter with souls in purgation. The first soul he meets, that of Casella, loves him, and he returns that love. This is not quite the love of Paradise, but it is a love which extends beyond the grave. Love in Limbo is admiration; in Hell, despairing pity; in Purgatory, true love; in Paradise, timeless love.

The souls of the dead crowd around Dante when they realize he is alive:

> *And as to a messenger with an olive branch*
> *The people crowd around to hear the news,*
> *And no one hesitates to join that throng,*
> *So at the sight of me stood motionless*
> *Those fortunate spirits, all of them, just as if*
> *They'd forgotten to go forth and take their beauty.* [70–75]

The gnostics bring the hope of consciousness to these souls; *gnosis* in its own way can also be a prayer for the dead. The olive branch, as a symbol of the peace of contemplation, represents the souls' hope for greater consciousness; the oil of the olive is a source of light. According to Tertullian, "the flesh [in Confirmation or Chrismation] is anointed that the soul may be sanctified, the flesh is signed that the soul may be fortified, the flesh is placed in shadow by the laying on of hands that the soul may be illumined by the Holy Spirit." But Dante, for those souls, is only the image of greater consciousness, not its realization; since they have become only partially conscious, the consequences of their former unconsciousness now begin to emerge, "as if / They'd forgotten to go forth and take their beauty." (Mandelbaum has "proceed to their perfection.")

The Ordeal of Mercy

As soon as the souls forget to pursue their course, they are ready to listen to Casella [lines 106–119]. His poetry has a celestial beauty which truly brings Paradise to earth, but this is not what they are there for. Casella's poetry reflects *gnosis*, but these souls look at him in the wrong way; they pay attention to him instead of to the Mountain of Purgatory. This shows how *gnosis* should keep its own place and not distract simple souls; the gnostic above all should know where the Mountain is and not divert others from it. If he divulges the secret of his insight, he runs the risk of dazzling and blinding the simple souls—and *also himself*. In these latter days this secret must be divulged, however, which means that great and destructive illusions will necessarily abound. Through the celestial beauty of Casella's songs, the aesthetic dimension is parading itself before those souls undergoing purification. But because they contemplate this beauty as something apart from themselves and the Purgation required of them, they enter into a spiritual stagnation which earns them the accusation of being "loiterers." Cato arrives in order to break this spell, so that they may go forth and become the beauty they are called to embody.

Dante attempts to embrace the shade of Casella, but his arms pass through him as if he were made of air:

> *O empty shades—in all except appearance—*
> *Three times over I clasped my hands behind him*
> *And three times brought them back against my chest.* [79–81]

When the deepest form of truth is openly revealed, it is sometimes accompanied by the greatest lack of substance; this is the perennial pitfall of art and aesthetics. As with a great deal of latter-day "esoterism," the spiritual understanding is there, but not much real benefit is derived from it. The will is not engaged.

And so Dante ends in a self-embrace: art falsely worshipped, or esoterism wrongly lived, is narcissism; it is related to incomplete cognition. There is an attempt to mentally grasp the fruits of love and *gnosis* before having gone through the refining fires of Purgatory. In a story which appears in many traditions, a man destined for sainthood is seen with a glowing light around him. When told of

Canto II

this by the onlookers he is ashamed, and lets them know that this means he has not yet reached perfection.

Casella questions Dante:

> *"As I loved you when I was in my fleshly body,*
>   *So, freed from mortal flesh, I love you still.*
>   *That's why I stay. But you, why do you travel?"*
> *"My own Casella, to return once more*
>   *to where I am, I undertake this journey. . . ."* [88–92]

Casella is saying: My soul has been saved without *gnosis*, without consciously traveling the spiritual Path—why, then, do *you* travel? The inner, "gnostic" answer is that Dante, who as a gnostic is "traveling" while still in the flesh, himself becomes the goal, in a certain sense, of the simple believer. To return to where one already is implies illumination. Because Dante is consciously returning to where he is, Casella can rest ("stay") in his presence, as if Dante were carrying the olive branch of peace. This reminds one of a statement by Martin Lings that "all who pass through the gates of Heaven incur thereby a tremendous responsibility: it is henceforth the function of each to be, himself or herself, an integral feature of the celestial Garden, a source of felicity for all the other inmates, a vehicle of the Divine Presence" [*Symbol & Archetype*, 53].

On the outer level, however, Dante is also saying that he must travel the spiritual Path in the flesh simply to be saved; if he doesn't go through Purgatory in this life, after death he will be damned. Greater spiritual capacity brings with it greater temptation: "To whom much has been given, much will be required" [Luke 12:48].

When Dante asks Casella why he has been tardy in reaching the shores of Purgatory, he answers:

> *"No injury has been done to me*
>   *If the one who takes up whom—and when—he pleases*
>   *Has kept me from this passage many times,*
> *Since from a Righteous Will his will is drawn."* [94–97]

The Ordeal of Mercy

Here Casella is beginning to intuit, and rest in, a justice that is beyond his mere individuality [the *Paradiso*, Canto III].

☖

As the Canto ends, Cato the Younger arrives, provokingly and deftly awakening the souls from their complacency, reminding them that for the ascent of the Mountain of Purgatory they will need aspiration, zeal, and the fear of God. Cato, as a suicide—though for reasons of honor, not despair—may be one of those souls who must wait in Purgatory until the end of time, but he has as compensation his position as Purgatory's "ruler." The souls who must wait until the end of time to enter Paradise are those who lack the ability to transcend time through intellectual intuition.

When Cato appears, the pride of love is transformed into love in the mode of fear.

Canto III

With Virgil's help, Dante begins to understand the ontological nature of Purgatory. Virgil surveys the Mountain so as to plan a route for their ascent. The travelers encounter the souls of those who repented late in life and who were also excommunicated; among them is Manfred, king of Apulia and Sicily.

Here Dante says of Virgil:

> *He seemed to me as if cut to the heart with remorse.*
> *O noble conscience, pure of any stain*
> *A trivial fault to you is a bitter sting!* [7–9]

As soon as Virgil embodies *conscience*, Dante sees Virgil's limitations for the first time. Virgil is the natural intellect come to its limit in conscience and morality, but Dante as a Christian is closer to grace and true Intellection; here Dante gives up the natural intellect (Virgil), at which point the Divine Intellect dawns upon him. This transition establishes Christ as the Divine Intellect, and is also a distant echo of Virgil's possible salvation. Conscience may be natural, but it carries the seed of supernatural Intellection within it.

> *Behind our backs the sun was flaming red*
> *But before me it was broken by the shape*
> *Of the only figure who blocked its rays—myself.*
> *And when I saw the ground before us dark*
> *Only in front of me, I turned to one side*
> *In sudden fear of being abandoned there;*
> *I saw my Comforter in the act of turning round:*
> *"Are you still without full trust?" he said to me;*
> *"Can't you see your Guide is still here with you?*

The Ordeal of Mercy

> *It's already evening where lies the buried body*
> *I used to walk around in, casting shadows.*
> *It was lifted from Brindisi; now Naples has it.*
> *And if now in front of me no shadow falls*
> *Wonder no more at this than at the heavens*
> *Where one ray of light cannot block another."* [16–30]

That Dante sees his shadow shows that he is gaining a permanent sense of the difference between shadow and substance. His shadow is his terrestrial life; his figure itself is his soul, his archetype. Dante is here realizing the essential shadowiness of life on earth, something he could not have seen from the standpoint of Hell.

That Dante casts a shadow proves that he has the stature of a man. According to Frithjof Schuon, "What above all distinguishes the human form from animal forms is its direct reference to absoluteness, indicated by its vertical posture" [*From the Divine to the Human*, 87]. The souls in Hell are animal-like because they are horizontal—which is why Hell is dark and skyless; its denizens cannot see in the vertical dimension. But now Dante is in Purgatory where the vertical dimension is clearly visible, where the sky, the sun, and his own shadow, are seen distinctly. Dante sees his shadow after first having glimpsed the entire form of Purgatory, which is higher than terrestrial existence.

> *"The man's insane who hopes that human reason*
> *Could somehow reach the end of the endless road*
> *That one Substance in Three Persons travels!*
> *Human race, be satisfied with quia* ['why'];
> *For if you'd had the power to see all*
> *There'd have been no need for Mary to give birth.*
> *You've seen the fruitless yearning of those men*
> *Who'd have satisfied that hope, if any could,*
> *And who now bear it as a grief unending.*
> *I speak of Plato and of Aristotle*
> *And many others too—"* he bowed his head,
> *And saying no more, withdrew into his sorrow.* [34–45]

Canto III

Mortals need the "why" because they need purgation; they require existential understanding to complement and fulfill their intellectual realization. Only the immortal angels can subsist on Intellect alone, but for mortals to believe that this is possible to them is, precisely, intellectual pride.

The "hope" which is a "grief unending" is a picture of despair, but hidden within it is the mystery of *conscience*, and the pangs of conscience are *not* fruitless yearning. The implication here is that if Virgil could participate in the Incarnation, he could reach salvation through the Divine Intellect.

To say that the Trinity travels a "road" is to imply that It is ultimately intelligible, though not on the plane of logic.

To ask "why?" is to fully accept what is, even before it is completely intelligible to you. If you don't accept what is absolutely given to you, you won't have any basis to ask "why?" Your *whys* will exist in a vacuum. The intellect cannot reach the end of the unending road through *why* without first existentially accepting *what*; if it attempts to do so, it becomes lost in abstraction.

The Incarnation is God giving Himself to the world. God says "here I am"—He is the *What* without which we would have been lost in the *Why*—but He is also the Divine Intellect, the all-seeing, the Sun of Righteousness, the eternal Word—the *Why* hidden in the *What*. When Joshua in Exodus ("Joshua" and "Jesus" are different forms of the same name) caused the sun to stand still, he was realizing the Divine Intellect. Likewise the blind man sitting on the way to Jericho [Luke 18:35–43]—the city Joshua conquered by God's power—waiting for Jesus to heal him, was waiting for the Savior to open the Eye of his Heart.

> *"Lift up your eyes" I said to my master then;*
> *"Here come ones with the power to give us counsel*
> *If now you cannot find such in yourself."* [61–63]

Dante, who possesses the insight of the saved, knows and informs Virgil that the souls they encounter can now guide.

These souls of modesty and humility manifest the lowest level of goodness. They have not fulfilled as much as those in Paradise, but

The Ordeal of Mercy

they are beautifully shy, and this is the basis of all the later flowerings of Goodness and Intellect:

> *As sheep who leave the fold will remove themselves*
> *By ones or twos or threes, while the others stand*
> *Timidly lowering their muzzles and their eyes,*
> *And what the first one does the others do,*
> *Huddling themselves against her if she stops,*
> *Simple and quiet and never knowing why,*
> *Likewise, moving forward in our direction,*
> *I saw the leader of that fortunate flock,*
> *Modest in face and dignified in gait.* [79–87]

These souls are like those who have to wait years to be granted initiation.

At the beginning of Hell [*Inferno*, Canto V] the futility of the romantic yet concupiscent love of Paolo and Francesca appears, just as in Limbo the futility appears of virtue without grace. But here in Ante-Purgatory, the noble Manfred is a positive manifestation of Divine Mercy. Paolo and Francesca's sin seems so insignificant as compared with Manfred's, which he describes as "ghastly." Likewise his openness to Mercy appears so slight; he seems to have touched it in such a little way. But for him Mercy is "green"—fertile; consequently the burden of earthly glory he bore during life gives way to the green river of Mercy.

Here we see the prayer of the living for "the good souls in Purgatory." Do you cease to love someone simply because they are dead? If the living and the dead had a true soul-affinity in life, death does not change this; the souls of one's loved ones are always present, in life or in death.[1]

---

1. Martin Lings composed a beautiful poem, "Requiem," on the subject of prayer for the dead in different religions, which, apparently, only the Protestants have rejected—unless the Catholics too have now abandoned it. It appears in his *Collected Poems*, Perennial Books, 1987.

Canto IV

The travelers now begin their climb with great effort, reaching the First Spur of Ante-Purgatory where they encounter those who repented late through negligence, among whom is the shade of Dante's friend Belaqua. The Canto begins with Dante's refutation of the doctrine of multiple souls, attributed to Plato, in favor of the orthodox (albeit esoteric) Christian doctrine of soul and Spirit.

> Whatever—by delight or else by pain—
>   Seizes upon some faculty of ours,
>   Wholly to that faculty the soul is gathered—
> So it appears to heed no other power.
>   This refutes the error that declares
>   That one soul above another takes fire in us.
> Therefore when a thing is heard or seen
>   Which concentrates all of the soul's perception,
>   Time passes but we're not aware of it,
> Because the power that pays attention differs
>   From the other power that keeps the soul entire;
>   The first is held in bonds, the other is free. [1–12]

Some critics, including Alan Mandelbaum, see in this passage a refutation of Plato's doctrine of multiple souls, in line with Aristotle's critique of that doctrine; the soul has several faculties, but all are subordinate to the soul itself, otherwise total concentration of attention upon a single object would not be possible. Yet clearly Dante is also positing a distinction between "the power that pays attention (or 'listens')," which is bound, and "the power that keeps the soul entire," which is free. This is perfectly in line with the following passage from the *Mundaka Upanishad*: "Two birds living together, each the friend of the other, perch upon the same tree. One eats the sweet fruit of the tree; the other simply looks on without eating." The bird who eats the fruit is the power that listens and pays attention to this or that powerful experience, and in so doing forgets the passage of time; the other who simply looks on is the power that "keeps the soul entire" in the face of that experience. The first is the soul or *psyche* itself; the second is the Spirit, the *Intellectus*, the *Nous*; in Hindu terms these correspond to *jiva* and *Atman*.[1] This subject is thoroughly dealt with by Frithjof Schuon in his essay "The Two Paradises" from *In the Face of the Absolute*.

> *A larger opening the villager often blocks*
>   *With just a little forkful of his thorns*
>   *When his grapes begin to darken in the fall,*
> *Than was the passage-way through which we climbed:*
>   *Only my Leader and myself behind him. . . .* [19–23]

This is the most difficult part of the strait and *narrow* path; remember that the entrance to the Inferno was *wide*. But without deep desire and spiritual aspiration, the necessary effort cannot be made—"Because strait *is* the gate, and narrow *is* the way, which leadeth unto life, and few there be that find it." [Matthew 7:14] The "strait gate" and the "narrow way" are symbols of the Christian spiritual practice called *recollection*, known in other systems as "one-pointedness of attention."

> *The summit was so high it conquered sight;*
>   *Far steeper rose the slope of the mountainside*
>   *Than the radius from mid-quadrant to the center.*
> *I was totally spent with fatigue when I cried to Virgil:*
>   *"Turn to me, sweet Father, see my state—*
>   *I'll be alone forever here unless you stay!"*
>   *"Son," he told me, "drag yourself up to that ledge—"*

---

1. Strictly speaking the *Nous* is more properly identifiable with the Vedantic *buddhi*, the intellectual faculty that transcends thought (*manas*), and the *Atman* with the Absolute Reality or *Brahman* considered as residing in the spiritual Heart or *Hrdayam*, and thereby functioning as the Universal Witness. *Buddhi*, however, may be seen as a kind of aperture through which the *Atman* witnesses the plane of the intelligibles, and below that the plane of the soul, and still below that the material plane, the world of sense experience.

Canto IV

> *Pointing to a slightly higher terrace*
>   *That circles the entire Mountain on that side.*
> *His words so spurred me to renew my effort*
>   *I strained every nerve, scrambling up behind him*
>   *Until the lower circle lay beneath my feet.*
> *On the edge of the cliff the two of us sat together*
>   *Facing the East, from which we had ascended*
>   *For all men take delight in looking back.*
> *First I turned my gaze to the lower shores*
>   *Then lifted up my eyes to see the sun.* . . . [40–56]

We can naturally see what is ontologically below us, not that which is above us. In order to witness what is higher than us on the Great Chain of Being we must be open to the mystery of spiritual Intellection, which transcends the natural intellect.[2] That Dante can raise his eyes to see the sun demonstrates that the travelers now possess a scope they couldn't support while traveling through Hell.

Here Dante is tempted to cling to his spiritual Guide in a false way [line 44] because he doesn't want to face the loneliness of purgation; but Virgil, like a true Guide, offers not security but rather encouragement and spiritual direction.

> *First I turned my gaze to the lower shores*
>   *Then lifted up my eyes to see the sun;*
>   *I wondered why it struck us from the left.*
> *When the Poet understood how bewildered I was*
>   *By the chariot of the light when I saw it pass*
>   *Between the north and the place where we now sat,*
> *He said to me: "What if the sign of Gemini*
>   *Were placed in conjunction with that mirror there*
>   *Which receives the light and guides it north or south?*
> *Then you would see the zodiac's crimson wheel*
>   *Turning even closer to the Bears—*

---

2. In our time the tendency to limit man to the natural intellect has resulted in the ideology known as "scientism," which is well-critiqued by scientist and metaphysician Wolfgang Smith in his book *Science and Myth*.

The Ordeal of Mercy

Unless it somehow left its normal track.
If you seek the power to think how that might be
   Then gather it to yourself and see this Mountain
   As placed upon the earth in such a way
That it and Zion share the same horizon
   Though each is seated in a different hemisphere.
   Then you'll know why the road which luckless Phaeton
So badly drove must pass us to the north
   Even as it skirts the southern side of Zion—
   If you rightly gauge the import of my words."
"Truly, my Master, at no time in the past
   Have I seen this matter so clearly as I do now,
   In the place where my discernment seemed deficient—
That the mid-point of the high celestial motion
   Which in a certain science is named 'equator'
   And which always remains between the sun and winter
Lies, as you said, just as far north from here,
   As south from the point from which the Hebrews
     viewed it
   While gazing towards the distant lands of heat." [55–84]

Here Dante realizes by the position of the sun that they are now in the southern hemisphere, where the Mount of Purgatory is situated at the exact antipodes of Jerusalem. The southern hemisphere, where everything is reversed, here represents the afterlife. Unlike Purgatory, however, Hell is not an *afterlife* in any complete sense, in spite of being a post-mortem state, because to say "afterlife" is to posit a mode of existence that can include earthly life while at the same time transcending it. Those in Hell have lost even the reality of earthly life, and so have fallen below it, into what René Guénon called "the realm of the infra-psychic." Purgatory too is incomplete, since the souls traveling through it are not yet reunited with their resurrected bodies, but it is more truly an afterlife than Hell is because it does not lie under the shadow of material existence.

   "Nonetheless, if it please you, I hope to learn
     How far we've yet to go—for the Mountain rises

Canto IV

> *Higher than my eyes have power to see."*
> *"The nature of this Mountain" he answered me*
>   *"Makes travel very hard on its lower reaches,*
>   *But the higher one climbs, the less one has to suffer.*
> *By the time it begins to seem so pleasant to you*
>   *That climbing up its slopes feels just as easy*
>   *As floating down the river in a boat,*
> *Then you'll be at the ending of your path;*
>   *There you'll be able to rest your panting breath. . . ."* [85–95]

The spiritual Path is experienced at the beginning as effort, at the end as Grace. And yet it is always *initiated* by Grace.

> *Close by a voice spoke up: "Of course it's possible*
>   *You first might have to sit and rest a while."* [98–99]

It will turn out that the voice is that of Dante's friend Belaqua. Belaqua has dampened his own aspiration, and so tries to throw a wet blanket over Dante's; as William Blake put it, "Corporeal friends are spiritual enemies." The souls here are stagnant, they can make no effort; it appears that they must wait until their allotted time is passed or until someone among the living prays for them; on the level of what these souls can see, this seems their only recourse. And yet, when Grace comes to them, unmerited, they will find within themselves a spiritual aspiration that can move their very being— an aspiration they were previously unable to recognize, since it resides in a part of themselves they have been blind to. Here the illusory quality of spiritual stagnation is shown. Sloth tries to tell us "there is no way," but there is always some way in which one's spirit can be receptive to Grace. If these souls were more open to Intellection, if they had more scope, their circumstances would be different because they would be conscious of the spiritual potentials inherent in them.[3] In the words of Maximos the Confessor:

---

3. Note that this is not the New Age doctrine which maintains that "you make your own reality." God is the only Maker, but without His help we remain blind to the true nature of His creation.

The Ordeal of Mercy

He who prays must never stand still on the steep ascent that leads to God. Just as he has to progress upward from strength to strength in the practice of the virtues [cf. Psalms 84:5-7], and to rise in his contemplation of spiritual truths from glory to glory [cf. 2 Corinthians 3:18], and to pass from the letter to the spirit of Holy Scripture, so he must advance in a similar manner within the realm of prayer. He must raise his intellect and the resolve of his soul from what is human to what is divine. [*Philokalia*, Volume Two, *Second Century on Theology*, 18]

> *We then made out on the left a massive boulder*
> *Which neither I nor he had noticed before.*
> *We approached it till we caught sight of some figures*
> *Who stood behind the rock in the shadow of it*
> *Slumped like people resting from fatigue.* [101–105]

The boulder is a symbol of these souls' closed-mindedness. These spirits possess Dante's potential for greater scope, but they are not tapping into it.

> *And one of them, who seemed to me exhausted,*
>   *Was sitting with his arms around his knees,*
>   *His face bent down between them, toward the ground....*
>   [106–108]

> *Barely raising his eyes above his thigh,*
> *He turned in our direction and saluted us:*
>   *"Go up, then, if you're both so keen to move!"*
> *He said to us—then I realized who he was....* [112–115]

> *When I came near he hardly raised his head:*
>   *"Have you finally figured out why the sun*
>   *Drives his chariot over your left shoulder?"*
> *His cocky tone and stagnant attitude*
>   *Brought a little smile to my lips.*
>   *"I'm not going to worry about you any more*
> *Belaqua," I let him know....* [117–123]

Canto IV

Dante smiles at the contrast between his friend's witty, ironic tone and his despondent posture. Here Belaqua repents of having hindered Dante; this is the very tail-end of all the vicious insults that filled the *Inferno*. In Purgatory, insults are transformed into friendly kidding and self-deprecatory humor.

Belaqua and the souls with him have nearly despaired of spiritual effort because they are almost blind to Grace. However, as Origen reminds us [*First Homily on Ezekiel*, 3]:

God did not create death; he did not create evil; but he left to human beings, as to angels, freedom in everything. Thus through their freedom some rise to the highest good; others rush headlong into the depths of evil. But you, man, why do you reject your freedom? Why this reluctance to toil, to fight, to become the artificer of your own salvation? "My Father is working still" it is written, "and I am working." [John 5:17]

Canto V

The ascent from the First to the Second Spur of Ante-Purgatory. Here Dante and Virgil meet the souls of those who repented late due to death by violence; these include Jacopo del Cassero, Buonconte da Montefeltro, and La Pia of Siena.

> I had already departed from those shades
>   And followed in the footsteps of my Guide,
>   When from behind, pointing his finger at me,
> One shouted: "See! It looks as if the sunlight
>   Does not shine below him on the left—
>   And when he walks, he walks like one alive!"
> I turned my eyes at the speaking of these words,
>   And saw them all now staring at me in amazement—
>   At me—and next to me, at the broken light! [1–9]

The broken light shows that the souls in Purgatory can indeed see the light, unlike those in the Inferno who could not see that Dante had traveled there from earth alive because they had no light to see by. The light shining on Purgatory is an otherworldly light, a celestial illumination; the souls there cannot at this point inhabit this light, but they can see it and anticipate it. A broken light is an incomplete light; the souls in Purgatory can understand the meaning of this incompletion, based on their lack of human bodies, because they can see both the light of Heaven and their own brokenness when measured against it. All souls in Purgatory are related to light because, though suffering, they are connected to Mercy; in Dante the light is "broken" in that he deflects grace and mercy in a way they do not; this is because he, as a living man, can still sin.

This soul sees Dante from below. Dante has ascended to a higher point because he has already done some of the work in this earthly body that the souls in Purgatory have yet to accomplish. He occupies a higher spiritual station than this soul, but because it is beyond death it can nonetheless see the earthliness in the figure of Dante, and the limitations of earthliness itself. Alvin Moore Jr. pointed out to me that these souls are seeing Dante's "etheric body," his passional body, called in scripture "the flesh": the *soul of his body*, not his soul as the "body" of his spirit.

The left side is the aspect of the soul that gravitates toward earthliness and darkness. Earthliness is not darkness in itself, but it can symbolize darkness, particularly to a soul in Purgatory, because the single work of a soul undergoing purgation is to conform itself to the celestial Light that it can now can see, and any attraction to earth such a soul may experience can only encumber such an effort. After all, earth is a place of exile. To be in Purgatory is also to be in exile, but unlike earth with its many choices, everything in Purgatory facilitates the work of conforming one's soul to that Celestial Light. Hence there is greater suffering in Purgatory; nonetheless this suffering helps the soul develop the ability to receive the light of Heaven.

> "Why does your mind so occupy itself,"
>   My Master said, "that you slowed your pace?
>   What does it matter to you what's whispered here?
> Follow me, and let the people talk;
>   Stand firm like a tower whose rafters never tremble
>   No matter how long and hard the wind might blow.
> Always the man in whom thought after thought
>   Keeps thrusting forward moves farther from the mark,
>   Because the force of one dilutes the other." [10–18]

Dante's tendency to immerse himself in thought is like a shadow of purgation. The souls in Purgatory, on the other hand, must at every second be aware of their existence with all its implications; when they become completely aware of it, they will have passed beyond Purgatory. Dante is impeded because he is chasing after thoughts, which are possibilities; he is focusing on possibility while forgetting his own existence, and is consequently paralyzed. The key to advancing in Purgatory is to rest absolutely in the Necessary, not pursue the Possible, and let the light of Heaven which has not yet been actualized in the soul nonetheless fall upon it, allowing it to become more and more receptive to that light, which is the light of Mercy. Thought, on the other hand, is here compared to *gossip*, which is vain conjecture; when we gossip we often say, "I'll bet you anything that so-and-so is doing this or that right now...." But when we are undergoing purgation we need to sit with the *one right thought*, and not try to escape it. And in this we are called to imitate the angels. Each angel, according to Thomas Aquinas, is in himself a single species rather than a member of one, which implies that each possesses, and is formed upon, a single idea. As Meister Eckhart puts it, "that's what an angel is: an idea of God."

Here Virgil is telling Dante not to let the wind of the Spirit fall to the mental level and degenerate into obsessive thought. The danger of pursuing truth by "thrusting forward thought after thought" is expressed by Frithjof Schuon as follows:

> The cult of intelligence and mental passion distances man from the truth. Intelligence withdraws as soon as man puts his trust in it alone. Mental passion pursuing intellectual intuition is like a wind which blows out the light of a candle.
> [*Spiritual Perspectives and Human Facts*, 139]

Likewise St. Maximos the Confessor says:

> If we persistently devote ourselves to God and keep a careful watch on the soul's passable aspect, we are no longer driven headlong by the provocations of our thoughts. On the contrary, as we acquire a more exact understanding of their causes and cut them off, we become more discerning.
> [*Philokalia*, Volume Two, *Third Century on Love*, 51]

The souls below must be ignored, for their own good as well as Dante's, but those above have ascended spiritually to the point where they can profit from dialogue with him: thus the whole of Purgatory is oriented toward ascent. The souls in Purgatory need the prayers of the living, but they also seek the intercession of Dante,

Canto V

who is alive though not *among* the living. And such compassion is only to be found in ascent; it's for the sake of compassion that Dante cannot remain on the level of the souls he is to aid. These souls want the prayers of the living, but they also need the prayers of the saints in heaven, which is Dante's destination. Dante helps these souls precisely through *vision*, the particular sort of vision that gives him the rare destiny of being, as it were, in two worlds at once. Suffering is existential prayer; Dante's journey through Purgatory is a prayer of this kind. It can only happen because he has had to live his life on earth as an exile—from his beloved city of Florence—and has come to know by this that earthly life is in itself an exile.

A crowd of spirits now accost the travelers, at which point Virgil instructs Dante: "Don't stop, but listen as you move ahead" [Mandelbaum, line 45]:

> "O soul that journeys to beatitude
>   With the same limbs that you possessed at birth,
>   Stop a while" they shouted as they came;
> "See if you recognize any one among us,
>   So you can carry news of him beyond.
>   Why do you hurry onward? Why can't you stay?
> It's a long time since we died by violence,
>   Sinners even to the final hour;
>   Then a heavenly light admonished us;
> By that light from earthly life we rose
>   Both penitent and forgiving, at peace with God,
>   Who stirs our hearts with longing to see His face." [46–57]

There is a great deal of stagnation being overcome in this Canto—a stagnation symbolized by the story told by one of these spirits, Jacopo del Cassero, of how he died in a swamp [lines 64–84]—so course Dante will be tempted to stop at this point. Jacopo even wonders, in lines 65–66, if Dante might lack the power to fulfill his intent to help them, as if trying to infect him with their own despondency. That Dante's thoughts were leaping ahead of each other, and of him, indicates that the totality of his soul was unconsciously falling under stagnation and thus being impeded in its ascent. The pull of carnality and earthly life was especially strong for these souls, so even though they are beyond that life now, they must intensely experience the limitation of having seen only earthly life while still in the body. St. Maximos the Confessor says that "A man engaged in the practice of the virtues is said to be 'sojourning' in the flesh [cf. Genesis 12:10], for by practicing the virtues he is severing the soul's relationship with the flesh and stripping from himself the deceit of material things." [*Philokalia*, Volume Two, *Second Century on Theology*, 18]

Jacopo entreats Dante to ask the people in his home town of Fano to pray for him after Dante's return to earth. In the state of purgation there can be an exchange of mutual help between the living and the dead, because all are moving toward salvation; Dante helps these souls mired in stagnation both by talking with them and by continuing without delay his own ascent, thus strengthening them and showing them the way.

The souls in this group, who died by violence, were denied the last rites; and this is no small loss. According to Rama Coomaraswamy in *The Problems with the Other Sacraments Apart from the New Mass*:

> As the Council of Trent explains, "this effect [of the Sacrament of Extreme Unction] is the grace of the Holy Ghost, Whose unction blots out sins, if any remain to be expiated, and the consequences of sin, and alleviates and strengthens the soul of the sick person, by exciting in him a great confidence in the divine mercy, sustained by which he bears more lightly the troubles and sufferings of disease, and more easily resists the temptations of the demon lying in wait for his heel [Genesis 3:15]; and sometimes, when it is expedient for the soul's salvation, recovers bodily health." These effects are usually grouped under four headings. The first effect is the remission of sins which follows from the passage in St. James: "If anyone be in a state of sin, his sins are forgiven him...."
>
> Secondly, this Sacrament remits temporal punishment due to us for our sins, which of course ordinary Confession and Absolution cannot do.... This doctrine must not however be

Canto V

construed to mean that when Extreme Unction is received, the remission of the entire temporal debt infallibly occurs. Often the subject blocks the completeness of the effect by defective and impeding dispositions. But, if the subject has in every way the correct disposition and devotion, it must be conceded that he receives the *plenissimam poenarum relaxationem*—the complete remission of temporal punishment. . . .

The third and terribly important effect is what is called the *comfortatio animae*: or the "Comforting of the Soul. . . ." The third effect of this Sacrament is "to free the minds of the faithful from [Satanic] solicitude, and to fill the soul with pious and holy joy. . . ." [125–126]

It is clear that we all must die, and indeed, in many ways this is the most important moment of our lives. It is at this time that one's entire life passes before one, and when final choices must be made, choices between despair and love, as so well exemplified by the two thieves crucified with Christ. It is a time when we need every available help—the prayers of loved ones, and above all the Sacraments which our holy mother the Church has for the past 2000 years so lovingly provided to the faithful. [124]

These souls have died without the last rites that facilitate the "normal" channels of grace, and so mercy must, as it were, laboriously find its way to them. Nonetheless they have already passed beyond the level of the natural man; they possess "perfect contrition," which alone, in the absence of the sacraments, can bring forgiveness.

> *Another [shade] said, "May that desire that draws you*
>   *Up this lofty Mountain be fulfilled,*
>   *As you in pious pity help me with mine.*
> *I was from Montefeltro, I'm Buonconte;*
>   *No one thinks of me, not even Giovanna;*
>   *That's why I wander in sorrow among these shades."*
> *"By what chance or what violence" I asked him*
>   *"Were you led so far astray from Campaldino,*
>   *That your final resting place was never known?"*

The Ordeal of Mercy

> "Oh," he answered, "At the foot of Campaldino
>   A river named the Archiano runs
>   Above the Hermitage in the Apennines.
> There where the name of that stream is finally lost
>   Wounded in the throat I made my way
>   Fleeing on foot, and bloodying all the plain;
> There I lost my sight—and when my voice
>   Ceased with the name of Mary on my lips
>   There I fell; my flesh remained abandoned.
> I speak the truth, so carry it to the living:
>   God's angel took me up—but he of Hell
>   Shouted: 'Why do you rob me, you from Heaven?
> You bear away the eternal part of him,
>   For just one tear; that's all that takes him from me.
>   But with the rest of him I'll deal in a different manner!'"
>   [85–108]

    Buonconte da Montefeltro is the son of Guido da Montefeltro who appears in Canto XXVII of the *Inferno* among the fraudulent councilors. Guido gave false counsel to Pope Boniface VIII (who is also damned) after the Pope absolved him in advance of a sin he was planning to commit; he believed that his mere membership in the Franciscan Order would be sufficient to blot out that sin. Guido was close to goodness—the Franciscans—but at the last minute evil overtook him; Buonconte was close to darkness—the Ghibelline army—but at the last minute Grace triumphed in his soul. These two stories show the primacy of intent over one's background and environment, and perhaps also over the kind of "profiling" that contemporary psychologists do, demonstrating that no matter how accurately one assesses another's personality, one cannot understand that person without knowing his true intent, and other deep aspects of the soul which are invisible to merely human eyes. And why didn't the long good life of the father "add up" to salvation, and the long evil life of the son to damnation? The father's goodness must have had some intrinsic defect all along that he was never able to heal; it was undoubtedly too centered in manifestation, too connected to the outer forms of the Church. Likewise the evil of the son was also intrinsically shallow, mostly affecting the outer man; it was not deeply rooted in his soul.

Buonconte at the point of death was deprived of both sight and speech. Both these faculties are essential to Dante's vocation: speech because he is a great poet, sight because his poetry is based on spiritual vision and is full of visual metaphors. St. Lucy, his patron saint, is a saint of spiritual vision who was also prayed to for relief from diseases of the eyes; the soul of Buonconte, though deprived of these faculties, is still able to pronounce the name of Mary. This is the Canto of *concentration on one thought*. From one point of view the whole purpose of the *Divine Comedy* is to invoke the name of Mary, who is foreshadowed by both St. Lucy and Beatrice; St. Bernard sings the praises of Mary toward the end of the *Paradiso*. All speech becomes concentrated in that single name, and all sight as well, because the name of Mary is the name of Wisdom. Mary translates the faculties of speech and sight to a higher level, beyond the limitations of the body, and saves the soul by means of them; thus even though Buonconte's body is destroyed, his soul is saved. Many of our contemporaries, both Christian and otherwise, seem to abhor stories like this; they fail to see that the soul's loss of the body is a necessary transitional phase for all but the saints. Buonconte has a long way to go before he can become one with his *resurrected* body; he cannot return to his earthly body, and must not attempt it.

The Devil complains, "why you do save him for just one tear?" But that tear was perfectly aligned with Mercy, and Mercy is limitless, while corruption is not. The Devil is implying here that long-winded prayers and multiplied penances should have had more power than that single tear, thus invoking "the reign of quantity" and the condition of "one thought outstripping another" that Virgil has just chastised Dante for falling into.

> "You already know how the atmosphere condenses
>   The humid vapor which must be turned to water
>   As soon as it rises to where the cold can seize it.
> He [the Devil] joined evil will, which is always seeking evil,
>   To intellect, and thereby set in motion
>   Wind and mist by the power of his own nature.

The Ordeal of Mercy

So later on, when the day was spent,
   The valley from Pratomagno to the highest ridge
   Lay choked with fog, so saturating the sky
That the pregnant air was transformed into water
   Which fell as rain, and so the gullies filled
   With whatever of it the earth could not absorb.
And as that water gathered into torrents
   It rushed so swiftly towards the royal river
   Nothing could hold it back. My frozen body
Was discovered by the mighty Archiano
   Which carried it to its mouth, where it joins the Arno
   And so unbound the cross my arms had made
Upon my breast when agony overcame me.
   It rolled me along its banks and on its bottom
   Till it girded me and buried me in its plunder." [109–129]

The Devil does what he can to defile Buonconte's body, but the soul is superior to the body, which is why it can still be saved; here the ontological precedence of soul over body is clearly demonstrated. The Devil wanted the image of the Cross of Salvation—represented by the corpse's arms crossed upon its chest—to be removed from him, but in doing this he ended by presenting an image of the soul, still symbolized by the body, as freed from constriction, which perhaps actually aided in the release of the soul from the body's prison, and also foreshadowed its final release from the "cross" of purgatorial suffering. So all the Devil's fury was in vain; his attempt to defile Buonconte's body only aided his soul in its redemption: "All things work together for the good to those who love God" [Romans 8:28].

The Devil acts through "Evil will joined with intellect." Demons have a certain level of intellect because they are fallen angels; however, an evil intent will eventually weigh down the intellect because if there is no spiritual detachment and ascent, the intelligence has no room in which to unfold. All true intellect has an objective quality; the traditional notion of the intelligence defines it as a reflection of *Nous* in *ratio*, of immediate spiritual knowledge in the mirror of the rational mind. The Devil tries to destroy Buonconte's soul but

Canto V

can only destroy his body, the emblem of his passions; thus Satan aids Buonconte in spite of himself. This illustrates the fact that there is an aspect of the Intellect—the *Nous* or *synderesis*—that cannot be darkened, cannot fall; as Meister Eckhart put it, "there is something in the soul that is Uncreated and Uncreatable; this is the Intellect." The Intellect in this sense—the *Nous*—apprehends Mercy directly. But if the will is perverted through rebellion against what the Intellect reveals, it turns in on itself, sabotages itself, and ends by doing the very opposite of what it wills; it does so through its attempt to deny or subvert the *Nous*, which is intrinsically impossible. The *Nous*, here, appears as immanent justice.

Canto VI

The travelers encounter more souls who have died by violence, including Dante's friend, the poet Sordello—though there is no historical evidence that he met a violent end. Dante learns more about the efficacy of prayer. He laments the corruption of Florence.

> *Whenever a game of dice is broken up,*
> *The loser stays behind; he feels despondent;*
> *He repeats the throws, and in sadness learns.*
> *The people all go off beside the winner*
> *One walks in front, one grabs him from behind*
> *Another at his side says "don't forget me."*
> *Never pausing he listens to one, and then another;*
> *They only leave him alone when he pays them off.*
> *That's how he defends himself from their advances.*
> *I felt the same in the middle of that crowd*
> *Turning my face first this way and then that*
> *Till I finally freed myself from them with promises.* [1–12]

Dante is the "winner of the game" because he is in ascent; the loser remains in the *Inferno* among the damned. Dante, here, must be bounteous for the sake of detachment. He must acknowledge and be generous to the various aspects of his own soul that are undergoing purgation, giving each the particular thing it demands, and thereby freeing himself from it. The purgatorial souls with their many demands remind one of the passions with their many temptations; one can certainly not free oneself from such passions by feeding them, though they often try to convince us that this is possible. Here, however, since those souls are close to the point where love supersedes justice, they can now (unlike the passions) be fed in a way that brings completion and so serves purification; they are no longer "under the curse of the law" [Galatians 3:13].

Canto VI

> *"I seem to remember, my Light, that you deny*
>   *Explicitly, in some text of yours,*
>   *That prayer can ever change what Heaven has written—*
> *But nonetheless that's what these people pray for.*
>   *So is their hope for an altered fate deluded?*
>   *Or am I not quite clear on what you said?"*
> *"My writing is unambiguous on that point"*
>   *He answered me, "nor is their hope deluded;*
>   *The sober mind will see no contradiction.*
> *The bar of Justice does not lower itself*
>   *Just because Love has the power to expiate*
>   *In a single stroke the sin that's placed one here.*
> *And in that passage where I expressed the principle*
>   *That prayer cannot cure a defect in the soul*
>   *I was speaking of prayer that could not rise to God."* [28–42]

This mention of prayers that can't reach to Heaven reminds us that we should't presume that our prayers will always automatically be inundated by Grace. We can prepare ourselves and do what seems necessary to call forth that Grace, but if Grace does indeed respond to our prayer, we should understand that this is a great blessing and not to be taken lightly. The very word "Grace" denotes a "free gift," an act of condescension that we can in no way deserve through our own merits.

Here Christian love overturns the law of karma; love is higher than justice, and therefore subsumes it. The Theosophist Madame Blavatsky, in *The Secret Doctrine*, characterized all prayer as black magic, since she viewed it as an impious attempt to subvert the law of strict cause and effect. William Blake, on the other hand, made the forgiveness of sins—the abrogation of the law of karma—the basis of the spiritual life: "Doth Jehovah forgive debt only on condition that it be Payed? . . . Such is the forgiveness of the Gods, the Moral Virtues of the Heathen whose tender Mercies are Cruelty. But Jehovah's Salvation is without Money and without Price, in the Continual Forgiveness of Sins, in the Perpetual Mutual Sacrifice in Great Eternity . . ." [*Jerusalem* 61:17]. This, we must note, is *real* love, not the kind of false love that hides situations that need to be put right under a veil of delusive sentiment. True love is hard to obtain. The early Fathers of the Church taught that there is no love without *apatheia*, dispassion. A passionate attachment to the *feeling* of love is not really love. Assuredly love will penetrate one's feelings as it does one's whole being, but this can only happen after the passions have been disciplined.

In the second half of this Canto Dante describes the conflict and corruption infesting Italy, even his beloved Florence, and laments the lack of an Emperor in the West who could play the role of secular guardian of Christendom, as the Byzantine Emperor and later the Russian Czar did for the Eastern Church. As a White Guelph, Dante was opposed both to a Pope who abdicates his spiritual function by allowing himself to be eaten up by worldly politics (which the Black Guelphs wanted), and to a weak Pope who would be forced to cede his independence to the Holy Roman Emperor (as the Ghibellines wanted).[1] Dante's ideal Emperor was one who would bring the kind of peace that would both ensure the Pope's independence and protect his spiritual function. Consequently, in his lament, he rails against both Guelphs and Ghibellines. In terms of the inner world of the soul, the "Ghibellines" symbolize the will in rebellion against the intellect, while the "Black Guelphs" represent the pride and aloofness of the intellect itself that, because it knows it is higher than the will, refuses to relate to the will and direct it, and so sinks by default into an inappropriate willfulness of its own that ultimately perverts its nature. The intellect, here, is not the Uncreated Intellect, but this Intellect as reflected in a soul ruled by the passions. Dante in these verses pictures how unbridled passion can destroy the object of its love, and with it, Love itself—and this just after the he has shown how Christian love supersedes and subsumes justice. Here, however, justice is not subsumed, but betrayed.

---

1. In our own time we are witness to Popes who combine both these deficiencies, both excessive political involvement and loss of their spiritual independence to the forces of globalism. Some have defined the contemporary Papacy as "the chaplaincy of the New World Order."

Canto VI

Editorial Commentary One:
The Symbolism of Clockwise and Counterclockwise

Counter-clockwise motion is in line with the motion of the turning heavens as seen when facing north toward their pivot, the Pole Star, while the motion of the heavens when facing south, away from the heavenly Hub and Source of their motion and toward their peripheral manifestation, is clockwise. This is why the motion of the two travelers through Hell is clockwise, and through Purgatory, counter-clockwise. Hell is reached through a descending motion away from spiritual Source and toward material dissipation, while Purgatory represents an ascending motion of return to that Source, via recollection. But in the religions of the Native Americans and the Buddhists, both of whom emphasize the Divine as immanent in conditions, the direction of sacred circumambulation is clockwise; the Lakota, who call south "the direction we always face," always move clockwise in their rituals to imitate of the motion of the sun in the northern hemisphere, which can be seen in its entirety only when facing south; the same can be said for the Hindus, the Buddhists, and the entire Amerindian collective in general. Conversely, the Muslims and the Christians, whose religions emphasize the Divine Transcendence, move in a counter-clockwise direction. Eastern Orthodox Christians circumambulate their churches counter-clockwise, as Muslims do the Kaaba; the "turn" of the Mevlevi ("whirling") dervishes is also counter-clockwise. Clockwise spiritualities recognize the Divine within conditions, and are consequently in danger (when they degenerate) of falling into identification with the outer surface of things, of capitulating to entropy, materialism and dissipation, and finally of worshipping the sub-human elements of nature. (We can see this in the case of modern science, which is based on an anachronistic revival of Paganism during the Renaissance, Paganism representing a degeneration of the archaic high spiritualities.) The opposite problem threatens counter-clockwise spiritualities in their degeneration—the danger that they will violently oppose and disturb the Divine order of the universe. The clockwise religions are closer to the primordiality of the Golden Age, when "the heavens declare[d] the glory of God and the earth show[ed] forth His handiwork" more obviously to the human race than they do today. The counter-clockwise religions came into prominence only after it had become necessary to recognize that humanity had fallen from the primordial state; the requirement now was not *first* to recognize God as manifest in conditions, but to understand Him, through faith and gnosis, as transcending the universe; only then could we contemplate Him as reflected in the forms and events of creation without falling into the kind of dissipation and incipient materialism that the Paganism of late antiquity represented.

This way of evaluating the significance of clockwise and counter-clockwise is further complicated by the fact that it was the traditional practice of witches to dance counter-clockwise or "widdershins," which means "as opposed to nature." In a time when the primordial clockwise religions were in force, this counter-clockwise dance would have represented the invocation of unnatural chaos; in our own time, when the transcendental counter-clockwise religions are dominant, the widdershins dance of the witches appears as a kind of parody of the transcendental Path.

So clockwise and counter-clockwise each have their positive and negative meanings. Cyclones turn counter-clockwise in the northern hemisphere, draw air in toward them, and produce an updraft. In the positive sense this represents recollection and ascent; in the negative one, a "calling-up" of infernal forces. On the other hand, fair weather anti-cyclones turn clockwise and produce a downdraft of air that moves out and away from their center. In a negative sense this indicates a sinking and dissipation of spiritual potency; in a positive one, the descent and dissemination of Divine Grace.

Canto VII

The travelers' conversation with Sordello. As night approaches he suggests that they rest and refresh themselves in the Valley of the Kings, where earthy rulers must expiate the "necessary" sins they were led into due to the responsibilities of their high position.

> After the glad and gracious salutations
>   Had been repeated three and four times over,
>   Sordello stood back and asked him, "But who are you?"
> "If ever to this Mountain were alotted
>   Souls deserving to ascend to God,
>   My bones were buried by Octavian.
> I am Virgil; and for no other crime
>   Than being without the faith did I lose heaven";
>   This is how my Leader answered him. . . . [1–9]
>
> "O glory of the Latins," he replied,
>   "Through you our language showed what it could do!
>   Eternal honor of my native city
>   [both Virgil and Sordello were from Mantua],
> What merit or what grace unveils you to me?
>   If you think me worthy to hear your words, then tell me
>   If you are here from Hell, and from what cloister."
> "Through all the circles of that sorry kingdom"
>   Virgil answered, "I have come this far;
>   Heaven's power moved me, and I bring it with me.
> Not through action but through neglect I lost
>   The sight of that high sun that you so long for,
>   Which I recognized at last—but all too late.
> A place below exists, not sad with torture
>   But through darkness only, where the lamentation
>   Is not expressed through wailing, only sighs.

The Ordeal of Mercy

I live there side by side with the innocent infants
  Snatched by teeth of Death before the gift was given
  To be liberated from the condition of human sin.
I live there with the ones who, though they're sinless
  Of the three high virtues never took the vestment
  Though they knew and fully followed all the others." [16–36]

If Virgil is personally guiltless, why was he not redeemed along with the other righteous Pagans when Christ harrowed Hell? Because he did not have the fullness of faith within himself. When Dante arrives in the Earthly Paradise, Virgil disappears, as if all along he had been a part of Dante's soul, and had in some sense been redeemed in the person of Dante; only through a Christian soul could Virgil arrive at true Christian faith. This is another and deeper aspect of what it means to pray for the dead.

The fact that Sordello, who is saved, makes obeisance to Virgil, who is not, indicates that, whatever the state of Virgil's soul, his writings had a deep spiritual import and were a precursor to Christ and the Christian era, and implies—though it does not state—that his soul is not entirely closed to salvation. When Sordello says "what merit or what grace reveals thee to me?", it is difficult to tell whether he is referring to his own merit or to Virgil's.

The place "not sad with torments but with darkness only" is Limbo, which is a realm of quiet despair. So long as the soul acquiesces to this despair it must remain at that level. But there's an implication that Virgil's soul no longer acquiesces; after all, if Cato could make it to Purgatory, why not he? Though he was late in recognizing the Sun he did in fact recognize it, indicating that he is no longer in despair and thus open to Grace. Virgil had to pass as Dante's guide through all the circles of Hell below Limbo, in order to see where despair and lack of faith finally lead; if he had not been called to something higher, he would have had no need to see the lower depths. Virgil is placed with the unbaptized infants because he was so near to the Christian dispensation, and yet so far. As a Pagan he was a man of mature character, but his Paganism itself was immature, like an infant.

Canto VII

But if you know and are able, then give some sign
   That might help us reach the point more quickly
   Where Purgatory has its true beginning.
He answered: "No fixed place has been assigned us;
   Here we can travel anywhere we like.
   As far as I can go, I'll be glad to guide you." [37–42]

Virgil asks Sordello to point out the door to Purgatory, but Sordello merely answers, "here we can travel anywhere we like." Virgil, as a Pagan, is under the yoke of necessity, while Sordello is wandering in possibility; he is under the regime of "with God all things are possible." But Sordello is also demonstrating a trap the soul can fall into; his ability to move is useless if he cannot find the door to Purgatory proper. For Virgil, the positive aspect of necessity is that he is very clear on what he needs to find, the door to true purgation; the negative aspect is that it is still uncertain as to whether the Grace that would open salvation to him is really available, and this is a serious barrier. For Sordello, the negative side of possibility is that he, like many poets, is mesmerized by the pure ability of his soul to be in motion, and forgets to ask what the purpose of that mobility might be; the positive side is that he is in touch with real Grace, and that Grace will inevitably bring him to the door of Purgatory, no matter how long he might delay.

The day is now coming to its end, so Sordello suggests that the travelers find a pleasant place to rest during the nighttime hours, seeing that travel in Purgatory is impossible by night. Virgil asks him if travel is then impeded by other spirits, but Sordello answers:

"Nothing beyond the darkness of night prevents you
   From making your way further up this Mountain;
   This is what entangles your will and weakens it." [55–57]

It's as if Virgil is wondering whether accounts of the afterlife like those that appear in *The Egyptian Book of the Dead* are true, where the soul's progress is impeded by various "guardians." Sordello answers that the only barrier is the darkness of the intellect, and—like some Eastern Orthodox theologians—traces all weakness of the

The Ordeal of Mercy

will to this very intellectual darkness. The power of the human will is *certainty*; without it, the will is crippled.[1]

> *Gold and fine silver, and scarlet and pearl-white,*
>   *Indian lychnite resplendent and serene,*
>   *Fresh emerald the moment it is broken,*
> *All these hues in color would be conquered*
>   *By herbs and flowers growing in that hollow*
>   *Just as the greater overcomes the less.*
> *Nor in that place had nature painted only,*
>   *But from the sweetness of a thousand odors*
>   *Made there a fragrance mingled and unknown.* [73–81]

In the valley where the travelers have sought shelter the plants are more luminous and colorful than gems and minerals are on earth; this indicates that Purgatory, for all its sufferings, is an ontologically higher state than earth is because it is informed by a higher life. Vegetable life is symbolic of Purgatory because it is a place of change and growth. In Catholic theology there are four final things: death, judgment, heaven and hell. But Purgatory is not final, only transitional. Like plant life, it appears and then is gone. The material plane, though lower ontologically, is a better symbol of the permanent realities of the spiritual world than the psychic plane is, due to its material stability, and to the fact that man, on earth, is a complete union of body and soul. According to Frithjof Schuon in *The Transcendent Unity of Religions* [62], "the highest realities are most

---

1. Whatever demonic "guardians" the soul may encounter after death in the "toll-houses" are essentially imaginal symbols of the various limitations of the intellect affecting that soul, which result in (and are reinforced by) the corresponding mis-applications of the will—a truth that is well-expressed by the Vajrayana Buddhists in their *Bardo Thödöl*, better known as *The Tibetan Book of the Dead*. This is not to say that angels and demons do not exist as objective entities, only that our encounters with them are mediated by our own states. Virgil's question to Sordello illustrates the literalism of his late Pagan mind-set, his polytheistic tendency to see the many manifestations of Divine Reality on the imaginal level as a pantheon of separate individuals rather than as multiple theophanies of the One God, or multiple states of the One Self.

Canto VII

clearly mirrored in their remotest reflections, namely, in the sensible or material order, and herein lies the deepest meaning of the proverb 'extremes meet.'" Earth, though lower than Purgatory, is complete, while Purgatory, though higher than earth, is partial; the point of the Resurrection where spirit and body are reunited has not yet been reached. Nonetheless colors are brighter in Purgatory because it's easier to receive higher spiritual energies there than within terrestrial existence.

The fragrance of the flowers growing in this valley is complex and mysterious. Their pleasant scent, like an "odour of sanctity," indicates purification of the soul; that's what Purgatory is for. The sense of smell has to do with intuition. These souls in Ante-Purgatory are experiencing "intimations of immortality," a foreshadowing of Purgatory itself in which the soul is prepared for Paradise. That the scent is "unknown" is like saying that it is unearthly, like nothing that can be experienced in this world. That it is a single odour mingled out of many fragrances makes it a symbol of the essential wholeness of a soul ready for Paradise. And this also indicates a redemption of the negative side of possibility; here is the point where many options, many possibilities, coalesce into a single choice.

> *There seated on the green grass and the flowers*
>   *Spirits I saw who sang "Salve Regina";*
>   *From outside the valley they could not be seen.*
> *"Before the feeble sun now seeks his nest,"*
>   *Said the Mantuan who'd led us there,*
>   *"Do not ask me to lead you down among them.*
> *From this ledge you'll more easily discern*
>   *The many acts and faces of that company*
>   *Than if mingled with them on the plain below."* [82–90]

Remaining on a point above these spirits so as to better view them symbolizes a higher spiritual perspective that gives the travelers a degree of objectivity in relation to them, and opens their vision to inner realities not visible from the "outside." In life these souls were kings, but in Purgatory they must inhabit not high places such as castles are built on, but rather a deep valley. Sordello, while naming them, laments that many of their descendents did not inherit their virtues.

He says:

> *Not often up from branch to higher branch* [of a family tree]
> *Rises the worth of man; this is the will*
> *Of He who gives, that we might ask it from Him.* [121–123]

This passage debunks the pride of genealogy and shows how we are individually responsible to God for our virtues, and cannot depend on the good spiritual qualities of our forbears. These kings waiting in Ante-Purgatory are reconciled with each other, even though they might have been killer and victim in this world. They are reconciled because all souls destined for purgation have at least a longing for Paradise, even if they do not yet have a vision of it, given that "faith is the substance of things hoped for, the evidence of things not seen" [Hebrews 11:1].[2]

Purgatory, unlike the Inferno [cf. *Inferno* 31:10], includes both night and day; this, like the presence of vegetation there, shows that it is in line with natural rhythms, unlike the unnatural fixity and chaos of Hell. Day and night in Purgatory are like the expansion and contraction, the *breathing* of the soul—a movement that purification requires. One is not purified of everything the soul contains, only of excesses, deficiencies and contradictions. The contraction of night moves the soul away from its impurities and allows for detachment from them; the expansion of day illuminates what needs to be purged and makes room for these residues to be released; it also illuminates and nourishes the virtues. Light is the goal of the ascent, but night and its darkness are necessary too; if the light were constant the soul would not be purified, only burned.

---

2. The Hindus make a distinction between the *pitri-yana*, the Way of the Ancestors, and the *deva-yana*, the Way of the Gods. Veneration of the ancestors leads to the round of rebirth, while veneration of the gods, ultimately resulting in the realization of the Nondual Absolute, leads to Liberation.

Canto VIII

Sunset in the Valley of the Kings. Two angels appear, and then a Serpent. The angels drive the Serpent off. Dante's vision of the three stars over the South Pole. His conversation with Currado Malaspina.

> *It was now the hour of longing for return*
>   *That melts the hearts of sailors on the sea*
>   *The day they've said to their sweet friends, "farewell,"*
> *When the new pilgrim's heart is pierced with love,*
>   *If he hears distant the tolling of a bell*
>   *That seems to mourn the dying of the day.*
> *That's when I began to let my hearing lapse*
>   *To better watch a soul who rose and beckoned*
>   *Gesturing with his hand for my attention.*
> *He joined his palms together and lifted them*
>   *Fixing his steady eyes upon the East,*
>   *As if saying to God, "I care for nothing else."*
> *"Te lucis ante" issued from his mouth*
>   *So piously, and with notes so sweet*
>   *It made me issue forth from my own mind.*
> *And the others too, in sweetness and devotion,*
>   *Accompanied that soul through all his hymn,*
>   *Resting their eyes upon the celestial wheels.*
> *Likewise fix your eyes upon the Truth*
>   *Dear Reader, for the veil has grown so thin*
>   *It will be easy now for you to pass within.* [1–21]

Te Lucis Ante Terminum is a traditional hymn sung at the hour of Compline, the end of the working day. Even though the light is now fading, this soul turns toward the East, the origin of light, instead of toward the west where the light sinks into matter; he has learned to place invisible Source above visible manifestation. He concentrates so devotedly that Dante participates in his devotion, and this raises him above human mentality so that he can perceive Truth directly, without the hindrance of his own mind. Darkness is coming; and this darkness has a double meaning: the darkening of the light of knowledge, but also apophatic mysticism, the knowledge of God by the complete negation of sense experience, imagination and intellect, which confers the sort of Divine Knowledge that remains after the human mind is extinguished.

Darkness is coming—so why does Dante tell us that the veil has become thin? Because the veil of shallow understanding is gone, and this is the moment when Dante reminds us to "look sharp," as if to say, don't think of yourself as in ignorance in the presence of this Darkness, but rather as now being able to unite with that higher and deeper apophatic understanding that is eternally present.

In Purgatory this alternation of night and day, negative and positive mystical understanding, apophasis and cataphasis, must happen because the soul isn't strong enough to hold to the positive perception of the mysteries without becoming attached to them; only the paradisical soul can see so much and still maintain detachment and dispassion. When darkness falls in Purgatory, the more superficial perceptions die, thus deepening the soul's understanding and ultimately leading it onward in its ascent.

> *Then I saw that company of noble spirits*
>   *Gathered there in silence, gazing upward*
>   *Pale and humble and filled with expectation—*
> *When from above, appearing, then descending,*
>   *I saw two angels, holding flaming swords,*
>   *But with the points of both blades broken off.*
> *Their garments were green as newly-sprouted leaves*
>   *Rippled and blown backward by the wind*
>   *Rising from the beat of their emerald wings.*
> *One assumed his station just above us*
>   *While the other descended to the opposite bank,*
>   *Till they encompassed all that group of spirits.*
> *The blond heads of them I could clearly see*
>   *But still my sight was dazzled by their faces*
>   *As any faculty is bewildered by excess.*

Canto VIII

"From Mary's bosom both of these have come,"
Sordello said, "so as to guard this valley
Against the Serpent that will soon arrive." [22–39]

These angels are the absolute arms of mercy protecting these souls against temptation, as they were not protected on earth. But souls in Purgatory cannot sin, so why does temptation have to appear? The fact that temptation (the Serpent) is crushed by the green angels symbolizes a constant renewal of the spiritual life at every second. The angels are protecting all the souls in Purgatory, not just those in the valley; these souls are simply placed where they can see this more clearly. This happens over and over only to the souls in this station; they have to fully see the form of the evil that tempts them; when that evil has fully taken form, and they finally understand it, they can move beyond it. The angels are green because they are emissaries of absolute Life; they are from the bosom of Mary because the Virgin is the vessel of God's Mercy for mankind, as is pictured in the Eastern Orthodox icon, "Theotokos of the Fountain." The principle of Life is Love, and green is the heraldic color of Venus, the planet of Love.

The angels with the flaming swords remind us of the cherub in the Book of Genesis set to guard the gates of the Earthly Paradise after the fall. But the tips of these angels' swords are broken off; they are not aggressors, but healers. (A motif widespread in myth and folklore is the notion that only the weapon that has dealt the wound is capable of healing it.) They are prefigurations of the fires of purgation that Dante will encounter on the terrace of lust, where Love is purified of worldly concupiscence. This is not the place where lust is expiated, however; the dwellers in this valley are not debauchees but imperfect kings. The perfect king would symbolize True Man, man as such; the imperfect king is someone with the potential to reach the stature of True Man, but with flaws that hinder this development. So the angels are here to heal the imperfections of kingship. That the tips of their swords are broken off symbolizes justice tempered with mercy; the besetting sin of kings, almost impossible to avoid, is an imperfect justice that, through excess, becomes merciless and cruel. The green angels have come to re-establish the

The Ordeal of Mercy

balance between justice and mercy; it's as if they represent the two pans of the Scales of Justice that appear in Libra, a sign of the zodiac ruled by Venus, indicating that the principle and source of Justice is Love itself. And that they have descended from the bosom of Mary recalls the Magnificat, indicating that the Virgin is not simply Mercy, but the perfect balance of Mercy and Justice:

> *He hath shewed strength with His arm;*
>   *He hath scattered the proud in the imagination of their*
>   *hearts.*
> *He hath put down the mighty from their seat,*
>   *and hath exalted the humble and meek.*
> *He hath filled the hungry with good things,*
>   *and the rich He hath sent empty away.* [Luke 1:51–53]

☩

I believe I'd gone down no more than three steps
  And stood below, when I saw a spirit looking
  Only at me, as if he hoped to know me.
Already by now the air was growing dark,
  But not dark enough to prevent it from revealing
  To his eyes and mine what first it had concealed.
He moved nearer to me, and I to him—
  The honorable Judge Nino! How glad I felt
  When I realized you weren't among the damned!
No cordial salutation was left unoffered
  Before he asked me, "How long has it been
  Since you crossed the wide waters to the Mountain's foot?
"Oh" I said, "I passed through the dismal regions
  Just this morning; I'm still in my first life
  Though I travel like this hoping to gain the other."
As soon as they had heard the reply I gave
  Both Nino and Sordello shrank back from me
  Like people who are suddenly confused.
One looked at Virgil; another turned to someone
  Sitting nearby and cried, "Stand up, Currado!

60

Canto VIII

> *Come and see what God's grace has decreed!"*
> *Then to me: "By the special gratitude*
> *You owe the One who so conceals from view*
> *His primal aim that none can cross that river*
> *When you shall stand beyond its spacious waters*
> *Ask my Giovanna to pray for me,*
> *There where the prayers of the innocent find their answer."*
>
> [46–72]

Dante takes three steps down into the valley at sundown; just as the sun is now setting, so something is setting in Dante's soul. Nino tells Dante that he should be grateful that he does not know God's primal aim; his knowledge of this aim would block his living out of the destiny God has ordained for him. This necessary ignorance has to do with the mysterious gift of free will, which must remain a mystery for the human mind. Not knowing God's primal motive also entails not knowing the evil that one will have to face in earthly life; if the soul about to be born were to foresee all its sufferings, it would despair and refuse incarnation.[1]

> *"Son, what are you staring at?" asked my Guide,*
> *"There in the sky?" "I'm watching those three torches*
> *From which this southern pole seems all on fire."*
> *"The four resplendent stars" he explained to me*
> *"You saw this morning have set now, nearer the pole;*
> *These three have risen up to take their place."* [88–93]

Dante looks toward the south pole and sees a constellation of three stars, which are usually said to symbolize the Theological Virtues: Faith, Hope and Charity, as the four stars in the first Canto represent the Cardinal Virtues, Prudence, Justice, Fortitude and Temperance. The constellation of four stars was visible at dawn, but these appear at dusk. The Cardinal Virtues depend upon natural perception, but the Theological Virtues need something like super-

---

1. Likewise Blake's Thel, his figure of negative innocence from *The Book of Thel*, rejects birth because she foresees the sufferings and privations of terrestrial life.

natural intuition or insight infused with Grace, which is darkness to the natural mind, in order to be understood and practiced. When day in Purgatory subsides, this indicates the closing of the natural perception so as to leave room for the infusion of supernatural perception, or at least as much of this as Purgatory allows. These three stars foreshadow the full personification of the Theological Virtues as three women in the Earthly Paradise.

> *As Virgil was speaking, Sordello suddenly drew him*
>   *To himself, and said, "Our Adversary arrives!",*
>   *Pointing with his finger to direct our gaze.*
> *On the side of that little valley that remained unguarded*
>   *A Serpent appeared—it might have been the same*
>   *That offered our mother Eve the bitter fruit.*
> *Through grass and flowers flowed that evil streak,*
>   *Sometimes turning its head to lick its back*
>   *Like an animal will that grooms and preens itself.*
> *Because I did not see I cannot say*
>   *Just how those heavenly falcons began to move*
>   *But I clearly saw that they were in fact in motion.*
> *When he heard the air being cut by those emerald wings*
>   *The serpent ran; then the angels wheeled around*
>   *And flew back up together to their stations.* [94–108]

   The Serpent has all the appearance of reality, but the angels are there to make sure that it is only an image of temptation and evil. The Serpent preening itself is the temptation faced by kings to vanity and self-aggrandizement, which Shakespeare perfectly analyzed in *King Lear*. Lear had the potential to embody true kingship, to be True Man, but instead of embracing that potential, he exiled his daughter Cordelia, the symbol of the Spiritual Heart, and sought power and vanity instead (represented by Cordelia's sisters) which ended up driving him mad. He believed that he was king in his own personality, not in his royal crown, his transpersonal function, and was consequently destroyed. Likewise the Serpent in Genesis, to which this Snake is compared, promised godhood but gave only despair. If the kings were to see the Snake in the wrong way, without

Canto VIII

angelic aid, it would tempt them to despair and evil, but since the angels have reduced it to an image, it works instead to reveal the darkness in their own souls and the places where purification is needed. This *catharsis* is one of the main spiritual functions of true art.

> *The spirit who'd drawn nearer to the Judge*
> *When he called, never for one moment*
> *Removed his eyes from me through the whole assault.*
> *"Then may the lamp that leads you ever higher*
> *Find enough wax within your own free will*
> *To let you reach that high enameled peak,"*
> *He said. "And if by chance you have true news*
> *Of Valdimagra and its neighborhood*
> *Then let me know, for there I once was great.*
> *Currado Malaspina was my name. . . ."* [109–118]

The will needs to be supple so that the purgatorial ascent may take place—not vague or inconsistent but rather malleable, capable of accepting the imprint of the Divine Will like sealing wax receives the pattern of the signet. The "enameled peak" is the Earthly Paradise, which represents the stability of the completed work. Wax is used in the enameling process, but it finds no place in the finished design. Likewise the individual will, through obedience, is necessary to the process of purgation, but it is no longer required when perfection is attained; its place has been taken by the Divine Will. The lantern that leads Dante on high is the *wisdom* or *working knowledge* that guides him in the process of purgation, as if the work of purifying the soul were a kind of alchemy, a spiritual craft or skill. Lanterns enclose wax candles; here the candle-flame symbolizes the Intellect, and the wax the personal will that, in allowing itself to be burned, feeds it. The Transcendent Intellect grows in radiance as the personal will is consumed.

The Ordeal of Mercy

Editorial Commentary Two:
The Symbolism of the Virgin and the Scales

Here the Virgin appears in the guise of Justice, who is traditionally represented as bearing both the Scales (the power to reach a verdict) and the Sword (the power to pass sentence). As René Guénon pointed out in *The King of the World* (63), the sign of Libra, the Scales, was once, according to Chinese tradition, a polar sign before it was placed within the circle of the zodiac; the Great and Little Bears were sometimes identified with the two pans of the Scales. This would relate the Virgin, as Justice, to the Pole, the fixed or *principial* point around which the universe revolves, and more specifically to the Pole Star in the tail of the Septentrion, the Little Bear; Mary, in her Polar or Hyperborean aspect, was indeed identified with this star by St. Bernardine [see *Editorial Commentary Eight*, 266]. The relationship of the Scales to the Pole is further reinforced by the fact that the English word "scale" derives from the Latin *scalae*, "ladder" (literally, "steps" or "stairs"): the Pole is the *axis mundi* which, in the form of the World Tree, is "scaled" by the shamans of Siberia [cf. Mircea Eliade in *Shamanism: Archaic Techniques of Ecstasy*]; it is also the ladder scaled by angels that Jacob saw in his dream in Haran [cf. Genesis 28:10–19]. In the liturgy of the Eastern Orthodox Church, this passage is often read on feast days dedicated to the Theotokos. The English word "scales" however, denoting the pans of a balance, is derived from the Old Norse *skal*, "bowl" (from which we get the toast "Skol!"), relating it more directly to the symbolism of the Virgin and the Cup [cf. *Editorial Commentary Eight*, 266]. The relationship between "scale" as *ladder* and as *cup* or *bowl* is difficult to establish etymologically; nonetheless their meanings converge, given that one meaning of *scale*-as-*ladder* is "a graduated series of magnitudes," and things are weighed in a balance using a graduated series of weights. Furthermore, several traditions place a cup or cauldron at the summit of the *axis mundi* [see *Editorial Commentary Eight*, 266]. "Scale" as *bowl*, said to be derived from the Old Norse "skell" = *shell*, is also undoubtedly related to *skull*; a skull is shell-like, and both shells and skulls (as with the Tibetans) can be used as bowls or drinking cups. It is also significant that Eastern Orthodox iconography, based on a commentary by Origen, shows the skull of Adam as buried at the foot of Christ's cross on Calvary or Golgotha—"the place of the skull." Academic etymologists tend to distrust correspondences like this; they forget that, unlike a human individual, a word can have many fathers: given a more symbolist relationship to words than we enjoy today, operating over millennia, "folk etymology" itself can shape language. Dante places the Mount of Purgatory in the Southern Hemisphere at the antipodes of Jerusalem, but later the northern polar constellations appear above the Mount; the effect of this is to bring together the Cross, the Mount and the Pole as three different symbols of the *axis mundi*.

Canto IX

Night in the Valley of the Kings. The Aurora Borealis. Dante's dream of the Eagle. The travelers reach the Gates of Purgatory and are accosted by the angelic Guardian, who inscribes seven P's on Dante's forehead. The Gates open.

> At that very hour, just before the morning,
>   When the little swallow her sad song begins,
>   Possibly remembering her ancient woes,
> And when the mind of man is free to roam
>   Farther from the flesh, less bound by thought,
>   Till it becomes almost prophetic in its visions,
> In a dream it seemed to me I saw suspended
>   An eagle in the sky, with plumes of gold,
>   And wings wide open, ready to swoop down,
> And it appeared to me that this was the very place
>   Where Ganymede abandoned his relatives,
>   When he was caught up to the high assembly.
> I thought within myself, "Perhaps his habit
>   Is to strike only here, and so from elsewhere
>   Disdains to bear up any in his claws."
> Then wheeling a bit, as it seemed to me,
>   He dove upon me, terrible as lightning,
>   And snatched me upward, even to the fire.
> It seemed that both of us were flaming in it;
>   And that visionary fire so sharply burned me,
>   My sleep was broken up, and I awoke. [13–33]

The swallow is apparently an allusion to the story, told by both Virgil and Ovid, of the rape of Philomela by Tereus, who cuts out her tongue to prevent her from implicating him—but she weaves the story into a piece of cloth and shows it to her sister Procne. The sisters revenge the rape and mutilation by serving up the flesh of

Canto IX

Tereus's son for him to eat, and when he discovers the deed and pursues them with murderous intent, Philomela is changed into a nightingale and Procne into a swallow. The swallow announces the Eagle that will appear in Dante's dream; she is sad because she is waning with the night to give place to the Eagle. That motive of revenge has to wane because in Purgatory one can only repent for one's own sufferings, not take revenge for someone else's. And if it be asked, how can one "repent" of suffering, the answer is that we are placed in Purgatory in order to attain perfection; the memory of suffering is an imperfection we must eventually be purified of.

Ganymede, son of the king of Troy and a youth of great beauty, attracted the love of Zeus in the form of an eagle, who snatched him away from his family and made him his cupbearer. Procne, on the other hand, is excessively attached to her family through the motive of seemingly just revenge. Eagles represent spiritual ascent; the constellation of Scorpio is symbolized by the Scorpion but is also related to the Eagle, the principle of spiritual aspiration, in this case symbolizing the sublimation of the passions. (The Eagle, as the bird of Zeus or Jupiter, is also related to the next sign, that of Sagittarius, which is ruled by the planet Jupiter; its ascent can thus be seen as representing the passage from one sign to the other.) This Eagle can only find its prey in Purgatory, not on earth or in hell, because Purgatory has to do with spiritual transformation. The fire the Eagle plunges into with Dante in his claws is the dawning of the spiritual Intellect that purges the soul of ignorance; this is why Dante awakens.

The Eagle is the Divine Intellect, the solar principle; gold is its proper color. Grace must be there for the ascent to be accomplished. Even while Dante is walking, grace is hovering over him. Effort is necessary for purgation, but not sufficient; this purification cannot be accomplished without the grace of God that lifts us beyond ourselves.

> *Just as when Achilles started up,*
>   *Darting his just-awakened eyes around him,*
>   *Not recognizing the place in which he was,*
>   *At the time his mother, stealthily from Chiron,*

The Ordeal of Mercy

> *Carried him asleep in her arms to Scyros,*
>   *(From which afterward the Greeks made him depart),*
> *Just so, when sleep had left my eyes, I started*
>   *And then turned cold and pale, just like the man*
>   *Who freezes when he feels the touch of fear.*
> *My Comforter alone was at my side.*
>   *Now the sun was more than two hours high,*
>   *And the sea it was to which I turned my face.*
> *"Do not be afraid" then said my Lord,*
>   *"Be reassured, for all is well with us;*
>   *Don't hold back, but put forth all your strength.*
> *You have arrived at last at Purgatory;*
>   *See there the cliff that encloses it in a circle;*
>   *See there the entrance, where the cliff is breached.*
> *Before the dawn, which ushers in the day,*
>   *When inwardly your spirit was asleep*
>   *Upon the flowers that carpet the land below,*
> *A Lady advanced, who said: 'I am Lucia;*
>   *Let me carry this one up, who lies asleep;*
>   *Thus will I make his journey easier for him.'*
> *Sordello and the other noble spirits*
>   *Remained while she took you; as the day grew bright*
>   *Upward she climbed; I followed in her footsteps.*
> *She laid you here, and with her lovely eyes*
>   *Pointed out to me the point of entry;*
>   *Then she and sleep together took their leave."* [34–63]

Here the Eagle is revealed as the dream-form of St. Lucy, emissary of the Intellect, who is sent by the Virgin to guide Dante. The Apostle John whom Jesus at His crucifixion called the son of the Virgin is symbolized by the Eagle—and the Virgin, of course, is Holy Wisdom. Entry into Purgatory is an initiation; the esoteric school aspect of Christianity is at the heart of the tradition, not on its periphery. Here Dante is initiated into this esoteric center, into the "Church of John."

Much as Dante would have liked to remain asleep and avoid the *agon* of Purgatory—as Achilles hoped, under his mother's influ-

Canto IX

ence, to avoid the Trojan War—now by command of the Intellect he must awaken to the unseen warfare and face the rigors of purification. But there is a great difference between the Pagan hero and the Christian one. Under his mother's domination, Achilles, hiding out on the island of Skyros and dressed as a woman, loses his manhood, which leads him to dally with his lover Patroclos before Troy instead of immediately entering the battle—whereas Dante, under the influence of St. Lucy and the Virgin, like the Christian knight who goes into battle carrying the standard of his lady, is awakened to the true war. To begin with Dante is afraid because of his ignorance—but certainty brings courage.

> ... there, where I first made out the rift
> Looking something like a crevice that splits a wall
> I saw a door with three stairs underneath,
> Of different colors, leading up to it,
> And a gate-keeper, who thus far spoke no word.
> And as more and more widely I opened my eyes,
> I saw him seated on the highest stair,
> With face so radiant I could not endure it.
> In his hand he held a naked sword,
> Which so powerfully reflected back the sunlight
> That as many times as I looked I could not face it.
> "Advance and be recognized: what is your purpose here?"
> He challenged us; and then: "Where is your escort?
> Approach with care, or else you might be injured!"
> "A Lady from Heaven, with knowledge this place,"
> My Master answered, "just a moment ago
> Directed us here, and pointed out the door."
> "Then may she speed your way in all that's good,"
> Our courteous porter immediately replied;
> "Come forward now; approach these stairs of ours."
> We did as he asked. The first stair we encountered
> Was marble white, so polished and so smooth,
> I was reflected in it exactly as I appear.
> The second stair, of scorched and crumbled stone
> Was of a color darker than deep purple,

The Ordeal of Mercy

And full of cracks both lengthwise and across.
The third which rested massively above
Seemed made of porphyry—as flaming red
As fresh blood spurting from a severed vein.
With both his feet firmly planted on this last
That Angel of God sat upon a threshold
Which seemed to me a stone of solid diamond. [74–105]

It is difficult for the travelers to develop their perception to the point where they can see the entrance to Purgatory as a gate; from a distance it looks like a breach in the wall. To see the entryway as a breach is to labor under the illusion that the passage into Purgatory is a kind of disorder or some act of Promethean self-assertion, but upon closer inspection it is seen to be entirely lawful.

The angel asks "where is your escort?" because if Dante had reached these gates through death he would have been escorted by a guard of angels. The angel's sword is a sword of discrimination; it determines who is barred and who may pass. It is too brilliant for Dante to look at because this sort of discrimination is angelic, not human; Dante cannot decide for himself whether he is ready to pass the Gate.

The first step of white marble, in which Dante can see his reflected image, represents the completion of earthly life, which, by a lifelong process of recollection, forms a soul destined for salvation. The second step of purple tending to black, cracked and crumbled, is the mortification of Purgatory. The red step is the Purgatorial Fire which brings transfigures the soul and fixes it in the state of redemption, whose final form is symbolized by the diamond, the perfect synthesis of hardness and translucency [cf. Plato's *Timaeus*], indicating that the rigor of purgation is Truth and foreshadowing the crystalline spheres of the *Paradiso*. Initially the soul must put out great effort because it is required bring out in itself its own quality of Necessary Being. This is the eternal and substantial aspect of it that needs to be transfigured from a degraded mortal condition under the whip of external destiny—Necessity in its fallen form—to the adamantine state of immortality, in which it partakes of the Necessary Being of God. The higher Dante ascends

Canto IX

up the Mountain of Purgatory, the less effort is required of him. In the words of the "Desert Mother" Amma Syncletica,

> Great endeavors and hard struggles await those who are converted, but afterwards inexpressible joy. If you want to light a fire, you are troubled first by smoke, and your eyes water. But in the end you achieve your aim. Now it is written: "Our God is a consuming fire." So we must light the divine fire in us with tears and struggle. [*Sayings of the Desert Fathers*]

Seven P's he inscribed upon my forehead
　With the point of his sword; and then he said:
　"When you've entered be sure to wash away these wounds."
The color of his robe was just the same
　As that of ashes, or dry earth excavated;
　He reached and took two keys from underneath it.
One was made of gold, the other of silver;
　First with the white, and afterwards with the yellow,
　He worked the gate—and so I was content.
"Whenever one key or the other fails
　So it will not turn correctly in the lock
　This entrance will not open," he said to us.
"One is more precious, but the other one requires
　A lot of skill and cunning before it will turn;
　This is the one with power to untie the knot.
I received them from Peter. He instructed me
　To rather err in opening than in keeping shut,
　For souls who prostrate humbly when they come."
Then he heaved the portals of the sacred door,
　Telling us "Enter—but also heed my warning:
　Whoever looks back must go back; that's the law."
And when the pivots of that sacred gate
　Slowly began to turn within their sockets
　Which are made of metal, resonant and massive,
Tarpeia itself did not rasp nor groan so loud
　When good Metellus was expelled from it
　Leaving that rock the poorer for his loss.

The Ordeal of Mercy

At the first peal of that thunder I turned, attentive;
I seemed to catch the hymn Te Deum Laudamus
Sung in voices mingled with sweet music.
What I heard then gave the same impression
As one will have when listening to the sound
Of people singing while an organ plays,
When at first we catch the words, and then we lose them.
[112–145]

The seven P's signify both the Seven Deadly Sins (the word for "sins" in Latin is *peccata*) and the purgation of them; here Dante is firmly *convicted* of his sins. The P's are like the ashes of Ash Wednesday, which signify death and mortification, but also life and redemption.[1]

The angel guardian of Purgatory is dressed in an ashen robe. Ashes in alchemy represent the stage of *calcinatio*, where all that is corruptible in the soul is burned away, leaving only that which is impervious to fire; as William Blake expressed it in his epic poem *Milton*, "All that can be annihilated must be annihilated!" What is mortal is destroyed so as to leave room for what is eternal.

The keys of Purgatory are the "keys of the Kingdom" given to Peter as the first pope, whose name means "the Rock"; here Dante is identifying the "church built upon a rock" with the Mount of Purgatory itself [Matthew 16: 18–19]. Since the two keys are mentioned in the Gospel in the context of binding and loosing, one might think that the silver key represents the impartial mirror of justice and the golden one, Divine Mercy. This is true on one level. But on a higher octave of understanding, the gold key is the Spirit and the silver key, the psyche. The gold, as a noble metal largely free from the possibility of adulteration (i.e., chemical combination), represents the crystallization of the soul in final redemption, its readiness for Paradise; the silver symbolizes the loosening of the psyche that

---

1. The five P's remind us of the Mark of Cain, an emblem of guilt. We should remember, however, that the mark placed by God on the forehead of the first murderer was put there for his protection. According to William Blake in his illuminations for the Book of Genesis, the Mark of Cain is a sign of the Forgiveness of Sins.

allows all the latent elements within it to come to the surface so as to be purified and transfigured. (Silver, according to one view of the alchemical art, is the stabilized form of the "universal solvent" Quicksilver, as Gold is of Sulfur.) In one sense the silver key is the principle of the poetic craft that allows it to align itself with the purposes of the Spirit, the key of gold. More universally, however, it is the receptivity of the soul to the commands of that Spirit; this is what unties the knot of sin. Such receptivity is not mere blind obedience, however, but requires intelligence. Receptivity is an art. And if gold is the Intellect, silver may be understood as the will: the first is more precious, but the second is the factor that determines the state of the soul, by how perfectly or imperfectly it conforms to the Intellect, the Spirit.

As if commenting upon the words of the angel, "he [St. Peter] bade me err/Rather in opening than in keeping shut," Martin Lings, in *The Secret of Shakespeare*, says [12] "The porter to Purgatory, that is, the gate of salvation, is by definition of unfathomable mercy.... But the porter to the Gate of Paradise, that is, the gate of sanctification, is relentlessly exacting...." When the angel warns the travelers not to look back, he is telling them to center their intent on the work of purgation itself, with no regrets; by this he foreshadows Lethe.

The opening of the gates recalls the time when Julius Caesar seized the Roman treasure that was guarded by the Tribune Metellus on the Tarpeian Rock. The Pagan Caesar as it were *breached* the gates by violence, which were opened to the Christian Dante by the power of humility. Here again the contrast between the Promethean dispensation and the dispensation of Grace is emphasized, a contrast expressed by Jesus in the following terms: "And from the days of John the Baptist until now (that is, until the advent of the new dispensation He represents) the kingdom of heaven suffereth violence, and the violent bear it away" [Matthew 11:13].

The voice is intermittently drowned in the music because it still remains unfinished; the passage through the whole of Purgatory is required to complete the human soul.

Canto X

The travelers enter Purgatory proper and find themselves at the First Terrace, the Terrace of Pride. Dante views a bas-relief depicting the Virgin Mary, David and Trajan as examples of humility. The souls of the Proud appear, carrying heavy stones.

St. Maximos the Confessor tells us:

The passion of pride arises from two kinds of ignorance, and when these two kinds of ignorance unite together they form a single confused state of mind. For a man is proud only if he is ignorant both of divine help and of human weakness. Therefore pride is a lack of knowledge in both the divine and the human spheres. For the denial of two true premises results in a single false affirmation.

Self-esteem is the replacing of a purpose which accords with God by another purpose which is contrary to the divine. For a man full of self-esteem pursues virtue not for God's glory but for his own, and so purchases with his labours the worthless praise of men. [from the *Philokalia*, Volume Two, *Third Century on Various Texts*, 64 & 65]

The astrological "planet" traditionally associated with Pride is the self-luminous Sun—but, ironically, Pride is perhaps the hardest sin to see for what it is. Vainglory, shameless social arrogance, is relatively easy to discern, but essential Pride—the root of vainglory, as well as of all the other sins—hides itself because it infects the totality of the soul, not just one part of it. As St. Augustine tells us, "all the other vices attach themselves to evil, that it may be done; only pride attaches itself to good, that it may perish." Pride is the source of all the other vices. St. John of Damascus says,

Canto X

We should commit no sin if these powerful giants had not appeared at the beginning, as Mark the wisest of sages says, namely forgetfulness, spiritual insensitivity and ignorance.... The primary cause, the baleful mother of them all, so to say, is *philautia*—love of self. [*On Virtues and Vices*, 88, 95][1]

Purgatory is the place where distorted love is set right. Part of the reason that all these paeans to the effect that "all you need is love" often ring so false is that no distinction is made between true love and distorted or false love. True love participates in a quality of goodness that false love cannot access, which is why distorted love brings destruction in its wake. And false love is also involved in error: when the will is distorted, the intellect is darkened—though one might also ask how the will could choose a false object if the darkening of the intellect had not already begun. These two aspects of the soul are in fact so intimately related that it is difficult to say which one initiates the process of the fall; all we can say for certain is that when they fall, they fall together.

> *When we had crossed the threshold of that door*
> *Seldom used due to souls with twisted love*
> *A love that makes the crooked way seem straight,*
> *Re-echoing I heard it close again;*
> *If I'd turned back my eyes upon it then,*
> *For such a fault what excuse could I have made?* [1–6]

When Dante hears the door to Purgatory slam shut behind him, but doesn't look back, he is setting his will in the right direction: toward the eternal truths of the Intellect. Dante cannot go back now because to do so would be to turn toward unreality, and perhaps be tempted to fill in with fantasy the void that remains now that the world of delay and ambiguity, represented by Ante-Purgatory, is closed to him.

---

1. These "giants," personifications of the passions, are the Titans; cf. *Inferno*, Canto XXXI and *Purgatorio* Canto XII. And the Buddhists certainly agree with John of Damascus when they name ignorance, *avidya*, as one of the prime causes of suffering.

The Ordeal of Mercy

We mounted upward through a riven rock,
  Swaying first to this side, then to that,
  Just as a wave will roll and then roll back.
"Here we must employ a little art,"
  Began my Leader, "that we may keep close
  First here, then there, to the receding side."
And this our footsteps so infrequent made,
  That sooner had the moon's decreasing disk
  Regained its bed to sink again to rest,
Than we came forth from out that needle's eye. . . . [7–16]

Here the travelers encounter cloven rocks that lean first to the right, then to the left, requiring them to pursue a wavering course. In Purgatory the soul's tendency to vacillation is overcome by allowing it to face its sins directly, and therefore harbor no ambiguous desires for them; here the desire of the soul learns to turn toward virtue completely. Before that point is reached, however, the soul needs the knowledge of good and evil, the pairs-of-opposites, even though it fell from Paradise precisely through such knowledge. This is the "art" of which Virgil speaks: the painstaking skill of discernment that allows one to pass through the narrow gate. Vacillation often presents itself as a meticulous and courageous search for truth, whereas it is really nothing but the ego jumping back and forth from one thing to another to escape its own annihilation. A constant ambiguity, never committing to anything, never certain of what is right, is the ego's counterfeit of the painstaking moral discernment to which Dante is called; as such, it is one of the major manifestations of pride. When the "inconstant" Moon reigns, so does ambiguity and reflective knowledge; this sort of knowledge must be darkened so that Dante and Virgil will be finally able to find the constancy of the Sun.[2]

---

[2]. The traditional doctrine of the pairs-of-opposites is thoroughly expounded by Ananda K. Coomaraswamy in his article "Symplegades," appearing in *Studies in Comparative Religion*, Volume 7, number 1.

Canto X

> *"Do not fix your mind on just one point,"*
> *My gentle Master said, who made me stand*
> *Upon that side where people have their hearts. . . .* [46–48]

For Dante to stand on Virgil's left side, the side of the heart, means that we are now getting to the heart of the matter, the point from which the whole condition of the soul can be witnessed. When Virgil advises Dante not to fix his mind on just one point, he is cautioning him not to let the contemplative practice of one-pointedness of attention degenerate into the sort of partiality or attachment to fixed ideas that compromises breadth of vision. The central point defines the whole field.

> *The angel who brought the decree of peace to earth*
> *Begged for in sorrow for so many years*
> *And opened Heaven from its long interdict,*
> *In front of us appeared so truthfully*
> *Sculptured there in gracious attitude,*
> *He seemed much more than just a silent image.*
> *You would have sworn that he was saying, "Ave";*
> *For there portrayed in effigy was She*
> *Who turned the key to unlock the highest love;*
> *By her stance she perfectly mimed the words*
> *"Ecce ancilla Dei," just as clearly*
> *As if she had been a figure stamped in wax.* [34–45]

It's striking for the Annunciation to be shown as an example of humility, since it represents the highest honor that can be conferred on a human being. St. John Climacus calls humility the Queen of the virtues. In some ways humility can be identified with outer meekness, but it isn't just that; according to Climacus, humility is ultimately something invisible and mysterious. Two people can perform the identical action, one with humility and one without, and it can be very hard to see the world of difference between them. In order to see humility we must be humble ourselves, and this is difficult for all of us. Mary totally submits her will to the will of God, like wax to the signet, which is what all souls in purgation must do.

The Ordeal of Mercy

But Mary is the Immaculate Conception, born without sin; she can give us a perfect example of the humility that purgation requires precisely because she herself, of all human souls, had no need of it—and this is a true mystery. As Climacus expresses it:

> You may be proud only of the achievements you had before the time of your birth. But anything after that, indeed the birth itself, is a gift from God. You may claim only those virtues in you that are there independently of your mind, for your mind was bestowed on you by God. And you may claim only those victories you achieved independently of the body, for the body too is not yours but a work of God.[3]

> *Sculpted in the same marble there appeared*
>   *A cart and oxen, drawing the holy Ark,*
>   *That makes one fear a task not in his charge.*
> *The crowd that appeared before it was divided*
>   *Into seven choirs, so one of my two senses*
>   *Said "No, they're silent" and the other, "Yes, they sing";*
> *The smoke of frankincense depicted there*
>   *Likewise caused the same uncertainty*
>   *The nose and eyes debated "pro" and "con."* [55–63]

People in certain mystical states will tell us that they "see sounds" or "hear colors" (the technical term for this is "synesthesia"); likewise when it comes to language, true mystical perception can often be expressed only in terms of paradox. Dante here is saying "yes" to his vision, even if his other, more outer senses contradict it; this contention between yes and no moves Dante forward on his path.

Here Dante encounters the effigy of Uzzah, who tried to catch the Ark of the Covenant when it was about to fall, and was struck down by God for violating the taboo that the Ark was never to be touched by human hand, but rather carried on poles. For Uzzah to attempt to support that object of holy power, no matter how good his inten-

---

3. The Taoists allude to an analogous truth when they speak of the highest form of action as *wu wei*, "doing without doing," as does the Zen roshi when he challenges the student to solve the *koan* "show me your original face before you were born."

tions apparently were, was for him to forget that the Ark, which is the Presence of God, was *his* support. To see ourselves as "co-creators" in partnership with the Almighty, to foolishly believe that He needs us as much as we need Him, is to fall into the error of the process and liberation theologians; it is to deny not only His omnipotence, but also His free gift to us of both salvation and existence.

The striking down of Uzzah is pictured as being viewed by a group of spectators who are separated into "seven choirs." If we take these as representing seven of the traditional nine choirs of angels in the system of Dionysius the Areopagite, and see the Ark itself as associated with the choir of the Cherubim (the second highest), since it was surmounted by two cherubs, then Uzzah himself would be emblematic of the highest choir of angels, that of the Seraphim, and specifically of the seraph Lucifer, the prototype of all Pride. Largely following Milton's *Paradise Lost*, we usually think of Lucifer as an angry rebel against God—but how much more arrogant it would have been for him to actually believe that God might need his help! The duty of the Seraphim is to remain rapt in the direct contemplation of God, in a perfect love that is inseparable from perfect knowledge—but if Lucifer really did fall into the delusion that God required his aid, then he "presumed below his station," falsely usurping the function of the Cherubim, in whom knowledge has begun to be differentiated from love. To become arrogant is to lower oneself; not every act of lowering oneself partakes of humility.[4]

> *Before that sacred vessel next appeared*
> *   The humble Psalmist, lifting up his robes;*
> *   Less and more than a king he was that day.*
> *Opposite him, pictured at the window*
> *   Of a great palace, Michal glared down at him,*
> *   The very image of a haughty, grieving woman.* [64–69]

---

4. William Blake, in *Milton*, pictures the Fall of Man as the product of a misplaced charity on the part of Satan, who offers to take over the harrow from Palamabron, the figure emblematic of pity for the oppressed. This is precisely an act of taking on "a task not in his charge." As the Hindus say, "It is better to perform your own duty (*dharma*), however poorly, than the duty of another, however well."

The Ordeal of Mercy

Uzzah ran to support the Ark of the Covenant when it was about to fall, an apparently virtuous act, and was struck down; David danced before the Ark after its return to Jerusalem clad only in an ephod (similar to an apron), an apparently shameful act that earned him God's favor.

It's often difficult to tell where true humility and true pride are; one can look like the other. David, in dancing before the Ark, had to temporarily give up his worldly kingliness (his robes and crown) and be a mere dancer. In this he was both "less and more than a king" because by this act he became a priest; the ephod later became part of the regalia of the Jewish High Priest. (In Ethiopia, where the true ark is supposedly housed, the Orthodox Monophysite priests dance on the feast of Theophany.) The reason that Michal despised him in her heart is that the important thing to her was to be married to a worldly king, not to a man like David who would humble himself to dance before the Ark; the fact that he was doing this in praise of God meant nothing to her. Michal is the part of the soul that wants to hold on to worldliness, to remain proud and unredeemed. In this she was truly "the daughter of Saul."

(Next Dante will view the effigy of the Emperor Trajan, and finally that of the Virgin Mary. Dante, as a Christian, can see more deeply into non-Christian realities than Virgil can, not only that of the Hebrews—Uzzah—but that of Pagan antiquity itself—Trajan.)

> *There the high glory of that Roman Prince*
> *   Was legendary, he whose famous courage*
> *   Inspired Gregory to his great victory;*
> *I am speaking of the regal Emperor Trajan.*
> *   On one occasion a poor widow stood at his bridle*
> *   In an attitude of weeping and of grief.*
> *Around him thronged his retinue of mounted knights*
> *   Bearing standards crowned with golden eagles*
> *   Visibly moving above them in the wind.*
> *This sorrowful woman standing in their midst*
> *   Seemed to be crying out, "Vengeance, my Lord!*
> *   For my dead son, for whom my heart is broken."*
> *In answer to her he replied, "Not yet;*

Canto X

> *You must wait for my return." But she retorted*
>   *Desperate with grief, "What if you don't return?"*
> *"Then my successor will satisfy your petition."*
>   *"What use to you is the good deed of another*
>   *If you neglect your own?" she answered him.*
> *"Be at peace," he said, "For now I see*
>   *I must fulfill my duty before I go;*
>   *Justice wills it, and mercy stays my course."*
> *These pictures were the visible speech of Him*
>   *Who has never gazed, nor will, on one new thing;*
>   *Since we've nothing like them, we experience novelty.*
>   [73–96]

   Dante is presenting Trajan to us as a perfect image of the Christian monarch, the first precursor in history of Christian kingship. And his virtue is all the more conspicuous because he is not a Christian—he would undoubtedly have disdained the title—and consequently he was not expected to manifest this depth of justice and mercy, virtues that later Christian kings would too often only mime in their hypocrisy, while in their hearts they were more Pagan than Trajan was. Trajan finally helped the poor widow when almost everything in him rebelled against this impulse because he intuited that to help her was to be faithful to his truest self, to the Self as such. This story enters Christian culture by virtue of that Self, which is the True Man, making null and void whatever lack of interest his little, outer man may have had in this high destiny.

   We usually think of humility and charity as "doings for others," and thus as rejecting all forms of *selfishness*. But in this case the Emperor, after refusing to perform an act of charity for another, finally agrees to do so *for himself*. To do good to oneself for the sake of the Self as such is to annihilate the outer man, the vanities and desires of the ego. Another Emperor might have helped the widow only out of human pity, but Trajan did so out of fidelity to the Real. And this is true humility.

   The widow demands justice, but the Emperor, while he acknowledges the justice of her petition, tells her he acts out of mercy, since it is mercy that finally stays his course. The same act appears as jus-

The Ordeal of Mercy

tice on a lower level but as mercy on a higher one. And this mercy doesn't exist in the world of time and motion but in the eternal present of God. Purgatory is based on motion, but there the motion of life is fleshed out in order for it to be overcome. Purgatory is the world of time as witnessed by Eternity.

> "Master," I said, "those that I behold
>   Coming toward us now appear inhuman.
>   I don't know what they are; my sight's unsure."
> He answered me: "The grievous quality
>   Of their torment bends them so far toward the earth,
>   That even I for a moment was confused.
> Just gaze at them, steadily, till you make out
>   The forms that now approach beneath those stones;
>   Already you can see how each is punished."
> O Christian pride! O miserable, weary ones!
>   You who in the sickness of your minds
>   Rely upon your own backsliding steps—
> Don't you understand that we are worms
>   Born to hatch angelic butterflies,
>   Who fly unveiled into the arms of Judgement?
> Why do your souls presume to soar so high?
>   You're like insects—defective caterpillars
>   In whom that metamorphosis is aborted. [112–129]

Secular humanist culture tells us not to look beyond the worm, and sees people who contemplate the formation of the butterfly as either fanatics or mentally ill. There is a hidden pride in this. Some people will say, "I accept that man is merely an animal crawling on a tiny mote in the vast cosmos," and think that by doing so they are humbling human pride; they consider those who say that man is also half angel and destined for Heaven to be the prideful ones. But the man who thinks "man is only an animal, only a machine, only matter" is trying to put a creature far greater than mere materiality into a narrow material prison; hence he must pridefully exalt the importance of materialism and material life. Not every abasement is an example of humility; not every exaltation is an example of pride.

Canto X

The terrace of Pride has a particular relationship to stone: the travelers must pass between tottering rocks; the three examples of the virtue of Humility appear as carved bas-reliefs; and the punishment of the prideful is to be forced to carry heavy stones, demonstrating how Pride often masquerades as "substance" or solidity of character. Dante once composed a series of poems dedicated to a woman named *Pietra*, "stone," who totally captivates his heart even though she is cruel and in no way returns his affections; *Pietra* seems to correspond in some ways to the Medusa in Canto IX of the *Inferno*. Since some maintain that one of Dante's terms for the esoteric spiritual Ecclesia, the Church of John, is *Pietà* (also symbolized by Beatrice), we are led to ask whether *Pietra* might symbolize the outer, worldly Church—the Church of Peter, the Rock. In the words of Frithjof Schuon:

> The Church of Peter is visible, and continuous like water; that of John—instituted on Calvary and confirmed at the Sea of Tiberias—is invisible, and discontinuous like fire. John became 'brother' of Christ and 'son' of the Virgin, and, further, he is the prophet of the Apocalypse; Peter is charged to 'feed my sheep,' but his Church seems to have inherited also his denials, whence the Renaissance and its direct and indirect consequences; however, 'the gates of hell shall not prevail against it.' John 'tarries till I come,' and this mystery remains closed to Peter. [*Gnosis, Divine Wisdom*, 102]

The Prideful want to be above it all, above the burdens of life—but one develops real substance only by confronting these burdens. Pride, on the other hand, flees from substance and virtue, and though it often wants to appropriate virtue, it can only destroy it. When the burdens of life arrive, the proud man has no real way of accepting them; as St. John Climacus says: "A proud soul is the slave of cowardice. Trusting only itself, it is frightened by a sound or a shadow." The stone the Prideful must bear on his back is the very life he refused to meet on equal terms.

Canto XI

The souls of the Proud, using a version of the Lord's Prayer proper to Purgatory, pray for the living. The travelers meet and speak with Omberto Aldobrandeschi, Oderisi of Gubbio, and Provenzan Salvani.

This Canto begins with Dante's exegesis of Matthew 6:9–13, his version of the Lord's Prayer:

> "Our Father, Thou who dwellest in the heavens,
>   Not bound by them, but from the greater love
>   Thou bearest to Thy first works on high,
> Praised be Thy Name and Thy omnipotence
>   By every living creature, since it is fitting
>   To give Thee thanks for Thy sweet influence.
> The peace of Thy dominion come unto us,
>   For unto it we cannot go of ourselves,
>   If it come not, with all our intellect.
> Even as thine own angels make sacrifice
>   Of all their will to Thee, singing Hosanna,
>   So may all men make sacrifice of theirs.
> Give unto us this day our daily manna,
>   Without which in this rough wilderness
>   Backward he goes who toils most to advance.
> And even as the trespass we have suffered
>   We pardon in one another, pardon Thou
>   Benevolently, nor judge us by our merit.
> Our strength, which is so easily overcome,
>   Do not try with the ancient Adversary,
>   But as he goads it to wrong, deliver us from him.
> This last petition verily, dear Lord,

Canto XI

Not for ourselves is made, who need it not,
But for the sake of those who've remained behind." [1–24]

Men on earth can pray both for themselves and for the souls of the departed, while the souls in Purgatory can pray only for the living, not for themselves. This shows how life on earth is more whole than life in Purgatory, while life in Paradise is more complete than either of them. Purgatory is the realm where souls must suffer not being fully themselves—a feeling that some who are going through purgation in this life may also experience.

God is the Most High, but He is not limited to this station, given that He is omnipresent. That He is high means that He deserves to be the goal of all our aspirations; that He is everywhere means that we can't hope to find a dark corner anywhere where we can hide from Him. "If I ascend up into heaven, thou art there: if I make my bed in hell, behold, thou art there" [Psalm 139:8]. He is worthy of praise due to His greater love of His first works because these are the secondary creative sources of the universe in the angelic domain, in which all creatures great or small may discover their eternal archetypes.

Here we offer up to God our sense of self-sufficiency, and along with it the sense that the contingent world we live in is also self-sufficient. We tend to see the world around us as existing in its own right; this is the idolatry that results in materialism and makes it such a difficult illusion to overcome.

The manna, our daily bread, is both the spiritual and the material sustenance we need to continue on the Path. If we offer up our own wills, Grace will come to us.

Judgment of others is inseparable from our attempt to establish our own worth, a work that is worthless in God's eyes; to pardon others is to free ourselves from the bonds of self-will.

Here "lead us not into temptation" is applied to the primordial temptation to rely upon our own strength rather than the power of God.

. . . praying for themselves and for us as well
God-Speed, those shades moved on beneath their burdens
Like the ones we sometimes bear in dreams,

The Ordeal of Mercy

Each in his degree, circling in their anguish
  But all of them weary, in that beginning circle
  Purging away the smoke-stains [caligine] of the world.
If these good souls are praying for us here
  Imagine what might be done by for them on earth
  By the prayers of men whose wills are good to the root?
Well may we help them wash away the stains
  They carried here, so that, clean and light
  They may ascend unto the starry wheels! [25–36]

In one sense the dross of the world has very little reality, but it does nonetheless weigh quite heavily on the soul. The burden bourn by these souls is that of unreality, the *caligine* or fog of this world. We usually think of reality as a heavy weight, and imagination as light and airy, but in reality the reverse is true. Here we can see how the sin of Pride inverts the true scale of things.

The will is rooted in goodness, in this world and the next, only if it is given to God; here Dante is saying that if the prayers of souls in Purgatory, who are not yet fully themselves, can be of such help to us, imagine how efficacious the prayers of those who are sanctified while still united with the body in this life can be for them.

"... if I were not prevented by the stone
  That holds down this stiff neck of mine
  Because of which I cannot lift my face,
This one who still lives, but does not name himself
  I would inspect, to see if I might know him,
  And make him pity me my heavy burden.
A Latin I was, born of an illustrious Tuscan;
  Guglielmo Aldobrandeschi was my father;
  I don't know if that name is still remembered.
The ancient blood and legendary deeds
  Of my ancestors so stoked my arrogance
  That, forgetful of our common mother
I held all men in contempt to such degree
  I died of it, as the Sienese well know
  Along with every child in Campagnatico.

Canto XI

> *I am Omberto; I'm not the only one*
>   *That pride has harmed, but all my family too*
>   *It's dragged as well into adversity.*
> *And here's where I must bear the burden for it*
>   *Among the dead, till God is satisfied,*
>   *Since I refused to bear it among the living."*
> *To better hear him, I bent down my face....* [52–73]

Omberto, because of the kind of pride that caused him to scorn his fellow countrymen, cannot see Dante, a fellow Tuscan. He is possessive of his lineage. He might have regarded his ancestry as something that involved him with many people and brought him into relationship with them; instead he essentially isolated himself from his ancestors and consequently became possessive of what he received from them; his pride inverted his sense of kinship and made it a source of alienation. If he could have taken what his ancestors gave him as a way of expanding his sympathy for others, it would have made all the difference in the world.

Dante must walk in a hunched-over position to be able to talk with the souls of the prideful; he can see and speak with these souls because he also has a degree of humility, though in doing so his own invisible pride is being humiliated at the same time; he lowers his head because he believes he will begin his afterlife at this point. In the *Commedia*, Dante is "I" as such. His is the only "I" that goes through the various states represented by the circles of *Inferno* and *Purgatorio*. The reader therefore tends to identify with Dante, which allows him or her to participate in the spiritual purification the *Purgatorio* dramatizes. When he points out the circle of Pride as a possible post-mortem destiny for himself, he is warning the reader not to enclose himself in his or her own "I"; whoever is unwilling to let go of the last vestiges of ego identity is trapped in this circle: "Thou shalt in no wise come out thence till thou hast paid the last farthing" [Matthew 5:26].

> *And one of them....*
>   *Twisting himself beneath the weight that crushed him*
> *Looked up, recognized me, and cried out*

The Ordeal of Mercy

Keeping his eyes arduously fixed upon me
  As, all bent over, I walked along beside them.
"Oh," I asked, "Are you not Oderisi,
  The honor of Gubbio, and honor of that art
  Which in Paris is called 'illumination'?"
"Brother," said he, "more joyous are the panels
  Touched by the brush of Franco Bolognese;
  Part honors I deserve, but he the whole.
In truth I never was so gracious to him
  While I lived, due to my great ambition
  For excellence, on which my heart was bent;
For such vainglory here the price is paid.
  And yet I would not be here, were it not
  That, still having power to sin, I turned to God.
O empty glory of merely human powers,
  How brief the green that lingers on your peak,
  Unless it's followed by an age of grossness!
Though in painting Cimabue believed
  He'd hold the field, now Giotto's all the rage;
  The other's former fame is growing dim.
So one Guido has taken from the other
  [Guido Calavcanti from Guido Guinizzelli]
  The glory of our tongue, and he who'll oust
  Both from their nest might already be born.
  [Dante Aligheri]
Worldly fame is just a breath of wind
  Blowing first toward this side, then toward that
  Which, when it changes sides, changes names." [74–102]

Here Dante encounters the pride of the artist. This form of pride in some ways demonstrates the ephemerality of vanity more than the pride of the politician does. The fame of the poet often outlasts the achievements of the man of action, but since it deals with insubstantial images it more clearly suggests the brevity of all worldly good.

"How brief the green that lingers on your peak / Unless it's followed by an age of grossness!" Here Dante seems to be saying that the fame of great art will only endure if it is not immediately overshadowed by succeeding works. A true spiritual light in a great work of art, however, will illuminate whatever worthy productions come after it, even if they are of lesser excellence, while a worldly glamour attaching to even the greatest achievement will obscure what follows it and make everything dull and opaque, ultimately concealing the significance of the great work itself. This has in many ways been the fate the *Divine Comedy*, which is so often reduced by modern criticism, incapable as it is of recognizing transcendent values, to the status of a "cultural" monument devoid of effective spiritual content.

Omberto speaks to Dante of another shade, traveling with them, whose earthly glory faded before his death:

> ". . . *who is he, of whom you just now spoke?*"
> "*That,*" *he replied,* "*is Provenzan Salvani;*
>   *He is here because he had presumed*
>   *To draw all of Siena into his hands.*
> *Never resting he has traveled thus*
>   *Ever since death; and with such coin he pays*
>   *The debt incurred for too much daring on earth.*"
> *And I:* "*If every spirit who waits until*
>   *The very lip of life before repenting*
>   *Stays long below before he can rise this far,*
> *As long as was the time he spent on earth*
>   (*Unless he's helped by good prayers in abundance*),
>   *How was this one's arrival here allowed?*"
> "*When that one lived in the greatest splendor,*" *he said,*
>   "*He placed himself, all shame being laid aside,*
>   *Willingly on the Campo of Siena,*
> *To take on himself the burden that his friend*
>   *Suffered in the prison-house of Charles,*
>   *Humbling himself, and trembling in every vein.*" [120–138]

Among the chief virtues of Purgatory are loyalty to others and a willingness to pray for them. Salvani expressed these virtues in life by publicly humbling himself to collect ransom for his friend; in reward for this he was admitted to Purgatory proper. Oderisi predicts that Dante will experience a similar humiliation in his coming exile, when he will be dependent upon the charity of others. Dante hints here that he will have to return to the circle of Pride when he dies; in saying this he stands in the place of everyman, since Pride is the root of all sins. Likewise exile is the mark of all earthly existence, even if this truth is not consciously felt. St. John Climacus says:

> ... exile [is] an irrevocable renunciation of everything in one's familiar surroundings that hinders one from attaining the ideal of holiness. Exile is a disciplined heart, unheralded wisdom, an unpublicized understanding, a hidden life, masked ideals. It is unseen meditation, a striving to be humble, a wish for poverty, a longing for what is divine. It is an outpouring of love, a denial of vainglory, a depth of silence.

Climacus speaks of obscurity as intrinsic to exile, but Dante achieved fame; the saint presents it in terms of a conscious choice to become a monk (from the Greek *monos* meaning singular, alone), whereas Dante's exile was forced upon him against his will. But what Dante was really going through was hidden from others despite his fame. No true exile can be based only on individual choice; it is a destiny willed by God.

Canto XI

Editorial Commentary Three:
William Blake and the Commedia

The system of William Blake comprises four ontological levels: Ulro, Generation, Beulah and Eternity; these are epitomized in the following verses:

> *Now I a fourfold vision see*
> *And a fourfold vision is given to me*
> *Tis fourfold in my supreme delight*
> *And three fold in soft Beulas night*
> *And twofold Always. May God us keep*
> *From Single vision & Newton's sleep.*

Ulro is the "single vision" of materialism, according to which even the existence of human consciousness is sometimes denied. Generation is made up of "contraries" or polarities, including male and female; it is the realm of development: "Without Contraries there is no Progression" said Blake in *The Marriage of Heaven and Hell*. Beulah is a dreamy lunar world where "contrarieties are equally true," a world of lyric beauty and sexual union; its threefold quality indicates that the union of opposites (though not their complete transcendence and integration) posits a third term, just as sexual union will produce a child. And Eternity is the Solar world of the Always So, the world of the Imagination, of the Human Form Divine, where all polarities are resolved, including the polarity of the sexes. In terms of the *Divine Comedy*, Ulro would then correspond to Hell, Generation to Purgatory, Beulah to the Earthly Paradise, and Eternity to the Celestial Paradise. In alchemical terms, Hell is analogous to Lead, the condition in which all possibilities and polarities are chaotically crushed together, including the polarity of Essence and Being; Blake's Satan is an *hermaphroditic* amalgam of all possible states. Purgatory would be the alchemical regime itself with its continuing process of *solve et coagula*, "dissolve and solidify," leading to the Silver of the Earthly Paradise. And Paradise proper would correspond to Gold, the *magnus opus* or final fruit of the alchemical process, the complete *androgenous* union of solidity and radiance where Essence and Being are not chaotically mixed together but rather exist in a *polar unity* in which form, rather than obscuring Reality, unveils It.

Canto XII

Now Dante surveys twelve examples of Pride carved into the pavement beneath his feet: those of Lucifer, Briareus (representing the Titans), Nimrod, Niobe, Saul, Arachne, Rehoboam, Eriphyle, Sennacherib, Cyrus, Holofernes, and the city of Troy. The appearance of the Angel of Humility. The travelers ascend to the Second Terrace, that of the Envious. The first P is erased from Dante's forehead.

> *Abreast, like oxen pulling in a yoke,*
> *I traveled on beside that burdened soul,*
> *As long as my kind pedagogue allowed;*
> *But when he told me, "Leave him, and pass on,*
> *For here it's best that with wings and oars together,*
> *Each one push his boat as hard as he can,"*
> *I stood upright again, as is appropriate*
> *For those who walk; nonetheless my thoughts*
> *Remained within me prostrate and ashamed.* [1–9]

The wings are aspiration, the oars are the will to follow aspiration's lead. Boats are normally moved by sails, not wings; that wings replace sails here suggests that the essence of spiritual aspiration is an openness to the wind of the Spirit.

Humility must be deeply interiorized. If we are asked to stand erect, it is for the sake of having been made in the image of God, not on account of our personal achievements. Although the act of prostration is important in Eastern Christianity, in the Orthodox liturgy the worshippers are exhorted over and over again to "stand aright"; on Sundays Orthodox Christians are required to stand, not kneel.

Now Dante sees the images of various figures emblematic of Pride; they are carved upon the pavement beneath his feet, beginning with Lucifer and the giant Briareus.

Canto XII

Upon one side I saw him who had been
  Created more noble than all other creatures,
  Down from heaven fall, flaming with lightnings;
On the other side I saw Briareus
  Lying smitten by the celestial shaft
  Heavy upon the earth in mortal cold. [25–30]

Lucifer represents the pride of being Godlike through knowledge; the Giants symbolize the pride of being Godlike through vast energies, through the appropriation of the Divine Uncreated Energies that St. Gregory Palamas speaks of by the individual self-will. According to Greek myth, the Giants or Titans were an earlier race of divine beings whom the Gods defeated. The Gods triumphantly surveying the Giants they have overcome represent the ego's attempt, through Pride, to appropriate and claim the virtues, thereby perverting them.

Lucifer and Briareus are succeeded by Nimrod, Niobe, Saul, Arachne, Rehoboam, Eriphyle, Sennacherib, Cyrus and Holofernes, and finally by the image of Troy; these twelve make up the "zodiac" of Pride.

Nimrod, the "great hunter" who built the Tower of Babel, is the pride of what René Guénon called "the counter-initiation," the Promethean counterfeit of the spiritual Path, as if man himself could construct a way to God instead of waiting for it to be given by God.

Niobe boasted that she was better than the Titan Leto, mother of Artemis and Apollo, because she had borne seven sons and seven daughters—an affront for which Leto killed all her children and turned her to stone. The pride of Niobe is to identify with Life itself, the Great Goddess. Even though her pride is that of a mother, it is similar in many ways to the pride of the feminists, whose battle-cry is "our bodies, ourselves!"; they attempt to own the Divine Creativity. The result of this pride is for Niobe to be turned to stone; all actual Life is being drained from her by her pride; her tears, mentioned by Dante, are the last remnant of this Life finally leaving her.

Saul, the first King of the Jews, later lost God's favor to David. Saul should have seen that his kingship was from God, that if God could give it he could also take it away, and that after God's anointing was removed from him and transferred to David he was no longer king, any more than Lear was king after he threw away his crown. This shows how we need to treat all our talents and whatever worldly position may come to us not as intrinsic to our characters but as gifts of God; there is no such thing as a "self-made man."

Arachne challenged Athena to a weaving contest, and won. In punishment the enraged goddess tore her cloth and struck her with the shuttle. Arachne then hanged herself, after which Athena changed the rope into a spiderweb and Arachne into a spider. Arachne's pride is a woman's pride; she believes that she herself is the Creator, the weaver of destinies and of the very matrix of things. This form of pride produces the kind of woman who puts all her energy into social manipulation as if it were her prerogative to assign fates to others. The fruit of this is for such a woman to lose her human characteristics and develop a cold-heartedness that is insect-like; she becomes an *arachnid*.

Rehoboam was a son of King Solomon. He was exiled because, in rebelling against the true king his father, he turned against his own people to rule over them as a tyrant. This is the pride that results in the use of authority for self-aggrandizement instead of for the care of the people placed in one's charge.

Eriphyle was bribed by the gift of a necklace to betray her husband Amphiaraus' hiding-place to his enemies; in revenge for this crime she was slain by her son Alcmaeon. Eriphyle's pride is the pride of possessiveness; she betrays the interiority of her relationship with her husband, the Spirit, for the sake of the outer ornament of social vanity. Her betrayal of Amphiarius is emblematic of the kind of spiritual divorce that robs so many children of their fathers, as we have seen in our own time. Eriphyle thought that if she got rid of her husband she could have exclusive power over her son Alcmaeon, but in betraying his father she robs him of the archetype of manhood, transforming him into a mad dog who ultimately destroys her. Here we start to see the beginning of the destruction not only of individual souls but of civilization itself.

Sennacherib was a king of Assyria who invaded the kingdom of Judah. In attacking Judah, Sennacherib is attacking those closest to God; this is a precursor of the persecution of the Church, and of

Canto XII

pneumatics everywhere, by materialistic civilization. In punishment, God smites his army with a plague during the siege of Jerusalem; he flees the field of battle, and is ultimately assassinated by his own sons. Here we can see how the bond between father and son, the chain of the generations, is broken in any civilization ruled by materialism; such a civilization will inevitably tear itself apart.

Cyrus was the greatest king of the Persians, the good king who defeated the Babylonians, released the Jews from exile, and sponsored the restoration of the Temple at Jerusalem. Later, after he slew the son of Tomyris, Queen of Scythia, the Queen had him beheaded and his head plunged in a basin of blood as an ironic tribute to his bloodthirstiness. The good and wise king is the virtuous example, the representative of the essential values that guide civilization; when he is destroyed, civilization is at a loss for guidance, and consequently perishes. Queen Tomyris here represents the lower soul in rebellion against the higher faculties; it was in a similar spirit that the Bacchae, the orgiastic female devotees of Dionysus, beheaded King Pentheus of Thebes. She immerses the severed head of Cyrus in blood as if to suffocate the higher qualities themselves in the flood of the passions; she does not mean to kill simply a man, but a principle.

Holofernes was the general of King Nebuchadnezzar of Assyria; he ordered the Jews to worship the king as a god. They prayed for his pride to be humbled, after which Judith entered his tent at the siege of Bethulia and beheaded him [Judith 13]. Holofernes, unlike Cyrus, is the servant of an evil ruling principle; now that the true king is gone, a false idolatrous king can be set up in his place, one who will seemingly give divine validation to the passions; the result of this is that Nebuchadnezzar goes mad and falls to the level of the subhuman instincts, crawling on all fours and eating grass like the beasts of the field [Daniel 4:31–33]. Judith represents the wholeness of the soul that rightly rejects the false idol that stands in the place of the higher faculties but in no way serves them; she is Holy Wisdom in the guise of Divine Justice.

"I saw there Troy in caverns and in ashes." The fate of Troy bespeaks the destruction of civilization. Was Dante predicting even the destruction of Christian civilization? We can't be sure, but he did understand that civilization as such, the entire human collective, can

The Ordeal of Mercy

be brought low through pride. The Roman Emperors, according to Virgil's *Aeneid*, traced their lineage back to Troy through Aeneas, as the English kings did through Brutus, as recounted by Geoffrey of Monmouth in his *History of the Kings of Britain*. And the Church adopted Roman civilization as a basis upon which to build western Christendom; thus all western civilization can be traced back, in mythical terms, to Troy. Here Dante shows how a civilization's pride in its exalted origins can be a worm within its collective soul.

Christian faith is a humble quality; it existed before Christian civilization came about, and in the form of a Christian Remnant it will survive this civilization's destruction. It will carry the Christian spirit, which was the spirit of that civilization, within its hidden soul. But the very humiliation of a civilization can sometimes preserve its spiritual essence; this in many ways was the experience of the Russian Orthodox Church under communism. The ruins of Troy are depicted as caverns and ashes. The caverns suggest the Christian catacombs—the ashes, humility and spiritual poverty.

> *What master of the stylus or the brush*
>   *Could render such fine outlines and such shadows*
>   *Enough to cause each subtle mind to wonder?*
> *The dead seemed dead, the living seemed alive;*
>   *Those who saw them directly saw no better*
>   *Than I who trod with bowed head on those scenes.*
> *With gaze held high, continue in your pride*
>   *You sons of Eve, and don't bow down your faces*
>   *For fear you might behold your evil ways!* [64–72]

The images Dante witnesses, carved in the pavement beneath his feet, are so true to life because he is confronted by the spiritual essence of the incidents they depict, which carry all the reality of the actual events, while situating them beyond time. This is what William Blake would call the Divine Imagination, and Henry Corbin (following Islamic cosmology), the *alam al-mithal*, the Imaginal Plane; any art drawn from this level of being is truly inspired. Dante walks upon these portraits instead of viewing them as in a gallery because the lessons they depict are a real path for him. According to earthly time, *all* the figures here depicted are among the dead, but according to a spiritual evaluation it's the damned who are dead, and the saved who are alive. Dante needs to distinguish between the two here, because what's alive will now help him in his ascent, just as what's dead will hinder him.

The sons of Eve (as opposed to the "sons" of the Virgin) are those on the path of *avidya-maya*. That Dante curses them to persist in their sin is ironic, since those on a truly evil path usually go deeper and deeper into ignorance come what may, and rarely see the road they have taken. So the curse is really an insight: if these souls were to see the evil of their path, that would already be the beginning of a *metanoia*, leading them to take a different road.[1]

> "Look, here comes an angel, hurrying
> To approach us. . . ." [79–80]

> *Towards us now the beautiful being advanced*
> *Dressed all in white, and his countenance*
> *Seemed to us like the twinkling morning star;*
> *He opened first his arms and then his wings.*
> *"Come," said he, "the steps are near at hand;*
> *The ascending path is easy from here on."* [88–93]

> *So few care to answer that invitation!*
> *Why, O human creatures, born to fly,*
> *Are you blown over by so slight a wind?* [94–96]

---

1. In the *Inferno* [III:64–69], Dante defines the practice of human art as an imitation of God's mode of creation rather than simply of the outer forms of nature—as a reflection of *natura naturans*, that is, not *natura naturata*. In line with this theory, the living images Dante now encounters in Purgatory should be seen not as the reproductions of historical forms and events but as their timeless prototypes; in Blake's terminology, they represent Inspiration, not Memory. Likewise the religious *exoterics* will imitate the outer forms of their religion, while the *esoterics* remain in touch with the ongoing flow of revelation that brought their religion into being and continues to maintain it, instant by instant. The present book follows Dante's method in that it treats the *Divine Comedy* not as a finished artifact but as a guide inviting the reader to open his or her consciousness to Dante's own sources of inspiration in the celestial order.

The Ordeal of Mercy

This angel, who is compared to the twinkling morning star, by opening his arms and spreading his wings is calling upon Dante to expand his vision; as is indicated by the bent stance the travelers must assume to view the representations of arrogance and its downfall, pride narrows one's vision and lowers one's aspirations. This angel is the true morning star because he empties himself and opens to higher vision, while Lucifer—who is identified with the morning star in scripture, the star closest to the sun just as Lucifer was the angel closest to God—though he originated from a high station, filled himself up with himself, and fell. The morning star is the perfect image of humility; even though it's in its own way glorious, it is nonetheless submissive. It heralds the sun, which is greater than it is—and when the sun rises, it must disappear.

"So slight a wind": This slight wind is the Spirit's call to the soul to become humble and receptive; the proud cannot withstand even the touch of it. Pride drives people back toward bestiality; it does not allow them to perform the spiritual ascent they were born for.

> *He led us on to where the rock was cleft;*
> *And there he struck my forehead with his wings,*
> *Promising me safe passage from then on.* . . . [97–99]

> *The bold abruptness of the ascent was broken*
> *By a flight of stairs, placed there in an age*
> *Before ledger and measure became corrupt.* [103–105]

That records and measures could be trusted in the ancient time when the Mount of Purgatory was constructed indicates that in those days the world was closer to the Logos as such, where the true measure and the true account of all things, past present and future, remains as it always was.

> *Now that we were upon the sacred stairs*
> *The climb appeared far easier for some reason*
> *Than it had been while traveling across the plain.*
> *"Tell me, my Master—what heavy weight*
> *Has been lifted from me, so that now I feel*

Canto XII

Hardly any fatigue as I keep walking?"
He answered: "When the P's that still remain
*   Upon your face, though they're more faded now*
*   Shall wholly be erased, as was the first*
Your feet will be so mastered by good will
*   That not only will they experience no fatigue*
*   But climbing up will give them great delight."*
Then I continued just like those who walk
*   With something on their head they cannot see*
*   Till other people's gestures rouse suspicion,*
To satisfy which the hand is better suited
*   To learn the state of things, and so completes*
*   The work that eyes themselves could not accomplish.*
So, spreading out the fingers of my right hand
*   I felt on my forehead only six remaining letters*
*   Of the seven that he who held the keys had carved;*
When he saw me doing this, my Leader smiled. [115–136]

   That the six remaining P's have become fainter now that the first P is gone indicates that when pride is removed from the soul, all the other sins lose part of their foundation. We commonly see pride as a power that helps us rise to higher things—but the truth is that it's much easier to climb without pride, which weighs us down and locks us in our lower selves.

   Now Dante can see himself as others see him whereas before he could not, because pride had locked him into himself; the essence of both gnosis and Liberation is to know yourself not as you appear in your own eyes, but precisely as you are known by God. Sight is the emblem of the intellective faculty, while touch is the most existential of the senses; Dante verifies that the first P has been erased from his forehead with touch not with sight because it is his being itself which has been unburdened. Only when he tries his will and finds it more responsive and submissive to the Will of God does he understand intellectively that the weight of pride has been removed from him.

Canto XIII

The Terrace of the Envious. Virgil praises the sun. The voices of two souls are heard, one of whom is Orestes. The punishment of the Envious: to have their eyelids sewn shut.

The envious, more than the proud, can draw one into their whirlpool. Envy is infectious; this is why gossip is so dangerous.

> *"If we linger here, hoping we might question*
>   *The people who pass," The Poet said, "I fear*
>   *Our choice of path will be too long delayed."*
> *Then steadfast on the sun he set his eyes,*
>   *And, guided by the right side of his body,*
>   *He turned his left side toward a new direction.*
> *"O thou sweet light! Trusting in you I enter*
>   *On this new path; along it may you guide us*
>   *As guided we must be when in this kingdom.*
> *You warm the world, shining over it;*
>   *Unless a different reason calls us elsewhere,*
>   *Your rays should be our guides for evermore!"* [10–21]

The sun is the most visible natural symbol of the Spirit. In the words of St. Dionysius the Areopagite:

> What praise is not demanded by the blaze of the sun? For it is from the Good that its light comes, and it is itself an image of the Good.... I am certainly not asserting in the manner of the ancients that the sun actually governs the visible world as god and maker of the universe. But since the creation of the world, the invisible mysteries of God, thanks to his eternal power and godhead, are grasped by the intellect through the creatures. [*Divine Names* IV, 4]

Canto XIII

In other words, the natural intuition of the Spirit must be followed until one is called to something higher, to full Intellection informed by Revelation. The sun gives its light and warmth—its insight and affection—to everything and everyone it looks upon, unlike envy which is partial rather than objective and withdraws affection out of spite.

> . . . *we heard spirits flying towards us—*
> *Though they could not be seen—spirits voicing*
> *Courteous invitations to the table of Love.*
> *The first of the voices flying past cried out*
> *"Vinum non habent. . . ."* [25–29]

By saying *Vinum non habent*, "they have no wine," the Virgin Mary prevailed upon Jesus to perform his first public miracle, the transformation of water into wine at the marriage feast of Cana [John 2]. A wedding is the height of worldly joy for the married couple, and as such can easily draw envy; the wine miraculously produced from water, however, manifests emotional openness and generosity, virtues in whose presence envy cannot develop. (Insofar as a wedding can symbolize union of the soul with God the Bridegroom, the envy of another's spiritual attainments may also be suggested here.)

One of these invisible spirits names himself as Orestes [line 33]. Orestes, a Mycenaean prince, killed his mother Clytemnestra for the murder of his father, King Agamemnon, upon the King's return from the Trojan war. During his absence Clytemnestra had been involved in an adulterous affair, and so we are being presented here with a situation obviously fuelled by sexual jealousy. When Orestes is tried for matricide, his companion Pylades attempts to impersonate him and be executed in his place. Orestes does not allow Pylades to sacrifice himself, however, but reveals his identity to the court. Envy involves the desire to be someone else. The envied person is the one who has "stolen" your sense of self; by being transformed into him, you hope—absurdly—to become yourself again. But in the case of Orestes and Pylades, the identification of one with the other, which in this case is based not on envy but on love, is rejected in the name of a still greater love. Each is content to be himself, and suffer his own destiny, without trying to steal a different destiny from the other, as envy will often attempt.

Pylades did not want Orestes to suffer for his crime; Orestes did not want Pylades to suffer for a crime he did not commit. This reminds us of Charles Williams's doctrine of "exchange and substitution," through which one can formally agree to take on the suffering of another, just as Christ suffered for all of us. In both cases these two friends wanted to spare the other the fate of death; Charles Williams would see this as an intrinsically Christian act. That Pylades was not prevented from taking on Orestes' fate served justice because it allowed Orestes be punished for his own crime; nonetheless, both friends strengthened the bond of friendship between them by being willing to die for the other: "No greater love hath a man than that he lay down his life for his friend" [John 15:13]. When Dante, as Ananda Coomaraswamy has pointed out, uses Pagan symbols to illustrate Christian truths, he demonstrates the universality of Christianity. The Christian revelation was not some strange eastern cult that imposed its worldview on the Pagan world; it was inherently universal from the beginning, which is why the Church calls itself "Catholic." This very universality is what enables it to bring salvation.

> ... *the third [spirit] was saying*
> *"Love the ones from who you've suffered evil!"*
> *And my good Master said: "This circle scourges*
> *The sin of envy—and that's the reason*
> *The lashes of the scourge are drawn from Love."* [35–39]

"Love your enemies" is in some ways an impossible command. If you recognize someone as your enemy, how can you love him? And we often envy or are jealous of people who have actually stolen something from us, not simply slighted us in our own minds. Envy has to do with a confusion in one's of sense of self, a loss of identity through identification with another; it's almost like a negative form of hero-worship. The radical command to love your enemies is a call to empty yourself of yourself; if you can accomplish this, your little ego-identity, your false self, will be annihilated. But no one can simply will to love his enemies; this command calls for a deeper change than personal will can produce. To pray for the power to forgive is necessary, but not sufficient; true forgiveness comes only by the Grace of God.

If someone is in a state of envy, that person's affections and perceptions have been displaced; he no longer feels what he really feels or sees what he really sees. He needs to ask himself not "how can I be like someone else or have what they have?", but "how can I be like myself? How can I *be* myself?" If he asks this question in sincerity, it will lead to self-acceptance; the burden of trying to be something that he is not, to be someone other than who he is—the burden of envy—is lifted from him. We cannot submit to or receive God's will for us, we cannot practice true obedience, if we are not willing to be ourselves.

That "The lashes of the scourge are drawn from Love" shows that the way to move beyond envy is to expand *into* love. If you are in a state of envy this expansion will inevitably bring pain; this pain is the beginning of the love of enemies. Those embedded in the state of envy who choose to expand through love are thus also being given an opportunity for deep self-sacrifice.

> *Then, even wider than before, I opened my eyes;*
> *Looking ahead, I saw souls dressed in mantles*
> *Identical in color to the surrounding rock.* [46–48]
>
> *I can't believe there's a man who walks the earth*
> *With heart so hard it wouldn't be pierced with pity*
> *To see what next presented itself to my sight:*
> *For when I had drawn near enough to those shades*
> *So I could clearly make out how they moved*
> *Heavy grief was wrung from my eyes in tears.*
> *They seemed to me to be covered with coarse burlap,*
> *And the one supported the other with his shoulder*
> *As all of them were supported by the bank.*
> *They looked to me just like blind men, fighting hunger,*
> *Who stand at the doors of churches begging alms,*
> *One leaning his head upon the other. . . .* [52–63]

The Ordeal of Mercy

These souls are the color of the surrounding rocks because they have lost their particularity through envy; they are no longer themselves. The shades are leaning upon each other because in losing their particular natures they have lost the independence they would need to stand on their own ground. On the other hand, the fact that they are able to help each other walk signals a reversal of the way they had been in life; envy entangles itself with the other only to hurt, not help.

> *. . . to the shades, of whom I just now spoke,*
> *The light of Heaven would not give itself;*
> *For their eyelids were sewn up with iron wire,*
> *Just as the eyes of untamed hawks are sewn*
> *Because their troubled spirit knows no rest.* [68–72]

The eyes of the envious are sewn shut because they have narrowed their perception through their sin, along with other qualities of the soul such as generosity and compassion; they have done this in order to protect their ego-identities, their little selves. That envy involves a misuse of perception is shown by the fact that envious people are continually imagining what the people they are envious of are doing and feeling and what their motives might be; envy is always involved with gossip, spying and paranoia. They are compared to hooded hawks because what they saw through envy, or thought they saw, deeply distracted these souls, causing them to fly off, looking for more "dirt" on the objects of their envy.

> *It seemed to me an outrage, while passing by*
> *To see the others without being seen. . . .* [73–74]

Those who are forced into obscurity through oppression, who see but are never seen, will often be tempted to the sin of envy. It is one of the ploys of rulers of the darkness of this world to "divide and conquer" their victims by flattering some so as to manipulate them through pride, and slighting others so as to control them through envy. In some ways envy is a form of negative or inverted pride; it is pride projected. In life these souls were compelled to "see" injustice,

Canto XIII

or what they took to be injustice, while not themselves being seen; they were forced to suffer in silence. But now they are in the opposite condition; though they are blind, they can be seen, and pitied. Dante feels he is being discourteous to these souls because he can see them while they cannot see him; he senses that he has an unfair advantage over them, and immediately renounces it. He is able to show them pity, and they, though blind, are able to receive it; through this compassionate attention they are being healed of the wounds to their self-respect that tempted them to the sin of envy in the first place. God's compassion is irresistible to those who choose not to resist it; it pierces all barriers, and when we are blind it penetrates the pores of our skin. Nothing in this world can deny us the vision of Paradise once purgation has made us worthy of it.[1]

The envious are unable to love; they have been wounded *through* love because they have not seen it for what it really is, and have therefore been led to misuse their faculty of spiritual sight. According to a convention of the courtly love tradition, love enters the heart through the eyes, but in this case love has entered not the heart but the ego, and been transformed into hate. They need to move *back* through this wounded love by expanding *into* love. The proud want to lord it over others; the envious simply want to protect themselves from emotional pain. Nonetheless both have departed from love and entered the ego in a vain attempt to achieve these ends. The envious are purged by temporary blindness because they must withdraw from sight for a time in order to learn to use sight more wisely.

> *I turned to them, and said: "You people, certain*
> *That one day you'll behold the highest light,*
> *Which in this place has become your sole desire,*
> *May grace most quickly clear away the scum*

---

1. It is one of the errors of Liberation Theology and other forms of the "social Gospel" to consider the envy that the oppressed feel for their oppressors as always justified and never sinful, simply because oppression also is a sin. But two wrongs don't make a right. If oppression generates envy, envy also supports oppression. How could envy serve justice? To envy one's oppressors is to wish to become like them.

The Ordeal of Mercy

> *Upon your conscience, so the stream of memory*
> *Can flow through it in perfect clarity. . . ."* [85–90]

Dante's mention of "the stream of memory" indicates that these souls no longer need to repress what has happened to them, but can easily accept it. They were envious because they had cut off part of themselves, but now they can remember themselves. To remember (the opposite of "dis-member") is to return to their wholeness, and consequently also to remember God.

> *"Tell me—for the news would be most welcome—*
> *If any soul among you is Italian;*
> *It may also profit him for me to learn it."*
> *"All of us are citizens, O my brother*
> *Of the one true city; but you mean to ask,*
> *Who may have passed through Italy as a pilgrim. . . ."*
> [91–96]

Souls undergoing purification—sometimes called "good" or "holy" souls—know that they were pilgrims in life because they are pilgrims now in Purgatory; Heaven is their true homeland.

> *Among the rest I saw a shade that waited;*
> *If any ask what gave me that impression,*
> *Its chin was lifted upwards like a blind man's.*
> *"Spirit," I said, "who humbles yourself to rise,*
> *If you're the one who made that answer to me,*
> *Make yourself known to me by place or name."*
> *"I was Sienese" she answered, "and*
> *With the others here I mend my guilty life,*
> *Weeping to Him that He grant to us Himself.*
> *Sapia—though sapient I was not—*
> *Was once my name, and at another's harm*
> *Much more than at my own good I rejoiced.*
> *And, lest you suspect I might deceive you,*
> *Hear if I was as foolish as I've told you.*
> *The arc of my years was already declining,*

Canto XIII

> *When my fellow-citizens in the region of Colle*
>   *Were joined in battle with their adversaries,*
>   *And I was praying to God for what He willed.*
> *They were routed—turned into the bitter*
>   *Passes of flight; and I, while watching them,*
>   *Felt a joy surpassing any other;*
> *So that I lifted high my defiant face*
>   *Crying to God, 'From now on I don't fear You!...'"*
>   [100–122]

> *"Peace with God I sought at the extremity*
>   *Of my life...."* [124–125]

Sapia has forsaken wisdom. It was her true destiny to embody wisdom, as is symbolized by her name—Sapia = *sapientia*. But as soon as she cries out that she no longer fears God, she departs completely from any wisdom that she might have partaken of; if "the fear of the Lord is the beginning of wisdom," the lack of such fear is the abortion of it. When she sought peace at the end of her life she took the first step toward regaining wisdom; her envy, and her wish for other people's downfall, indicates that she thought she didn't need them, that she considered herself self-sufficient; so part of the restoration of her soul consists in her gratitude that someone else had been willing to pray for her sake: gratitude is the direct opposite of envy.

> *"My eyes," I said, "will here be taken from me*
>   *For only a little time; my sin is small*
>   *Measured by the times they turned to envy.*
> *A far greater fear holds my soul suspended,*
>   *Fear of that heavier torment underneath;*
>   *Even now its load weighs hard upon me."*
> *She questioned me: "Who led you, then, among us*
>   *This far up, if you fear to return below?"*
>   *"The spirit who, in silence, walks beside me.*
> *I walk alive; therefore you may ask me*
>   *Chosen spirit, if you'd have me take*

The Ordeal of Mercy

> *My mortal steps beyond on your behalf."*
> *"This is such a rare and wondrous thing"*
>   *She answered, "It must stand as a great sign*
>   *Of God's love for you: so help me in my prayer.*
> *I beg you now, in the name of your heart's desire*
>   *If ever again you walk the Tuscan soil*
>   *To see my name restored among my kindred.*
> *You will find them, friend, among that foolish people*
>   *Who trust in Talamone, but there will lose*
>   *More than they did when digging for Diana—*
> *Though the admirals will lose the most of all."* [133–154]

Dante speaks here only as a penitent, making no mention of his worldly identity; he has learned to put first things first. And how courteous Dante is to Sapia; instead of mentioning the fact that he will soon ascend to higher terraces than the one in which she is undergoing her trials, he only mentions lower terraces and the sins he will have to expiate there. Neither does he reveal Virgil's identity to her; at this point Virgil is merely his silent Guide; he has begun to leave his personal identity behind in Hell.

Dante's encounter with Sapia establishes what Purgatory really is: a deep relatedness between souls who are connected in inner ways that have no necessary outer expression. Dante is saying that he has enough of an affinity with Sapia to meet her in his vision of Purgatory, and that the best use of this meeting is to allow him to complete his journey, return to mortal life and pray for her. And his simple ability to ascend means that he has more strength to aid her. The envious do not want to see others rise above them, and so can receive no help from them, whereas this soul is learning from Dante that it is in her best interest for him to ascend the Mountain, to progress on the spiritual Path, so that he can help her.

Talamone was a small Tuscan harbor, bought by the Sienese in 1303. They tried to convert it into a major seaport to rival Genoa, an expensive operation that ultimately failed. The Diana was an underground river which, according to legend, flowed beneath Siena; the Sienese poured a lot of time and money into an attempt to find it. Sapia is able to predict a loss that will be coming to the Sienese due

Canto XIII

to their envy of Genoa's commercial success. Siena wanted to *be* Genoa as it were, and so instead of the Sienese looking to what they really possessed, they simply tried to imitate her, and therefore suffered loss. They are shown as being driven by *fantasy* to exhaust their resources, first by trying to set up a port in an unsuitable location, then by digging for a mythic river; the sin of Envy, as a misuse of the faculty of spiritual perception, is based on fantasy and supposition.

Canto XIV

The travelers encounter Guido del Duca and Riniero de Calboli. Guido, at some length, denounces various Italian cities and individuals. The travelers hear the voices of spirits who fell through Envy: Cain and Aglauros.

Here Dante is accosted by two spirits:

> *The first one said: "O soul who, still enclosed*
>   *Within the body, travels toward the heavens,*
>   *For charity's sake console us, and declare*
> *Where it is you come from, and who you are;*
>   *We marvel at the grace that you've received*
>   *As at a wonder never before beheld."*
> *And I: "Through midst of Tuscany there wanders*
>   *A little stream that is born in Falterona,*
>   *Its course is done in less than a hundred miles;*
> *From by its banks I bring this body to you.*
>   *To name myself would be to speak in vain,*
>   *Because that name is not yet widely known."* [10–21]

Dante alludes of course to the river Arno, which waters Florence; one of the spirits now discourses on the spiritual state of that city:

> *"It's best that the name of such a valley perish;*
> *For from its source at the point where towering mountains*
>   *Are split from Pelorus—and few the ranges*
>   *That reach such altitude, much less surpass it—*
> *To the place where it yields itself in restoration*
>   *Of what the heavens have sucked up from the sea,*
>   *To replenish what is carried by the rivers,*
> *Everyone there sees virtue as a foe*

Canto XIV

And flees from it as if it were a snake,
  By evil custom, or else the land is cursed,
Which is why they've all so changed their nature
  The residents of that God-forsaken valley,
  It seems as if Circe kept them in her sty.
Past ugly pigs, better fed on acorns
  Than finer food for human use created,
  It starts to take its poor and meager way.
Next in its descent it encounters dogs,
  Whose snarling bark is much worse than their bite,
  And turns its muzzle away from them in scorn.
It keeps on falling, and the more it grows,
  The more it finds the dogs becoming wolves—
  This hopeless ditch, luckless and accursed.
Flowing down through many a hollow gulf,
  Next it runs into foxes so fat with fraud,
  The trap has not been made they cannot slip." [30–54]

The people there flee from virtue, from the higher vision which is related to the sky, and place their attention on the earth, the serpent; their "supernaturally natural" attraction to the Spirit, diverted to false ends, is the very thing that inflames their materialistic obsessions. This reminds us of how some Christians are deeply suspicious of metaphysical ideas and spiritual wisdom, which they see as intellectual pride, if not "Gnosticism"; they flee them, not understanding that they are the fruit and fulfillment of the Christian life. In Eden the Serpent appeared as wisdom, but was really deception and subversion; here it appears as an enemy, whereas in reality it is virtue. This inversion indicates how in Purgatory the effects of the Fall are reversed. And just as the water of the Arno must flow downward and return to the Ocean before the sky, the realm of the Spirit, can sublimate it and return it to its Source to fall as pure rain, so the souls in purgation must get to the very bottom of their sins before they can be purified of them.

When the human population of a region degenerates, nature degenerates along with it. Humans overcome by their passions have lost the use of reason, like Odysseus' men when they were trans-

The Ordeal of Mercy

formed into pigs by the witch Circe. Here the pigs are concupiscence; the dogs, meanness; the wolves, organized predation; the foxes, low cunning in service to criminal ends.

> *The speech of the one and aspect of the other*
>   *Had formed in me the desire to know their names;*
>   *So, somewhere between question and entreaty*
> *I asked, at which the spirit who'd spoken first*
>   *Began again: "You're asking me to perform*
>   *For you a thing you would not do for me;*
> *But since God wills that in you should shine forth*
>   *Such grace of His, I will not be ungenerous;*
>   *Know, then, that Guido del Duca is my name.*
> *My blood was so set on fire with burning envy,*
>   *That if ever I saw another making merry*
>   *You would have seen my own face turning pale.*
> *From my own sowing, here's the straw I reap!*
>   *O human race! Why do you place your heart*
>   *Where equal sharing is prohibited?"* [73–87]

This soul is beginning to grow beyond itself here, to overcome envy by being willing to reveal its identity even though Dante enjoys the privilege of not having to reveal his. In regarding the Spirit in Dante, it is coming into the presence of the Spirit as such, the Power that can lift it out of its misery. Dante is in Purgatory as an esoteric pilgrim, a spiritual traveler; to identify himself under these circumstances would go to build a separate identity and thus block his path, whereas the soul he encounters, in revealing who he is, "gives himself away" as it were. What this soul accomplishes by confession, Dante achieves through discretion. In the words of Christian writer Walter C. Lanyon, apparently paraphrasing a verse from Proverbs, "He that holdeth his tongue shall take a city."

Guido del Duca now recites a long litany of Tuscan political and social degeneracy, and ends by saying,

> *"But go now, Tuscan; it delights me more*
>   *To weep at what we've said than to keep on talking,*
>   *So much has our discourse disturbed my mind."* [124–126]

Canto XIV

Envy pushes us toward pettiness and worldly concerns, and this whole recitation of political recriminations and bitter gossip perfectly illustrates such pettiness. Perhaps it bored the contemporaries of Dante as much as it bores us today to hear it—or perhaps it drew from them the kind of low fascination that is often produced in our own time by shallow celebrity gossip. When they are finished, Virgil chides Dante for paying attention to them, saying that although the sky filled with spiritual beauties stretches above them, he spends his time staring at the ground, chewing over grudges and low concerns that prevent him from placing his attention upon higher things—a failure that God immediately chastises by sending the voices of Cain and Aglauros like lightning. Through gossip and pettiness he is close to falling under the power of the Adversary.

Cain's is the deepest and most impious envy: to envy someone because he is accepted by God. By the mark God places on Cain's forehead He protects him from actually being slain, but He does not protect him from being the one that others *want* to slay, since the mark reveals his identity and his sin; it is as if the mark that protects him also petrifies him within his own envy. Nonetheless Cain is also to be envied: first because he is inviolate—God has declared that whoever slays Cain will be punished seven-fold—and secondly because he is successful in worldly terms, since after his murder of Abel he goes on to found the first city; his ability to build in brick and stone is like a sign of his inner petrification.[1]

So it would seem that to envy Cain is entirely justified: what could be more unfair than for the first murderer to be exalted as the founder of civilization itself? Abel, since he enjoys God's favor, is emblematic of the children of the Spirit, while Cain represents the children of this world. For the materialists who give all their life to the ego, the outer man, to murder the spirituals who cultivate the inner man is a great crime; but for the spirituals to envy the worldlings in turn and seek revenge against them is seven times worse: *corruptio optima pessima*. The worldlings, for all their limitations, have a part to play in God's plan, but for the spirituals to become

---

1. Cain represents agricultural civilization, and Abel the pastoral culture that agricultural city culture eventually marginalized and supplanted.

The Ordeal of Mercy

worldly themselves through envy of the materialists is both a spiritual and a material disaster.

Aglauros too is petrified. She had wanted, like her sister Herse who had a love affair with Mercury, to participate in a mercurial destiny; but instead, through envy, she encounters the opposite fate: as punishment for her interference with their love, the god turns her to stone. Mercury, the patron of merchants, scribes, thieves, spies and traffickers in information, is traditionally associated with the sin of envy.[2]

Mercury is the principle of volatility, yet his curse turns Aglauros to stone. Titus Burckhardt, in *Alchemy: Science of the Cosmos, Science of the Soul*, speaks of the affinity between volatility and petrification in terms of the wrong relationship between Sulfur and Quicksilver, *forma* and *materia*:

> When sulphurous dryness joins one-sidedly with mercurial coldness, so that coagulation and contraction come together (without the action thereon of the expansive heat of Sulphur or the dissolving humidity of Quicksilver), a complete *rigor* of soul and body ensues. In terms of life, this is the torpor of old age, and on the ethical level, avarice. More generally and more profoundly, it is the wrapping up of ego consciousness in itself, a mortal condition of the soul that has lost its original receptivity and vitality, both spiritually and sensually. The other way round, a one-sided conjunction of heat and humidity (i.e. expansion and dissolution) results in a volatilization of powers. It resembles the condition of consuming passion, vice and dissipation of spirit. Characteristically, the two types of disequilibrium are usually found together. One begets the other. The numbing of the powers of the soul leads to dissipation, and the fire of passion lived out regardlessly brings inward death. [127–128]

---

2. See Martin Lings, "The Seven Deadly Sins in Light of the Symbolism of Number" in the anthology *Sword of Gnosis*, edited by Jacob Needleman.

Canto XV

The travelers climb to the Third Terrace, that of the Wrathful. Virgil analyzes anger as based on the sense of insufficiency sinners feel when cut off from God's bounty and the love between souls that exists in Paradise. Dante has a vision of three examples of mildness and long-suffering in the face of insult and injury: the Virgin Mary, Pisistratus and St. Stephen. His vision causes him to weave and stagger. The travelers become immersed in the black smoke of anger.

> *Now that we'd gone far enough around the Mountain*
>   *So we were walking directly toward the west,*
>   *The sunbeams struck the middle of our faces.*
> *That's when I felt my forehead overpowered*
>   *By all that splendor far more than at first*
>   *Till unknown things had filled me with amazement;*
> *So next I joined together my hands and raised them*
>   *To the top of my brow, using them as a visor*
>   *To shade my eyes from that excessive glare.*
> *As when from off the water, or a mirror,*
>   *A sunbeam takes the opposite direction,*
>   *And rises at an angle that's equal to*
> *Its angle of its descent—and also equal*
>   *On both sides from the line of a dropped stone*
>   *(As experiment and science demonstrate,)*
> *So it seemed to me that I was struck*
>   *By a reflected light that flashed before me;*
>   *Before it my vision swiftly turned away.* [7–24]

    Dante overwhelmed by the radiance of the setting sun reminds us of the state affecting people overcome by anger; they are filled with fire. St. Paul was purified of his anger against the Christians by just such a brilliant light on the road to Damascus. Anger is a misapplication of a power—the incensive faculty—that is essentially positive, an energy that is received or understood in too narrow a way. That this light comes from the west indicates that it is not the direct radiance of Heaven, but rather the heavenly light as reflected by the world of outer manifestation; the west symbolizes materiality, just as the east represents spiritual revelation. Manifest existence reflects Divine Reality but does not embody it. The light is here pictured as reflected off of a horizontal surface; this represents the Substantial Pole—the "face of the waters" in the first chapter of Genesis—where the invisible realities of the Essential Pole, the archetypes of all things, appear as if in a mirror.

> *"What wonder if your eyes are still bedazzled*
>   *By the family of high heaven," he answered me;*
>   *"It is an angel, who comes to invite us upward.*
> *Soon to behold these things will be no hardship*
>   *But rather an entire delight to you,*
>   *As much as nature has fashioned you to feel."*
> *As soon as we had reached that blessed angel,*
>   *With joyful voice he told us: "Enter in;*
>   *The stairs here are less steep than those behind."* [28–36]

Virgil explains to Dante that the light he sees, which appears to his eyes as the setting sun, is really the light of an angelic messenger. The Sun represents manifested, cosmic light; the angel, the Source of light itself; the sun of outer manifestation is setting so as to give way to the Divine light. Dante assumes that he is seeing the light of manifestation, but he is actually being dazzled by the light of heaven. Manifested existence is distinct from the Divine Reality, but if we know how to see using our spiritual faculties we can see through the veils of existence to the Divine Reality itself.

The line "As much as nature has fashioned you to feel" indicates that the human form was designed by God to know Him directly. This is our true nature, which we have fallen away from through Adam's sin. The western Church has emphasized the distinction between the natural and supernatural orders so as to guard against pantheism, but this very distinction is, in another way, a product of the Fall: in the words of Frithjof Schuon, the human faculty of spiritual perception is "supernaturally natural," though this natural faculty is rarely awakened without access to revelation.

The shallower stairs indicate that Anger, for all its difficulty, is easier to deal with than Pride and Envy because these sins tend to hide themselves more completely than anger does. When anger does attempt to conceal itself, it often turns into either pride or envy or both, which only results in greater anger later on. As William Blake wrote in his poem "The Poison Tree": "I was angry with my friend / I told my wrath / My wrath did end. / I was angry with my foe / I told it not / My wrath did grow...."

> "What did that spirit of Romagna mean,
> To say that 'equal sharing is prohibited'?"
>   [cf. Canto XIV: 73–87]
> Then he to me: "Of his own greatest failing
>   He knows the harm; therefore do not wonder
>   If he reprove us, to save us from regret.
> Because your desires are directed to that place
>   Where the act of sharing lessens every share
>   Envy works the bellows of your sighs.
> But if the love within the Supernal Sphere
>   Should upwardly direct your aspiration,
>   That fear would not remain within your breast;
> For there, the more that each of us says 'our'
>   That much more of good each one possesses,
>   And greater love within that cloister burns."
> "I am hungrier now to be satisfied," I said
>   "than if I had not opened my mouth to speak
>   And greater uncertainty gathers in my mind.
> How can it be, that good distributed
>   To more recipients will make more wealth
>   For them, than if it's held by just a few?"
> And he to me: "Because your mind's still fixed
>   entirely upon the things of earth,
>   You gather darkness from the very light.

The Ordeal of Mercy

That ineffable and endless Good
   Which lies above us, runneth unto love,
   As to a lucid body flows the sunbeam.
So much it gives of itself as it finds warmth,
   So that, as far abroad as love extends,
   Over it increases the eternal worth.
The more numerous the loving souls above,
   The better they love, and the more of love they share
   Like mirrors, each reflecting all the others.
But if my explanation's missed the mark,
   Beatrice you will certainly see, and she
   Will satisfy this need, and every other." [44–78]

Material goods diminish when shared; spiritual goods increase. This principle was illustrated by Jesus in the miracle of the multiplication of the loaves and fishes [Matthew 14:13–21]. Kindness and compassion are deeply regenerative. If we try to "redistribute the wealth" in a clinical or socialistic way, everyone ultimately has less; envy cannot be overcome by pandering to it. The real spirit of giving is not utilitarian; it might even sometimes exhibit an "impractical" quality of extravagant generosity. But materialistic giving, as Virgil points out, is based on fear—the fear that if our goods are not given they will later be stolen. We don't pay taxes out of a sense of generosity, but only because we fear the consequences of failing to do so. Furthermore, if we were to seek only our own spiritual destiny, our *swadharma*, instead of comparing our fate to the fates of others, envy would be impossible to us. In order to do this, however, we must realize that while the collective good is a very real value, only individual souls—not collectives—can be saved.

This hunger for knowledge on Dante's part invokes greater knowledge—a knowledge inseparable from love—which will ultimately manifest as Beatrice. But hunger for quantitative, materialistic knowledge ultimately diminishes even the knowledge one already has; the soul becomes burdened by facts and assumptions and loses its spiritual insight. Such insight is cultivated partly by overcoming one's greed for worldly information; as the *Tao Te Ching* puts it, "Knowledge is gained by daily increment; the Way is gained by daily loss, loss upon loss until at last comes rest." (A good example of the hunger for worldly, materialistic knowledge is *curiosity*, which is a kind of envy.) Virgil is saying here that Dante has a certain amount of materialistic greed in his desire for knowledge, but that since the knowledge he seeks is spiritual in essence, it will ultimately heal this greed; his hankering for information, based upon doubt, will be put to rest by spiritual certainty. It's easy for us to understand how doubt arises from and produces faithlessness, but Virgil implies that Dante's doubt is fertile since it has to do with facing the unknown. False certainty, on the other hand, is based on an idolatry of what is already known, and is therefore sterile.

The Good here is the Good as such, which is a name of God. Just as polished bodies reflect light, so hearts polished and purified by Love give back the light of the Good. Because they face it directly, not obliquely, they immediately return it to its Source, and in so doing become luminous bodies in themselves; this is what the Virgin Mary was alluding to in the Magnificat when she said "My soul doth magnify the Lord" [Luke 1:46]. And sanctified souls can also be mirrors for each other because each soul is so close to its own essence that it is able to immediately acknowledge the essence of the souls it encounters. This is the meaning of deification or *theosis*; the essence of all souls lives in the being of God. On one occasion St. Seraphim of Sarov and another monk were sitting together in a snowy forest, when the saint was transfigured; his companion saw, shining out from him, the Uncreated Light. As the saint questioned him about what he was seeing, he addressed him as "Your Godliness," indicating that one can see the light of God only *by* the light of God. If the power to witness the glorification of another only comes by virtue of one's own glorification, spiritual envy is at an end.

> *"Strive, then, that the five wounds you still bear*
>   *May quickly be removed, just like the first two—*
>   *Such wounds as heal themselves through suffering."*
> *I was just about to say "I'm satisfied"*
>   *When I saw that we had reached another circle;*
>   *The eagerness of my eyes had made me silent.* [79–84]

The Ordeal of Mercy

The "five wounds," the five sins yet to be expiated, suggest the five wounds of Christ. Pride, with its excess of self-involvement, and envy, which entails an excessive involvement with another, render the soul too opaque for it to achieve contrition by meditating on Christ's passion; these sins absorb the self and destroy all objectivity. It is easier to be objective about the last five sins, however—that is, to clearly understand them as transgressions—which is why it is easier to see beyond them to the saving wounds of Christ.

> *There it appeared to me that in a vision,*
>   *Or ecstasy I was suddenly caught up:*
>   *I saw a crowd of people in a temple,*
> *And at the door a woman, with the sweet*
>   *demeanor of a mother, who was saying:*
>   *"Son, why have you treated us in this way?*
> *Behold, your father and myself in sorrow*
>   *Have sought you everywhere." Here she ceased;*
>   *What had first appeared now quickly vanished.* [85–93]

Jesus, disputing in the Temple with the doctors of the law—the episode that is being alluded to here [Luke 2:41–50]—raises anger to a higher level because He is disputing over Truth. We all know how anger blinds, but it may also sometimes bring insight: if there is such a thing as righteous anger, there is also something that we could call *gnostic* anger, the struggle against falsehood. In order to "hate the sin not the sinner," we must understand sin not purely as a transgression on the part of the will, but also as the orientation of the will to intellectual error. And the expiation of an attachment to falsehood is accomplished in part by Divine Wrath. As St. Maximos the Confessor tells us, "He who loves falsehood is handed over to be harrowed by it, so that by suffering he may come to know what it is he willingly pursued, and may learn by experience that he mistakenly embraced death instead of life." [*Philokalia*, Volume Two, *Second Century on Various Texts*, 43][1]

---

1. This gnostic or prophetic anger was alluded to by William Blake in *The Marriage of Heaven and Hell* when he presented his method of printing using acid-

Canto XV

Mary is gentle to her son Jesus because she has sublimated anger to such a degree that it has become in her a search for God; when she finds Jesus in the Temple, her search is fulfilled; "the finding of the Lord in the Temple" is one of the joyful mysteries of the rosary. Perhaps all anger is really a frustration at being alienated from God, which we project on any object we feel is somehow blocking us in life, not realizing that the barrier to be found within ourselves.

> *Then I beheld another with those waters*
>   *Coursing down her cheeks which grief distills*
>   *When it is born from great disdain of others,*
> *Who said: "If you are ruler of that city*
>   *Whose name produced such strife among the gods,*
>   *Who sends forth shining sparks of every science,*
> *Avenge yourself on those audacious arms*
>   *That clasped our daughter, O Pisistratus";*
>   *Yet that lord, benign and mild, appeared to me*
> *To answer her with serenity in his gaze:*
>   *"What shall we do to those who wish us ill,*
>   *If we even dare to condemn the one who loves us?"* [94–105]

Here the mother, wife of Pisistratus the ruler of Athens, entreats her husband to kill the young man who's had an affair with their daughter. In doing so she seems to be defending her daughter, but this defense is also filled with great anger at her, as Pisistratus understands. (Women in folklore will sometimes represent the lower impulses of the soul—as in the Grimm's tale "The Fisherman and the Fish," for example—as men will sometimes embody the Spirit, as in "Snow White," "Sleeping Beauty" and "Cinderella." The *Divine Comedy* however, in line with the exaltation of the Lady in the Courtly Love tradition, reverses this symbolism.) Not every-

---

etched plates as a symbol of "melting away apparent surfaces and exposing the Infinite which was hid." Blake characterized War and Hunting as the greatest delights of Eternity. Hunting symbolizes the quest for Truth, and War the intellectual struggle over the nature of Truth, reminding us of Ibn al-'Arabi's teaching that "there is war between the Names of God."

The Ordeal of Mercy

thing that presents itself as righteous anger is truly righteous or disinterested.

> *Then I saw a people on fire with wrath,*
>   *Stoning to death a young man in their anger,*
>   *Crying to each other, "Kill him! kill him!"*
> *I saw that man bow down, because of death*
>   *That already weighed upon him, to the earth,*
>   *But he raised his eyes, that were the gates of heaven,*
> *Praying to the high King in the press of battle*
>   *That He would pardon all his persecutors,*
>   *With the look that must unlock the rains of mercy.*
>   [106–114]

St. Stephen fixes his eyes on Heaven, and so brings heavenly grace to earth; he truly illustrates the sublimation of anger. Through his eyes, which transmit heavenly compassion, the recipients of this compassion can gaze into heaven itself; that the grace of God is given and received by the eyes indicates that compassion is not merely a sentiment, but a transcendental way of knowing. (I have always wondered whether the compassion of St. Stephen, which was witnessed by St. Paul who held the garments of those stoning the him to death, was the real seed of Paul's encounter with Christ on the road to Damascus.)

> *As soon as my soul returned to the outer world*
>   *To meet those things outside it which are true,*
>   *I understood the truth of my former errors.*
> *My Leader, who could see me carry myself*
>   *Like a man just then awakening from sleep,*
>   *Said: "What's wrong with you? Why can't you walk?*
> *For more than half a league you have been trudging*
>   *With eyes clouded and with stumbling legs,*
>   *Like someone who's oppressed by wine or sleep."*
> *"O my kind Father, if you'll listen to me,*
>   *I'll tell you all the things I saw within me,*
>   *When my legs were stolen from beneath me."*

Canto XV

> *"Even if you had a hundred masks*
>   *Upon your face they could not hide from me*
>   *Even the slightest of your thoughts"* he said.
> *"You saw what you saw to make sure you wouldn't fail*
>   *To open up your heart to the waters of peace,*
>   *That flow from the fountains of eternity.*
> *I did not ask 'What's wrong?' as someone does*
>   *Who only looks with eyes that lose their sight*
>   *When the body lies abandoned by the soul;*
> *I asked it to give energy to your feet.*
>   *This is how we need to prod the lazy*
>   *Who are slow to use their wakefulness when it returns."*
>   [115–138]

For Dante's attention to return to the outer world of reality from his inner world of vision represents the attainment of objectivity. His visions were erroneous in that they were hallucinatory and thus had a certain subjective element; they were "not false" [Mandelbaum, line 117] in that they were representations of actual truths, witnessed through valid though imperfect intellection. Attachment to such imperfect visionary states is a common weakness of artists. Dante here is beginning to understand the nature of what the Hindus call *Maya*, the truth that manifestation is both a revelation and a veil. The manifest world possesses much less intrinsic being than the realities of Heaven, but it is nonetheless able to reveal them to us; this is precisely its function.

Virgil reproves Dante for his weak and wavering steps during his visions. He has witnessed them in a state of spiritual drunkenness, but Virgil reminds him that if he remains in this state he will lose his way. In order to walk the spiritual Path he must return to a state of sobriety so as to existentially realize, by the conscious submission of his will, what he has seen in the inner world. He needs above all to go forward, even if he must temporarily depart from the inner world of vision; he must enter the black smoke of anger.

Canto XVI

The Wrathful punished by black smoke. The travelers meet Marco Lombardo, who lectures them on free will and the causes of corruption, and extols the virtues of three aged men now alive in Italy: Currado da Palazzo, Gherardo da Cammino, and Guido da Castel.

> *Darkness of hell, and of a night bereft*
> > *Of every planet under a meager sky,*
> > *As overcast as any sky could be,*
> *Even these had not had power to blind my eyes*
> > *As did the smoke which now enveloped us,*
> > *Nor against my eyelids had they felt as rough as this;*
> *It did not let a single eye stay open.*
> > *That's when my wise and faithful Guardian,*
> > *Came near to me and offered me his shoulder.*
> *Even as a blind man goes behind his Guide [I walked]....*
> > > [1–10]

Here anger is described as being even darker than Hell; in its fury it may invoke and make a covenant with the Powers of Darkness, even if a particular soul infected by anger has no awareness that this has taken place; this is one of the meanings of "blind anger." [Cf. Psalms 6:8: "My eye is troubled from anger."] In the thrall of anger Dante has to look to spiritual guidance, his only hope of liberation. The heavenly spheres disappear in the black smoke of anger because the souls on this terrace are being called on to see the negative aspects exhibited by celestial influences when they are mediated through the psychic domain, the level of dealt with by the science of astrology. The mystery of free will these souls are striving to realize derives from a realm higher than the psychic plane, the world of the natural man.

Canto XVI

> *Voices I heard, and every one appeared*
> *To pray for peace and mercy to the Lamb,*
> *The Lamb of God who takes away our sins.* [16–18]

The spirits they encounter are chanting *Agnus dei, qui tollis peccata mundi, miserere nobis*: "Lamb of God, who takest away the sins of the world, have mercy on us." It is as if the sin of anger in particular is a burden that must be lifted through mercy. Since it is an inflammation and perversion of the will we cannot easily *will* to overcome it, and more than any of the other deadly sins, it calls upon the human will to aid and support it. All rage, while we are in the throes of it, appears justified, even if it is the furthest thing from justice; this is the great seduction of anger. "Hearing," in scripture, often refers to obedience and receptivity to guidance; to "heed" is not simply to listen, but to hear and obey. Seeing, in a state of anger, is susceptible to distortion by passions and worldly influences; we are "blinded," we "see red." Hearing, on the other hand, can invoke the soul's response to true guidance even in the midst of this distortion. Jesus doesn't say "he who has eyes to see, let him see," but "he who has ears to hear, let him hear." [Matthew 11:15 et al.]

One of the spirits asks,

> *"Who are you, whose presence splits the smoke,*
> *Who speaks of us as if you were still a man*
> *Who uses months to divide the course of time?"* [25–27]

Dante answers him:

> *". . . Clothed in those same swaddling-bands*
> *Which death unwinds I take the upward path;*
> *After passing through the pains of Hell, I come.*
> *God has so enfolded me in His grace,*
> *That it's His Will I behold His heavenly court*
> *In a way that modern men so rarely do. . . ."* [37–42]

Earthly time is different from purgatorial time; time in Purgatory is measured by suffering, not by any external criterion. To measure time by "months" is to exist in the earthly or "sub-lunary" world, beneath the sphere of the Moon and ruled by its cycles. The swaddling-bands represent the mortal flesh, which Dante carries with him since he is passing through Purgatory alive. But they also symbolize the spiritual mortality that sin imposes on the soul, enclosing it and preventing it from seeing its eternal destiny; as they are unwound, they release that soul to follow the upward path. Dante is making an analogy here between the soul's release from the flesh through death and these souls' release from the *spiritual* death that is sin. Souls in Hell may exist in perpetuity but they are not immortal; they have not escaped the death of sin, whereas the good souls in Purgatory are in the process of being released from it.[1]

That Dante mentions Hell to these spirits reiterates just how dark anger can be. Dante in the *Inferno* was able to detach from hellish suffering through witnessing it; unlike the damned, he knew he was only a visitor there. If he had identified with hellish states and felt at home in them, he would not have sought the path of salvation. According to Emmanuel Swedenborg in *Heaven and Hell*, "...a man who is in evil is bound to hell, and is actually there as to his spirit; and, after death, desires nothing more than to be there where his evil is. Consequently, after death, it is not God who casts the man into hell, but the man himself." No-one in terrestrial existence is irrevocably damned, however, whatever John Calvin may have believed; they can always seek, and find, the way to purification. Dante is seeking an extraordinary knowledge, rare for moderns, of the other world while still within this life. Since terrestrial life, even though it is under oppression by sin, is fully incarnate and complete like the life of Paradise, not partial as existence is in Purgatory, Dante must completely know the other world—Paradise, Purgatory and also Hell—in order to see it as it really is; this is why the passage through Hell is, for him, a step on the road to Paradise.

The soul who has addressed Dante is revealed as that of Marco Lombardi. "The world indeed has been stripped of every virtue" Dante says; "as you said to me, it cloaks—and is cloaked by—perversity" [58–60]. "Brother," Lombardi replies, "the world is blind"

---

1. When Hamlet, in his soliloquy, speaks of "shuffling off this mortal coil," he is employing almost the same image.

Canto XVI

[65–66]. The world hides its perversity, and this perversity also hides the true, God-given nature of the world. The world was created by God to mirror Him, but to the degree that it becomes perverted it loses this ability; the reason that it does not appear to us as perverse without special spiritual insight is that the essence of its perversion is its commitment to illusion.

Dante asks Marco Lombardi about the causes of the perversity of the world:

> "Some attribute the cause to heaven, others place it
> At a lower point: I beg you to define
> The true cause, so I can enlighten others." [61–63]

"You the living," says Marco,

> ... continue to attribute
> Every cause to heaven, as if it was
> The necessary source of every motion.
> If this were true, your free will would be lost
> Nor would there be any equity or justice
> In returning joy for good and grief for evil.
> The heavens move your appetites alone—
> Not all of them, but even if they did
> Nonetheless you've still received the light
> To tell good from evil; thus the sovereign will
> Though at first it struggles hard against the stars
> If well nurtured, finally conquers all. . . . [67–78]

> Issuing from [God's] hands, the soul—on which
> He thought with love before creating it—
> Is like a playing child who laughs and cries;
> Such a soul is simple, unaware;
> But since a joyful Maker gave it motion
> It willingly turns to all that brings delight.
> At first it has a taste for trivial goods
> Running after things that might beguile it
> Unless there's a guide or rein to turn its love. [85–93]

The Ordeal of Mercy

"Heaven" or "the heavens" in this passage are not God per se, but they are permeated by the life of God and nothing in them can exist without His permission; in this context they include both the celestial and the psychic domains. Our free will, however, is higher than these "heavens" because it is close to the spiritual essence of the soul that only God can see. Those aspects of our lives that are determined by the influences of the astrological heavens, in terms of either outer events or inner impulses, can hide this freedom from us, but they cannot destroy it. Throughout the *Purgatorio* "the stars," *stelle*, represent the promise of Paradise; here, however, *cielo*, "heaven," or *ciel*, translated as "the heavens," indicate the celestial spheres not in their Paradisical essence, but more in terms of their influence upon the psychic or natural man, via the appetites, to which the spiritual or pneumatic man, whose will is free, is not subject:

> *To a greater Force and to a better Nature,*
>   *Though free, you are subject; that is what creates*
>   *The mind in you that the spheres cannot control.*
> *So if the present world has gone astray,*
>   *The cause is in you: seek it in yourself.* . . . [79–83][2]

The Intellect as such is beyond the created universe; in the words of Meister Eckhart already quoted above, "there is something within the soul that is Uncreated and Uncreatable; this is the Intellect." The freedom of the will is intrinsically identical to the Uncreated Intellect because it is based on *certainty*. The will as we know it, however, must undergo purification in order to find its home in this Intellect; otherwise it will only live on the exterior of the psyche, defiantly asserting itself.

That God gives the soul "light on both good and evil" means that the soul in the state of nature is attracted to both because both can bring delight. But even though the newborn soul has a freshness and innocence about it, it cannot learn to will the good without spiritual guidance. The soul's *war against the heavens* is its struggle

---

2. Cf. Shakespeare, from *Julius Caesar*: "The fault, dear Brutus, is not in our stars but in ourselves."

Canto XVI

to unite itself to the Good by its free will in opposition to the passions, which in their darkness attempt to drag it to perdition. In the words of St. Paul, from Romans 8:38–39:

> For I am persuaded, that neither death, nor life, nor angels, nor principalities, nor powers, nor things present, nor things to come, nor height, nor depth, nor any other creature, shall be able to separate us from the love of God, which is in Christ Jesus our Lord.

And from Ephesians 6:12:

> For we wrestle not against flesh and blood, but against principalities, against powers, against the rulers of the darkness of this world, against spiritual wickedness in high places.

This is the battle against the passions of the unredeemed soul spoken of by Lorenzo Scupoli in his book *Spiritual Combat*, which in its Eastern Orthodox rendition, as edited and expanded by St. Nikodemos of the Holy Mountain, is entitled *Unseen Warfare*. The battle is not carried on only against our own instinctive impulses, however, but also against actual demons. This "war in heaven" is always going on because it transcends time; in our own spiritual lives we are even now fighting on the side of St. Michael and his holy angels against Satan and his fallen ones. After all, the war in heaven and the casting out of Satan appear not in book of Genesis but in the last book of the Bible, the Apocalypse; this is in order to demonstrate their timeless, eternal quality.

About this unseen warfare St. Maximos the Confessor says:

> Those who still fear the war against the passions and dread the assault of invisible enemies must keep silent; in their struggle for virtue they must not enter into disputes with their enemies but through prayer must entrust all anxiety about themselves to God. To them apply the words of Exodus: "The Lord will fight for you, and you must be silent" [Exodus 14:14]. [*Philokalia*, Volume Two, *First Century on Theology*, 30]

The Ordeal of Mercy

Thus it was necessary to establish laws
  For limits, and to have a king who might
  At least make out the tower of the true city.
The laws exist, but who administers them?
    No one does, because the shepherd who leads
    Does not have cleft hooves, though he chews the cud.
Therefore the people, who can see their guide
    Grab only for the goods that greed presents,
    Feed on these, and so seek nothing else.
Thus it should be clear that evil guidance
    Is the cause that brings corruption to the world;
    This, not nature, breeds the same in you. [94–105]

Dante is asking here about *collective* perversity; is this too a product of individual free will? Collectives cannot commit themselves to acting on the basis of clear intent like individuals can; this is why salvation pertains only to individual souls. A collective, though it may be improved, cannot be *saved* like a soul can. Dante certainly had his own ideas about what would be good for the Christian collective: it should follow a Christian law promulgated by an independent Pope and administered by an independent Emperor, not solely by a Pope acting without the protection of imperial authority, who may be able to promulgate the law ("chew the cud") but cannot enforce it because he is without "cleft hooves." Leviticus 11:3 allowed the Jews to eat only animals who both chew the cud and have cloven hooves. Here *chewing the cud* represents speech and the *hooves*, action. (Allen Mandelbaum sees *cleft* hooves as representing the principle of the two powers, the Pontifical and the Imperial.) Unfortunately, many people nowadays tend to put their heart and soul into the attempt to "save" collectives, at the same time considering their individual souls to be essentially worthless. Traditionalist writer and Catholic priest Rama Coomaraswamy would always counsel traditional priests that it is not their responsibility to save the Church, but God's; their duty is to be good priests and save their souls. Dante failed in his attempt to restore the Church as a social collective; the *Divine Comedy*, however, preserves and perpetuates his vision of the true path of salvation and enlightenment for individual souls. And just as his *Commedia* is a greater achievement than anything he was able to accomplish in political terms, so the salvation of the soul is intrinsically higher than the "improvement" of conditional life; according to St. Thomas Aquinas, a single human soul is of greater value than the whole world. Collective corruption does not exist because of fate imposed by the stars, nor as a direct expression of fallen human nature—which, after all, has been redeemed through Christ's atonement—but because of a wrong use of free will on the part of corrupt leaders. Following the bad example of the popes, the people only run after the worldly goods they can identify with; they expand and inflate the value of these things, blinding themselves to all higher Good.

> *Once Rome, who made the world good, had two suns*
>   *Each of which gave light to a different road:*
>   *One the path of the world, and one of God.*
> *Now one has quenched the other, till the sword*
>   *Is joined to the shepherd's crook. How wrong it is*
>   *That one should force the other to follow it*
> *Because mutual fear is cancelled through their union.*[3]
> [106–112]

Once there was both a real Emperor and a real Pope in Christendom, but because there is no true Emperor now like Constantine or Charlemagne—a role later fulfilled by the Czar of "Holy Russia," the Third Rome, the heir to Byzantium—a deep imbalance exists that forces the Pope to seek worldly power, and thus embrace corruption. To pray that God will send a true Christian Emperor to take care of the worldly dimension is to give the Pope a deeper spiritual role than he can exercise if he is forced to take the reins of secular power. Likewise if the outer, visible church is not protected and

---

3. In this passage we can see both the principle of the separation of Church and State—which can only happen in a fundamentally Christian context, however, since no balance or alliance is possible between the Church and the underlying principles of the modern secular world—and the doctrine of checks and balances between the branches of government: two central principles of the U.S. Constitution.

defended, then the inner Church, comprising the paths to the depths of the Christic revelation, is lost, partly because it must attempt to fulfill the role of the outer Church, which it has inherited by default, without the Divine permission to do so; this was precisely Dante's objection to the papacy of Celestine V in the third canto of the *Inferno*.

Marco Lombardi mentions three righteous men who still reside in the corrupt Lombardy of his birth: Currada da Palazzo, Gherardo da Cammino and Guido da Castello, commenting that "they find God slow in summoning them to a better life" [122–123]. These three are called upon by God to witness the corruption of Christendom, which is probably not a vocation they would have chosen for themselves. To be called to be a witness to an evil one cannot change means that one's very being must stand with what is being corrupted *as if it were inviolable*—which, in the eternal order, it actually is. This is the mystery of the Remnant.

Canto XVI

Editorial Commentary Four:
On the Aggiornamento of the Catholic Church and the Giant of the World

Protestantism tried to lay claim to the reality of the inner church—we can see this clearly in the writings of Jacob Boehme and the other early Lutheran pneumatics—but ended by becoming more external, more swept away by history, than even the Papacy at its most corrupt... at least before Vatican II. This is why the traditional Catholics of today, radically marginalized though they be, must do all they can to retain the traditional forms of the *outer* church. Only by attempting to fulfill this nearly impossible task will they be able to preserve the inner dimension of the Christian tradition. Today, however, the Church since the Second Vatican Council has rushed to become as Protestant as possible—in so doing becoming even more worldly and time-bound than the Protestants ever were—until it finally came to the point, under Benedict XVI, of offering itself as something resembling "the chaplaincy of the New World Order." Instead of preserving the remnants of Christian Empire, Benedict XVI, in his encyclical *Caritas in Veritate*, called for a "true world political authority," a secular One-World Government that some believe will be dominated by Satanic elites. As René Guénon predicted in *The Reign of Quantity and the Signs of the Times*, the regime of Antichrist will take the form of "an organization that would be like the counterpart, but by the same token also the counterfeit, of a traditional conception such as that of the 'Holy Empire,' and some such organization must become the expression of the 'counter-tradition' in the social order...." This call becomes even more explicit in "Towards Reforming the International Financial and Monetary Systems in the Context of Global Public Authority," a paper produced by the Pontifical Council for Justice and Peace, October of 2011, which contains the following passage:

> ... one can see an emerging requirement for a body that will carry out the functions of a kind of "central world bank" that regulates the flow and system of monetary exchanges similar to the national central banks... [the stages in the creation of this bank] ought to be conceived of as some of the first steps in view of a public Authority with universal jurisdiction.... In a world on its way to rapid globalization, the reference to a world Authority becomes the only horizon compatible with the new realities of our time and the needs of humankind. However, it should not be forgotten that this devel-

opment, given wounded human nature, will not come about without anguish and suffering. Through the account of the Tower of Babel (Genesis 11:1–9), the Bible warns us how the "diversity" of peoples can turn into a vehicle for selfishness.

A universal world authority brought about through anguish and suffering, where diversity is in effect outlawed—a true imposed unification—is what the post-conciliar Church is openly calling for in this document. Here the failure of the Tower of Babel is used as an image of the evils of diversity, symbolized by "the confusion of tongues." What these post-conciliar Catholics conveniently forget is that the Tower was the emblem of Nimrod's Promethean rebellion against God, and that the confusion of tongues was ordained by God Himself [see Genesis, chapter 11].

Canto XVII

Examples of those who sinned through anger: Procne, Haman and Amata. The Angel of Mildness. The travelers ascend to the Fourth Terrace, that of the Slothful. Virgil's speech on the nature of Purgatory, in which he defines the three lower sins—Pride, Envy and Wrath—as based on perverted love, the three upper ones—Avarice, Gluttony and Lust—on excessive love of earthly goods, and the sin of Sloth itself on defective love.

> *Remember, reader, if ever in the mountains*
>   *A mist overtook you, through which you could see*
>   *Only as a mole sees, sensing through his skin,*
> *And how, when those vapors, moist and thick,*
>   *Began to thin out, till at last the sphere*
>   *Of the sun entered weakly in among them,*
> *Then your imagination will be quick*
>   *In coming to understand how once again*
>   *I saw the sun, that was just about to set.* [1–9]

To see through one's skin is to apprehend the whole environment or context one is immersed in; to see the whole of any situation is to exclude or dampen anger, which is *partisan* by nature. It is based on partiality; it is partial rather than whole. The hour of sunset symbolizes finality; when the sun is setting, a certain maturity and completeness have been realized. This is the time when a full understanding of the light of knowledge transmitted by virtue of the sun can come into being.

> *O power of Imagination that sometimes takes us*
>   *So far from the outer world we can't perceive it*
>   *Though a thousand trumpets thunder all around us,*

The Ordeal of Mercy

If it isn't sense that moves you, then what does?
You are moved by a light that finds its form in Heaven,
Or by a heavenly will that guides you downward. [13–18]

Here Dante describes the inner images he sees as deriving directly from spiritual vision, the vestibule of pure Intellection, not from the senses or from any memory of sense experience. Heaven is the plane of the Intelligibles, but Purgatory is a realm within the intermediary or imaginal dimension, which is like the objective aspect of the world of dreams.[1] Like the imagination, Purgatory is volatile and incomplete. If one is in the Celestial realm, the Intelligibles are as concrete as anything we know; we think of them as abstract only because this is how they appear to us in earthly life. But in the imaginal realm, the Intelligibles appear as the *dramatis personae* of a symbolical drama. Dante is saying here that the imaginal plane is like the Sun of the Intellect as seen through the clouds of psychic world.

The "will that guides you downward" is the creative Will of God; what forms itself in Heaven is thereby incarnate on the earth—an incarnation that is perpetually recapitulated in the act of perception, as the scientist/metaphysician Wolfgang Smith so brilliantly demonstrates in the chapter "The Enigma of Visual Perception" from his book *Science and Myth* [Angelico Press, 2012]. The eye/brain complex participates in revealing the true nature of the object of perception by means of the image it forms of it. This image-formation is stimulated by the physical world and presents us a true picture of that world, but we don't just see with our eyes, we also see with our brains, which must help to form the true image of what we perceive, always aided by something which transcends the brain, that being the Intellect per se. And this Intellect, as Plato taught us, is also capable of receiving perceptions directly from the transcendent spiritual world—of being "moved by a light that finds its form

---

1. The French Islamic scholar Henry Corbin and the Russian Orthodox writer Pavel Florensky have both transmitted doctrines relating to the ontology of the "imaginal plane."

Canto XVII

in Heaven"—and of transmitting these perceptions to the mind of the perceiver.[2] As Dr. Smith explains:

> ... what renders the world perceptible to sentient beings and intelligible to man is the presence therein of *forms* precisely. It is moreover to be understood that these forms are not subject to the bounds of space and time, and must be distinguished categorically not only from the physicist's particles and fields, but from corporeal entities as well [i.e., real existing things capable of being perceived by the senses]: in a word, they are not "things." Yet *it is forms that constitute things and bestow upon them such reality as they possess* ... to conceive of authentic perception one requires a notion of *morphe* or *eidos*: only a *form* is able to join a subject to an object so that "in a way" the two "become one" as Aristotle declares. ...

The empiricist mind is able, certainly, to envision a psychosomatic domain; and [perceptual psychologist James J.] Gibson, for one, has maintained that perception constitutes neither a physical nor a mental act, but pertains indeed to the psychophysical organism. One needs however to realize that the psychosomatic realm, by virtue of its somatic and hence material base, is subject to the temporal condition; in this realm "everything flows," as Heraclitus observed. But this implies that the *nunc stans* [the Scholastic "standing now," the eternal present]—and hence the act of perception—is not to be located in that domain. However "supra-temporal" the disembodied soul may be, the fact remains that, in union with the body, the soul becomes subject to time ... [however] the fact that perception takes place in the *nunc stans*, and thus "above time," entails that perceiving is not, strictly speaking, a psycho-

---

2. Aristotle's contribution to the metaphysics of perception was the realization that our very ability to "make sense" of sense experience ultimately derives from the Intellect's capacity to see the corporeal world through the lens of the forms or Ideas; his notion of *forma* (to use the Scholastic term) was precisely the Platonic Idea considered as incarnate in this or that real existing thing. Thus, in lines 17–18, "finds its form" alludes to Plato and "will that guides you downward" to Aristotle. We must never forget that Aristotle himself was a Platonist.

somatic act: the faculty by which we perceive proves not to be psychosomatic, but *spiritual*, and that spiritual faculty is what tradition terms *intellect*.

The objective nature of true perception is unveiled by Dante at this point in order to overcome the self-willed subjectivity of partial perception which is the basis of all anger.

Next Dante alludes to three episodes, two from classical antiquity and one from the Old Testament, which appear to him before the inner eye of Imagination. The first is the legend of the rape of Philomela, which is recounted both in Ovid's *Metamorphoses* and Virgil's *Aeneid* and *Georgics*. Philomela is raped by her brother-in-law Tereus, who cuts out her tongue; nonetheless Philomela reveals to her sister Procne what has happened by weaving the story of it into a piece of cloth. The sisters take revenge on Tereus by killing his son and serving up his flesh for his father to eat. After he learns what what they have done, Tereus tries to kill them, but during the pursuit all three are transformed into birds: Philomela into a nightingale, Procne into a swallow, and Tereus into a hoopoe. (Dante, however, recounts an alternate version where Philomela becomes the swallow and Procne the nightingale.)

Philomela, whose tongue was cut out by her brother-in-law Tereus to hide his rape of her, is like someone who is oppressed but has no language to describe her violation, reminding us of the seal of silence often placed on violated children by their tormentors, as well as of society's tendency not to believe such children's stories. That Philomela weaves images into the cloth in order to communicate what has happened to her sister Procne implies that she must learn the language of symbols in order to communicate to others the reality of what has happened—and even to herself. We often need to develop an understanding of these realities in order to come to terms with and understand certain deep violations; the "bare facts" do not tell the whole story. And that she becomes a nightingale after her revenge on Tereus, when the real import of his violation has been revealed, suggests of the myth of Solomon when he learned the language of the birds. i.e., the science of symbols. Poetic symbols can communicate realities that our senses do not immedi-

Canto XVII

ately apprehend—in this case the truth that Tereus, in raping Philomela, actually killed his own son: his innocence and spiritual potential. Certainly Philomela's anger and revenge are mortal sins; nonetheless the *meaning* of anger must be understood before it can be transcended. Upon seeing this vision Dante "withdrew to the within, to what imagining might bring" [Mandelbaum, lines 22–23], just as Philomela did so as to heal the wound of her violation. Dante himself was violated in this way when all his political hopes were disappointed and he was exiled from Florence—the city that had almost been his *shakti*, his "emanation" in Blake's terminology, his *Beatrice*. After this loss he could only seek Beatrice in the other world, the imaginal world of his *Divine Comedy*.

In the second story, from the Book of Esther, the Jew Mordecai refuses to bow down to Haman, minister of Ahasuerus, King of Persia, because Haman had ordered all the Jews of Persia massacred—a fate they escaped through the intercession of Esther, the Jewish wife of the king, after which Ahasuerus ordered Haman to be hanged. (Apparently Dante drew the notion that Haman was "crucified" from the word *cruci*, meaning "gallows," which appears in the Latin Vulgate.)

Haman's anger, oddly enough, though it is more intense than Philomela's, is also more volatile, which is why it ends by breaking like a bubble [lines 31–33]. It appears more fierce but it actually has less depth because it has less justification. Philomela's anger is a perversion of justice, Haman's an outright betrayal of it.

The third story is that of Queen Amata of Latium and her daughter Lavinia from the *Aeneid*. When Latium was burned, Amata mistakenly believed that Turnus, Lavinia's fiancée, had died in the fire, and so hanged herself; she did so because she was bitterly opposed to Lavinia's proposed marriage to Aeneas, which she now believed was inevitable. (He was finally slain by Aeneas, who then married Lavinia.)

The image of Haman's anger and its retribution "rains down" from above [line 25] because his type of anger is visible and collective; Amata's anger "rises up" from below [line 33] because, since it is based on her jealous possessiveness over her daughter, it is hidden and personal—jealousy being the one sin we are most ashamed of revealing. This is a poisonous anger because she is angry at something that would be a future good: the marriage of Aeneas the Trojan to the Latin princess Lavinia, leading to the establishment of the Roman world, the very world in which Christianity would later flourish. Philomela's anger is against a real transgression; Haman's is a transgression in itself, or rather a defense of one; Amata's is the worst of all because it is an anger against a potential good, which already exists in both in her soul and in that of her daughter, operating on a level deeper than conscious desire. By her possessiveness she attempts to interfere with the flow of life and destiny, thus in a sense murdering her own soul; her suicide is like a hidden hatred of Lavinia projected on herself. Lavinia mourns the loss of Turnus, but nonetheless accepts Aeneas; she submits to Providence and in so doing affirms life.

> *Just as sleep is shattered, when suddenly*
>   *New light hammers in upon closed eyelids,*
>   *And as, now broken, it quivers before it dies,*
> *So this inner vision of mine collapsed*
>   *As soon as that effulgence hit my face,*
>   *Far greater than any light we're familiar with.*
> *I turned around to determine where I was,*
>   *When a voice spoke out, "The passage up is here";*
>   *It wrenched me away from every other purpose. . . .* [40–48]

> *Exactly as if I were blinded by the sun,*
>   *That hides within its own excess of light,*
>   *Just so my power of sight was overcome.*
> *"This is a divine spirit, who points the way*
>   *Of ascent without our even asking him,*
>   *And who in his own light conceals himself. . . ."* [52–57]

Dante's vision is shattered by a light so bright that it is hard for him to see. That Dante experiences this brightness indicates that he is intuiting the fruits of the spiritual ascent. He is seeing beyond this particular place he has gotten to, this particular level of purgation; he has glimpsed the end of the spiritual Path. This is why he puts

Canto XVII

ascent on the Path before everything else, and most particularly before *curiosity*. That the spirit is hidden by its own light indicates a reality too high for Dante to see in his present state; that the angel comes unasked means that he has nothing to do with the subjectivity of Dante's soul and its various needs; his light is a totally objective reality and must be accepted as such. Dante now feels the brush of a wing on his forehead—perhaps the 3rd P is being erased—and hears the words "blessed are the peacemakers." Anger is being overcome.

> *Already over us were so uplifted*
>   *The last beams of the sun, pursued by night*
>   *That the stars appeared around on every side.*
> *"Why now do you dwindle away, my manhood?"*
>   *I said within myself; for I perceived*
>   *The vigor of my legs was held in check.* . . . [70–75]

The setting of the sun begins to reveal the stars, the world of Eternity, which at this point can be finally seen during the *day*—that is, consciously. Day is the objective aspect of life, unlike the night which, in certain contexts, can represent the subjective aspect, the world of dreams. First Dante's strength melts away—only then he sees; his energy is turning away from the will and toward the Intellect, away from struggle and toward perception.

> *"Son" he began, "never was Creator nor creature*
>   *Ever without one form or another of love,*
>   *Whether natural or subjective; this you know.*
> *The natural remains forever without error;*
>   *But the other may err by choice of evil object,*
>   *Or by falling into deficiency or excess.*
> *While properly directed to the Primal Good,*
>   *And moderate in pursuit of the secondary,*
>   *It cannot be the cause of sinful pleasure.*
> *But when it turns to evil, or with greater care*
>   *Or lesser care than it should pursues the good,*
>   *Creation works against its own Creator.*

The Ordeal of Mercy

Thus you can begin to see how only love
   Is the seed within yourselves of every virtue,
   And every act that merits punishment.
Now given that love can never turn aside
   Its gaze from the welfare of its proper subject,
   No thing can ever truly hate itself;
And since we can't conceive of any being
   Standing alone, nor from its Cause divided
   No creature has the power to hate its Maker.
Therefore if my discrimination is sound,
   Evil love is directed to one's neighbor,
   And this is born in three modes in your clay." [91–114]

The natural dimension possesses its own objective measure, but on the level of the soul, in terms of love of a particular object, the realm of psychic subjectivity comes into play. For example, our natural appetite for food never exceeds or falls short of proper measure; our mental relationship with food, on the other hand, amplifies and distorts its significance, attributing a meaning to it that it does not in fact possess. This produces gluttony, as well as such disorders as anorexia and bulimia. "Soul-love," *amore d'animo*, relates to the realm of the psyche, not the Spirit; in Purgatory, the psychic realm, this subjectivity is dramatized so that the soul may be purged of it. Hatred of one's neighbor takes three forms: the "pure" ability to take delight in another's hurt; the feeling that any advantage to another must be a disadvantage to oneself; and the desire to revenge oneself for an injury at the hands of another.

Dante emphasizes that *amore d'animo*, love on the level of the soul, is not evil in itself, that it remains good "when properly directed to the Primal Good." Likewise Frithjof Schuon writes:

> An indispensable condition for the innocent and natural experience of earthly happiness is the spiritual capacity of finding happiness in God, and the incapacity to enjoy things outside of Him. We cannot validly and persistently love a creature without carrying him within ourselves by virtue of our attachment to the Creator; not that this inward possession must be perfect,

Canto XVII

but it must at all events be present as an intention which allows us to perfect it. [*Esoterism as Principle and as Way*, 144]

Love is much more than a positive feeling; it is close to our essence. There is no such thing as a neutral love; our love belongs either to salvation or damnation.

Virgil says that we are all barred from actually hating God; if we really knew Him, we could not hate Him. Alongside this one could place Meister Eckhart's statement that "the more he blasphemes the more he praises God." Whatever we do, God is inviolable. He gives us everything, even the energy to hate. The life he gives us will go to feed either love or hatred, depending on our intention; we cannot really hate God, however, and it is not in God's nature to hate Himself. Nor can we really hate ourselves, because we are made in the image of God; as Eckhart says, "my truest 'I' is God"—and on some level, the level of the *synderesis*, we know this. Virgil explains that we cannot really hate ourselves because ultimately we cannot truly see ourselves as apart from God; He is both our Creator and our Essence.[3] It is certainly possible, as we all know, to feel hatred for God or for ourselves, but these feelings are basically unreal; when we put energy into these hates, we are only feeding illusion. It is impossible to hate anything we recognize as real; the only thing we actually can hate is illusion itself. Our illusory mental image of a God capable of being hated is totally unreal, consequently our hatred has no effect on its true Object. Likewise our hatred for ourselves is illusory because we can only hate ourselves on behalf of ourselves. Only hatred of our neighbor is capable of mushrooming into a complete hatred, an open field for anger. There is illusion in such hatred as well, but to the degree that our neighbor is actually hostile to us, or we to him, this illusion has a certain reality to draw upon. The hatred of one's neighbor is based on the sense of separateness. We can feel hatred for another because we can conceive of him as

---

3. The principle that the Absolute is the One Self of All, paradoxically experienced by each of us as his or her own private and unique identity, is elucidated by Frithjof Schuon in his essay "The Enigma of Diversified Subjectivity," which appears in his book *The Roots of the Human Condition*.

separate from us, but in reality that separateness is also illusory; our neighbor, like us, is made in the image and likeness of God.

Virgil continues his discourse by distinguishing the sins of Pride, Envy and Anger, purged on the three lower terraces, from Avarice, Gluttony and Lust, expiated on the three higher ones. The three lower sins result from a self-contradictory and self-sabotaging love, while the love represented by the three upper sins involves a misuse of energy in the mode of excess. Those on the lower three terraces do not see the import of their own love, while those on the upper three love the good, but love it so excessively that they forget God. They mistake the relative for the Absolute. Here, however, on the terrace of Sloth, a lack of energy is being expiated; its occupants love the good, but love it in a lax fashion. Sloth is an attempt to reach a state of contemplative peace too easily, without first having satisfied the demands of discipline, which is inner activity. This, in Hindu terms, is to mistake *tamas*—ignorance and stagnation—for *sattwa*—clarity and equilibrium; as Frithjof Schuon taught, it is impossible to repose in something ontologically lower than oneself. And there is no way to move from *tamas* to *sattwa* without *rajas*, activity. Excessive *rajas*, however, misses the attainment of *sattwa* and turns toward *tamas* again; Anger, exhausted, becomes Sloth. Furthermore, Pride, Envy and Anger are the principles of the three modes of hatred of the neighbor as explained by Virgil. The unmixed delight in another's harm is based on Pride, the fear that the advantage of another must be a disadvantage to oneself on Envy, and the desire for revenge for injury suffered on Anger.

On this terrace Dante finds it useful to delay for a night so that he may learn more from Virgil—even though the sin being purged here is Sloth, which is *heedless* delay. In heedless delay one is actually sinking back into obsessive activity without knowing it. The contemplative, on the other hand, reposes in stillness of mind, but it takes effort and good will to reach this kind of stillness. The slothful soul is filled with unconscious activity; the contemplative soul rests in Pure Act.

Canto XVIII

Virgil speaks on love, free will and responsibility. The Slothful are punished by being made to run without rest; while running, they name Caesar and the Virgin Mary as examples of zeal. The travelers interview the Abbot of San Zeno. The Slothful then present examples of their own sin: the Jews in the wilderness and the Trojans in Sicily. Dante is overcome by sleep, during which he dreams of the true nature of Sloth—a dream recounted in the next canto.

St. Maximos the Confessor says of Sloth:

While passions such as forgetfulness and ignorance affect but one of the soul's three aspects—the incensive, the desiring or the intelligent—listlessness alone seizes control of all the soul's powers and rouses almost all the passions together. This is why this passion is more serious than all the others. Hence Our Lord has given us an excellent remedy against it, saying: "You will gain possession of your souls through patient endurance" [Luke 21:19]. [*Philokalia*, Volume Two, *First Century on Love*, 67]

The idea that the sin of Sloth, which includes such things as fear and sadness as well as complacency, is actually a *passion* is foreign to the contemporary mindset. We can easily understand Anger and Lust as passions, but it is harder for us to see Sloth as such, because it reveals the passions to be essentially "passive," whereas we like to think of them as vital and dynamic. According to the Church Fathers, the passions take control of our will and force us to *passively* act according to their agendas instead of being true to ourselves. Thus the cure for them is *action* in its truest sense. Pure action is to center in God—who, according to Aquinas, is Himself "Pure Act." The essence of pure action is prayer.

The Ordeal of Mercy

The traditional term for the sin of Sloth is "acedia," a general deadening of all life; one has "lost the taste for life." Acedia is characterized by a deadness of the senses, and even more so by a deadness of the feelings. A person afflicted by acedia has great difficulty in finding any meaning in life. In an article entitled "A Requiem for Friendship" [*Touchstone: A Journal of Mere Christianity;* September, 2005], Anthony Esolen complains that the youth of today are no longer as alive and "youthful" as young people once were; this could certainly be classed as a form of acedia. Acedia is a passion that pervades the modern world. It lowers spiritual expectations and thus draws people into an acceptance of hopeless materialism, resulting in such things as the obesity plague that now besets us. And since it pervades every aspect of life, its origin is difficult to isolate. It is in the very nature of acedia that its victim should be relatively unconscious of it, since it always produces a decrease in awareness, and even on occasion a physical sleepiness. It is clear that the term acedia covers much of what we would define today as depression.

If acedia is a particularly modern malaise, it may be because we moderns are emotionally isolated by our conditions. The great temptation when confronting acedia is to distract oneself by seeking novelty. *Restlessness* is a major symptom of it—and who could be more restless than modern man? A special case of this restlessness is dissatisfaction with the place where one lives, which of course makes it difficult to establish domestic roots and thereby overcome social isolation. Jungian psychologist Marion Woodman, in a lecture given in San Francisco in the early 1980's, commented on the tendency among many of her clients to spend their spare time in restaurants, bars, coffee shops, anywhere but at home—and this was even before the spread of laptops and the internet. Part of the reason for this behavior is that such people are trying to heal their acedia through contact with others (which, of course, the use of laptops and smart phones acts to block). Jean-Claude Larchet, however, in his book *Mental Disorders and Spiritual Healing*, maintains that this condition can only be healed through solitary struggle. One must directly resist the tendency to sleepiness, lack of awareness and loss of energy, not simply run from it.

Another result of acedia is our inability to value our homes, our

Canto XVIII

habit of considering them merely as places to "crash." Many of our contemporaries who groom themselves impeccably for the workplace will allow their places of residence to fall into disarray and even squalor. If we could live content within our homes, we would be far less tempted to turn our houses into mere economic commodities. People who can only be responsible and diligent when under supervision may be affected by the sin of Sloth without realizing it. And whether we are solitaries or live in communion with others, Sloth can be overcome only by Love. Just as it is in the nature of a flame to ascend, so it is in the nature of Love to make the soul restless until the Beloved has given it joy.

> "*The soul, which is created quick to love,*
>   *Quickly follows anything that pleases,*
>   *As soon as pleasure awakens her to act.*
> *Your apprehension from some real object*
>   *Takes an image, which is then displayed within you*
>   *Until the soul turns toward it; after that*
> *If she conceives a firm desire for what she sees,*
>   *That desire is love, through power of which your nature*
>   *Is re-unified within you by means of pleasure.*
> *Then even as the fire must travel upward*
>   *By virtue of its own form that's born to rise,*
>   *Till it finds the place where it can last the longest,*
> *So the soul when seized by pleasure enters*
>   *The spiritual motion of desire, and never rests*
>   *Till she has found delight in the thing she loves.*
> *Perhaps you can now begin to see how hidden*
>   *The truth is from those people who still claim*
>   *All love must be praiseworthy in itself*
> *Because its matter happens to appear as good.*
>   *Not every impression the wax receives is good*
>   *Even though the wax itself is always fine.*"
> "*Your word, along with my own wit to follow*
>   *Have unveiled the truth of Love*" *I answered him;*
>   "*Yet now I'm filled with even greater doubt:*
> *If Love is offered to us from without*

The Ordeal of Mercy

> *And with no other foot the soul can travel,*
>   *How can her choice of path determine merit?"*
> *He answered me, "Whatever reason knows*
>   *That I can tell you; for more you must still wait*
>   *For Beatrice, who can speak the truths of faith.*
> *Every substantial form, both separate*
>   *From matter and united with it as well,*
>   *Collects in itself its own specific power,*
> *A force which can't be seen until it acts,*
>   *Nor show itself except by its effects,*
>   *As green leaves demonstrate the life in plants.*
> *But as for the source in man of his discernment*
>   *Of first principles, as well as of his love*
>   *For love's prime objects, this he does not know;*
> *These things are in you like instinct in the bee*
>   *To make its honey; and this primal will*
>   *In itself is deserving of neither praise nor blame.*
> *And so that all may be gathered to this will,*
>   *You have innate within you the power of judgment,*
>   *To act as threshold-keeper of your ascent.*
> *This is the principle chosen to decide*
>   *What destiny you merit for a given work*
>   *Since it reaps and winnows the good work from the bad.*
> *The ones who followed their reason to its root*
>   *Were well aware of this inborn liberty,*
>   *Which is why they could offer Ethics to the world.*
> *So even if you say that every love*
>   *Takes fire within you from Necessity,*
>   *Still in yourselves you hold the power to curb it.*
> *This noble virtue Beatrice understands*
>   *By the name Free Will; therefore you must be sure*
>   *To remember this, if she chooses to speak of it."* [19–75]

We are not the puppets of beauty; beauty embodied as an outer object must call to the inner dynamic, the specific *intention*, which can unite with it. We, as lovers of beauty, are not called to be simple-minded devotees; this isn't merely a case of the emotions of the

Canto XVIII

devotee being mindlessly drawn to the object of beauty or worship. As we apprehend this object of beauty, an alchemical transformation happens in the soul, and this releases the intention, the "ruling love" that guides us toward union with that object, which is at the same time a union of form and matter within the soul itself. Here is where Virgil prepares Dante to meet Beatrice, who herself *is* this union of form and matter.

One mistake some modern Perennialists will make is in giving everything to this primordial will to seek beauty, whereas Virgil makes it clear that this is neither praiseworthy nor blameworthy. What is all-important to us is the inner conscience, the *synderesis*, an aspect of the indwelling Transcendent Intellect, that can weigh truth and falsehood, good and evil; this is the root of free will.

Free will is there to constantly guard the primordial love of beauty, to curb it when it moves in wrong directions so that it might more fully travel along true paths; this is perhaps the real meaning and nature of the *daimon* of Socrates. Love for any object can always seem good because it draws upon energies of the soul that are innocent in themselves, symbolized here by the wax that is "always fine." But it's crucial to understand that false love draws the soul into disintegration, while true love leads it toward integration and fulfillment.[1] The difference between true and false love lies neither exclusively in the object nor exclusively in the intent, but in the presence or absence of the right union between the object and the intent. There is no intent, however, until the soul is confronted by the object; it is the choice of the right object of love that forms the right intent.[2]

> *And that noble shade, for whom Pietola*
> *Is more renowned than any town in Mantua,*
> *Had freed me from the burden of my doubt.*
> *Therefore I, who by now had gathered*

---

1. Certain pedophiles, for example, appear to be *seeking innocence* in hopes of possessing it, but in such a way that innocence is destroyed.

2. This marriage between object and intent is also the basis of all true Knowledge, a doctrine that is suggested here by the union of Dante's *wit*, his receptive intelligence, with Virgil's *word*, a manifestation of the Active Intellect. Knowledge,

The Ordeal of Mercy

His clear and open answers to my questions,
Stood like a man on the edge of empty sleep.
Then my drowsiness was lifted from me
Suddenly by a people, who behind us
Had already turned themselves in our direction. [82–90]

The souls who now appear protect Dante from the randomness that is about to tempt him [see lines 143–145]; they are a force acting to hold him to what he has truly understood through Virgil. Zeal implies being in touch with the meaning and import of what you are doing; it's not just "will power" operating in blindness, but the true union of will and knowledge. Likewise Dante will resume his ascent as soon as the sun's light strikes him, the sun being symbolic of the Intellect [lines 109–111].

Soon they were upon us—because, running
All that mighty multitude approached;
And two souls in the vanguard cried out, weeping,
"Mary ran in haste unto the mountain;
Rushing to conquer Lerida, Caesar thrust
First at Marseilles, then pushed on into Spain." [97–102]

These lines allude to the Virgin Mary's eagerness to bring news of her pregnancy to her cousin Elizabeth, herself pregnant with John the Baptist, and to Julius Caesar's lightning campaigns against Pompey in the Roman Civil War, when he left the bulk of his army behind and attacked Marseilles and Spain with a smaller but more

---

like Love, is both intentional and objective; the power of the Active Intellect, which is pure *forma*, draws the *materia* of the soul out of its subjective self-involvement and allows it to submit intentionally to objective Truth. Just as the freedom of the will arises as if out of nothing, so the inborn ability to recognize the truth of axioms or principles appears fully formed, previous to all dialectic; it is unveiled, not constructed. Here Dante's theory of Love develops directly out of the Aristotelian hylomorphic theory that Wolfgang Smith, in his book *Science and Myth*, applies to the nature of visual perception. Nor is this correspondence as far-fetched as it might seem, in view of the fact that, according to an axiom of the Troubadours, Love enters the Heart through the Eye.

Canto XVIII

mobile force. Mary after the Annunciation is filled with joy; this is the very opposite of the kind of slothful indifference that can turn against fertility. Pregnancy appears heavy and slothful, but in fact it is a dynamic affirmation of life. In the case of Caesar, something that seems smaller and less powerful compensates for its limitations by being swifter and more dynamic. To overcome Sloth we must not try to leap over every obstacle at once; instead we should downsize the task, being careful to avoid fantasy and grandiosity, and pinpoint the immediate necessity that must be addressed. This is what allows us to access the Spirit; it is the Spirit of God which has the power to overcome Sloth, not forced human effort. One of the most common yet least obvious aspects of Sloth is self-will; self-will makes excessive and ponderous demands on the situation it confronts, but is unwilling to really see it as it is and respond to it.

> *And one from among those spirits told us, "Come;*
> *Follow us and you will find the gap.*
> *We're so full of zeal to make our way,*
> *We cannot stop, so therefore pardon us,*
> *If you for discourtesy mistake our justice...."* [113–117]

These souls point out to Virgil and Dante the passage to the next terrace, but they do not linger to speak with them. In the process of overcoming Sloth they have overcome the attachment to being looked at as helpers, or even as those who, like some purgatorial spirits, can foretell the future. Because their dedication to accomplishing their purgation is entirely one-pointed, all they tell to Dante they tell merely "in passing." One of the most insidious manifestations of Sloth for the spiritual traveler is the temptation to *teach* what he knows before he has *realized* what he knows.

> "I was Abbot of San Zeno at Verona,
>   Under the rule of our good Barbarossa,
>   Of whom Milan still speaks with so much sorrow.
> He already has one foot in the grave,
>   Who shall soon regret that monastery,
>   And repent of all the power that he held there,

The Ordeal of Mercy

Because his son—sick in his whole body,
　And sicker still in mind, the evil-born,
　He raised above the true shepherd of that place." [118–126]

The abbot was slothful because he did not work to develop within himself the understanding of who would have the spirit to be worthy of that position, instead choosing someone who simply happened to be available, no matter how unworthy.

Those in the rear then shouted: "That first people
　For whom the sea was parted all were dead,
　Before its inheritors ever saw the Jordan;
And those who were not willing to endure
　The struggle to the end with Anchises' son,
　Gave themselves up to a life bereft of glory." [133–138]

The Children of Israel became mired in depression, ambiguity and regret for what they had lost in Egypt rather than focusing on the goal of entering the Promised Land; this is why it took them forty years to pass through the wilderness. "Anchises' son" [line 137] is Aeneas; the *Aeneid*, like the *Odyssey*—and like the *Divine Comedy*—is a fable of the journey of the soul. In the course of his difficult homecoming to Ithaca to be reunited with his wife Penelope, Odysseus had to progressively leave behind all his companions; likewise Aeneas abandoned those of his followers who were reluctant to press on to Latium, where he would ultimately marry Lavinia. The soul in its journey must divest itself of extraneous tendencies and desires in order to become the "simple" soul of theology—the soul of one essence, of one will, of one mind. If it can do this it will reach Paradise, which is its true homeland.

Sloth is not simply laziness, but also cowardice and a tendency to shirk responsibility. It often expresses itself as false forgiveness (especially *self*-forgiveness), a passive tolerance for present evil that invites the arrival of greater evil in the future. Sloth allows us to stifle the voice of conscience and helps us cultivate a deliberate unconsciousness for the purpose of attacking or manipulating others—particularly those who challenge us to awaken from our slumber. It

Canto XVIII

is not just weakness of the will but also darkness of the mind, a truth alluded to by the saying "the sleep of reason begets monsters."

> *And when those souls were so far in the distance*
>   *It was possible no more to make them out,*
>   *Then a new thought rose within me, and another,*
> *And from that, others, so many and diverse*
>   *That I wandered on from thought to random thought,*
>   *Till I closed my eyes in vagrant reverie,*
> *And all those thoughts were transformed into dreams.*
>   [139–145]

Sloth breaks down order in our circumstances, and order in our thoughts as well; this demonstrates just how deluded we are when we think of chaos as liberating. We may consider this randomness as somehow "natural," but it is no more natural than form is, and in fact is centered in a plane of being lower than form, specifically the plane of *materia*, which is lower than the realms occupied by conscious beings, biological life forms, and even sensible physical objects. (For an exhaustive treatment of the difference between the physical plane perceived by the senses and the material plane posited by modern physics, where random indeterminacy and statistical probability rule, see Wolfgang Smith's two books *The Quantum Enigma* and *Science and Myth*.)[3]

The random thoughts that beset Dante draw him into the dream state. According to St. Maximos the Confessor, "Thoughts which are not impassioned are simple. Impassioned thoughts are composite, consisting as they do of a conceptual image combined with [a]

---

3. Too much externally-imposed order is oppressive, but so is chaos when it goes beyond its proper role of breaking down the excesses of artificial order and becomes excessive in itself. The legitimate role of thought is to function as the active *forma* of our experience, in relation to which our circumstances function as *materia*. But in a condition of Sloth, thought becomes random—that is, unintentional—through an imitation of *materia*, which is properly passive, thus illegitimately positing *materia* as the active pole. This is the point at which Necessary Being, manifesting though intelligible forms, degenerates into the blind necessity of circumstances that Blake called "the female will"—the regime of Fate.

passion" [*Philokalia*, Volume Two, *Second Century on Love*, 84]. Such thoughts often appear as verbal chatter, which St. John Climacus relates to Sloth: "Despondency or tedium of the spirit [*acedia*] is frequently an aspect of talkativeness, and indeed its first child." In the next Canto, however, these random thoughts, even though they have led Dante to a lower state of consciousness, produce a dream that reveals the true nature of Sloth by demonstrating its seductive nature.

Canto XVIII

Editorial Commentary Five:
"Achilles and the Tortoise" as a Parable of Sloth

It may be more than coincidental that San Zeno of Verona bears the same name as the Greek philosopher Zeno of Elea, one of whose famous paradoxes, that of Achilles and the Tortoise, presents the perfect picture of effort hampered by mental scruples, which so often produce a condition of Sloth in those affected by them. The paradox is as follows: Achilles challenges the Tortoise to a footrace. Achilles can run ten times as fast as the Tortoise, so the Tortoise gives him a head start of ten yards. The Tortoise runs the ten yards, and Achilles then begins. Achilles runs ten yards, during which time the Tortoise, one-tenth as fast as Achilles, runs one yard. Achilles runs the one yard, during which time the Tortoise runs a tenth of a yard. Achilles runs the tenth of a yard, during which time the Tortoise runs a tenth of a tenth of a yard, etc., etc. So it appears strictly logical that Achilles will never catch up with the Tortoise—though of course we know that he must in fact pass him and win the race. Furthermore, the Achilles of Homer's *Iliad*, for all his heroic prowess, may be taken as a type of Sloth, in view of the fact that his wounded pride after being slighted by Agamemnon, and his subsequent dalliance with his lover Patroclus, caused him to delay entering battle during the Trojan War. Here, perhaps, we can see how obsessive competition and effort can be a hidden form of Sloth insofar as they divert one's attention from one's true responsibilities. And one relationship between male homosexuality and Sloth—a condition that of course does not affect all male homosexuals—is its tendency to become drawn to the aesthetic surface of things rather than to real fertility. The pursuit of the aesthetic surface seems liberating since it is detached from the hard necessities of life represented by the "feminine" world of reproduction and child-rearing; and certainly this pursuit is capable of making valuable contributions to society. Yet to the degree that it is not grounded in the full reality of human earthly life, it is cut off from the deeper aspects of God's Grace and Will which are the animating principles of that life, and thus is tempted to indulge in the "lighter" and more volatile aspect of Sloth we call *frivolity*—and one aspect of frivolity is *obsessive intellectualizing*, a vice that is obviously not limited to male homosexuals, or even to the male sex. The self-involved individual intellect, pursuing mental abstraction while alienated from the substance of life, is like *forma* divorced from *materia*; likewise *materia* without the animating influence of *forma* must sink into the slothful obscurity of matter. This is why the attempt to escape the *tamasic* quality of the maternal, feminine principle through mental self-indulgence, which is a common expression of the masculine principle separated from its feminine counterpart, is doomed to failure; when Climacus speaks of the relationship between talkativeness and Sloth, he is discerning the effects of a divorce between form and matter.

Canto XIX

Dante's dream of the Siren of Sloth. The Angel of Zeal appears. The travelers climb onward to the Fifth Terrace, that of the Avaricious and the Prodigal—the misers and the spendthrifts. The Avaricious are punished by being bound face down to the earth. Dante and Virgil converse with Pope Adrian V.

There came to me in dream a stammering woman,
    With squinting eyes and two misshapen feet,
    With crippled hands and sickly yellow face.
I gazed at her; and as the sun revives
    Cold limbs made numb by darkness of the night,
    In just that way my gaze revived her tongue,
And after a time her limbs became straight as well,
    Till my look at last transformed her countenance
    Until it assumed the color that's most loved by love.
And when her speech had fully come to life
    Then she began to sing, which might have made it
    Hard for me to turn away from her.
"I am that sweetest singer, called the Siren,
    Who leads astray the sailors on the sea
    So delightful is my song to them.
I drew aside Ulysses from his path
    Unto my song; who comes to live with me
    Seldom leaves, so wholly do I content him."
Her mouth had not yet closed again, before
    A Lady appeared, vigilant and holy
    Close by my side, and put her to confusion.
"O Virgil, Virgil, tell me, who is this?"
    Sternly she spoke; and as he approached
    That honest one, his eyes fixed firmly on her

The Ordeal of Mercy

She seized the other and stripped her all in front
Tearing her dress till her belly was exposed;
The stench that wafted from it woke me up. [7–33]

This figure is distorted because Sloth is intrinsically related to chaos, which produces random, unformed thought. Dante sees that something is wrong with the figure, so he focuses his intellect upon it. However, his intellect is misplaced in this case, in much the same way as the intellect of someone who thinks of intelligence as if it were part of the natural order, and interprets nature as if it had no relationship to God. This is an entirely deceptive way of perceiving, and will lead anyone seeing and thinking in these terms into illusion. Virgil, because he is listening to the saintly woman—and it is sanctity that will save one at this point, not cleverness—is able to unveil the true ugliness of the "siren" and so draw Dante's attention away from her. The true nature of Sloth is ugliness, but when Dante misuses his intellect—or rather relies solely on his *individual* intellect which is ruled by the ego and thus subject to the passions—he sees her as beautiful; he has projected the intrinsic beauty of the Intellect as such upon an unworthy object.

Very often a sin is healed by its opposite (lust by chastity, anger by kindness etc.), but in this case the opposite of Sloth is a kind of fruition of that sin; according to some commentators, the figure in Dante's dream represents not so much Sloth, which is based on a deficiency of love, but rather the "higher" sins of Avarice, Gluttony and Lust, based on excessive love. In this Canto Sloth announces Avarice, which is often used as a false way of overcoming laziness; someone who has wasted his or her youth, for example, or is reacting against an inner spiritual passivity, may try to "make up for lost time" by obsessively making money. Sloth may also bloom into Lust; our word "slut," which seems to be a combination of the words "sloth" and "lust," denotes a girl who is lazy but also promiscuous. In the words of Climacus, "Alertness keeps the mind clean; somnolence binds the soul. The alert monk does battle with fornication, but the sleepy one goes to live with it."

A further aspect of the "siren song" of Sloth is that it can sometimes masquerade as spiritual detachment or *apatheia* and contemplative repose. The essence of Sloth, however, is not the intuition of Eternity, as contemplation is, but rather the fear of spiritual change. (That *apatheia* has been transformed into our word "apathy" shows how the worldly mind, when it looks at contemplation, can see only Sloth.)

> *I turned my eyes; then good Virgil said:*
>   *"At least three times I've called you; rise and come;*
>   *Let's find the opening that will let you enter."*
> *When I rose I saw in broad daylight already*
>   *All the circles of that Holy Mountain;*
>   *On we went with the new sun at our backs.*
> *Following him, I felt my forehead burdened*
>   *Like one who bears the weight of heavy thought,*
>   *And bends down like the half-arch of a bridge;*
> *Then heard the word: "Come close, the pass is here."* [34–43]

The travelers are then addressed by a guiding angel:

> *He who spoke to us had wings wide open*
>   *Like those of a swan; with these he pointed us*
>   *Upwards between two walls of solid granite.*
> *Then he beat those wings, and fanned us with them,*
>   *Confirming that those* qui lugent [the meek] *will be blest,*
>   *And have their souls filled full with consolation.*
> *"What's wrong with you, that you always watch the ground?"*
>   *My Guide began to say, when both of us*
>   *Had climbed a little higher than the angel.*
> *I answered, "This new vision that I've had*
>   *Keeps hold on me and makes my steps uncertain;*
>   *Somehow I can't shake off the thought of it."*
> *"Didn't you see that ancient witch," he said,*
>   *"For whom alone the slopes above must suffer?*
>   *Didn't you see how man is freed from her?*
> *That's enough—it's time to move your feet,*
>   *To lift your eyes to the lure that's whirled about*
>   *On his massive wheels by that Eternal King."*

The Ordeal of Mercy

Just like a hawk, who first inspects his feet,
  Then turns to the falconer's call and stretches forward,
  With longing for the food made ready for him,
So I became.... [46–67]

After Virgil awakens Dante he moves forward again, but under great oppression; he describes himself as walking bent over like the half-arch of a bridge. This indicates that his sense of oppression is not ultimately an obstacle, but rather something he must pass through consciously in order to continue on his journey. This vision of materiality has come to him just as he is about to rise above it, when he is on the point of breaking the spell of that witch, an aspect of the Darkness of This World, who wants to enforce the materialistic view of things upon which Sloth is based. The lesson is: don't try to analyze or immediately attempt to atone for an attraction to lower things, but rather give yourself to the lure of the upward path. Don't fear that this might represent imbalance or one-sidedness, hatred of the material world or rejection of the body; an exclusive concentration upon elevation, represented by the swan-wingéd angel, is precisely what is needed here. Dante is learning, like the falcon responding to the voice of the Falconer, to listen for the call of *vidya-maya*, rather than to the siren-song of *avidya-maya*. As St. John Climacus says in his chapter "On Mourning," "Blessed is the monk who can lift up the eyes of the soul to the powers of heaven." Below this point, the will had to work *against* desire to accomplish purgation; but now, after beholding the *lure* of the Divine, will and desire are one.

Now the travelers come upon the souls of the Avaricious, lying face down on the ground and singing *adhaesit pavimento anima mea*, "my soul cleaves to the dust."

According to St. Maximos the Confessor, Avarice is related to Pride: "Self-esteem and avarice produce each other. Those who are full of self-esteem acquire riches and those who are rich become full of self-esteem." He also sees Avarice both as the seed of spiritual hypocrisy and as a way by which such hypocrisy is often exposed: "Whenever a lover of riches [who] feigns virtue by an outward show of devotion finds he has procured the material possessions he

Canto XIX

desires, he repudiates the way of life that made people think he was a disciple of the Logos." [*Philokalia*, Volume Two, *Third Century on Love*, 83; *First Century on Theology*, 64]

The souls of the Avaricious cleave to the dust, to this material world, and so also to sorrow, because in life they rejected what might have lifted their souls up and consequently brought true happiness. Mourning, here, is a deep lamentation that produces depth and receptivity in the soul. In the words of Climacus, "Mourning is a golden spur within a soul that has been stripped of all bonds and ties, set by holy sorrow to keep watch over the heart." Avarice in particular must be *mourned* in order to be overcome because in life it cuts the soul off from spiritual elevation. Avarice doesn't necessarily lead to chaos as Sloth often will, but it does lead to a strict substitution of material concerns for spiritual ones.

Mourning, here, is grief for what has been lost through an avaricious evaluation of things, for one's separation from the whole spiritual dimension. As Climacus says, "We have not been called here to a wedding feast; He who called us has summoned us to mourn for ourselves ... those gifted with the heart's depth of mourning turn away from their bodies as if from an enemy."

Among the souls of the Avaricious the travelers encounter the soul of Pope Adrian V; Virgil gives Dante permission to interview him. Adrian reminds Dante that in the next world they neither marry nor are given in marriage; he does this in order to emphasize that in the Resurrection the soul is married to the Spirit, not to the corpse. The soul must divorce this world of materiality so as to participate in the wedding feast of the Lamb. The resurrection of the body happens not within the context of earthly materiality, but within that of the marriage of soul and Spirit. In the words of Climacus, "The man wearing blessed, God-given mourning like a wedding garment gets to know the spiritual laughter of the soul."

The very fact that the Papacy is a spiritual office blocks the descent of the Spirit when that office is given over to worldliness, and so pulls the soul into worldly concerns. It is striking that all that matters to the soul of Pope Adrian now, all he values in the world of the living, is his pious niece Alagia [lines 142–145], not all the memory of his accomplishments, status and possessions.

Canto XX

The Virgin Mary, Fabricius and St. Nicholas are given as examples of Poverty and Generosity, the virtues that are directly contrary to Avarice and Prodigality. Hugh Capet, the founder of the Capetian Dynasty, condemns his descendents. Pygmalion, Midas, Acan, Sapphira, Heliodorus, Polymnestor, and Crassus are given as examples of the sin of Avarice. The entire Mountain trembles at the release of a single soul from Purgatory—which will turn out, in the next Canto, to be the soul of Statius.

> *The will that fights a better will is helpless;*
>   *Therefore, so as to please him against my pleasure,*
>   *I drew my sponge from the water not yet filled.*
> *Onward I moved, as onward moved my Leader.* . . . [1–4]

Dante must pass by the sorrowing of the Avaricious without burdening them further with his queries, and without his own soul becoming entangled with the weight of the material values they had clung to in earthly life, lest both he and they fall into the abyss. The sin of Avarice can easily make one fall; its materiality has a kind of gravitational pull to it. The sorrow of these souls is in the process of liquefying and loosening that pull of Avarice, not just for themselves but for the whole world, and this touches on the mystery of how the souls in Purgatory, who need the prayers of the living, can nonetheless pray for the world and for us. These souls fulfill the task of love through sorrow, and love-through-sorrow leads beyond itself always; this love is allowed to die in the process of purgation so that a higher love, imbued with light, can be born. This is why the soul of Hugh Capet tells Dante that the light he sees in him now is more helpful to him than Dante's prayers will be after he returns to earth. The love these souls experience through mourning allows itself to be annihilated. They don't let their love become enshrined; they don't hold on to it, but yield it to higher states of being. By this they are purged of the sin of Avariciousness-in-Love, the temptation to turn love into a possession.

> *O heaven, by whose turnings many think*
> *Things here below are changed.* . . . [13–14]

Here Dante debunks the idea of astrological influences as the true causes of events to show how the Avaricious habitually "play the odds" and rely upon trends and projections instead of recognizing all events as the will of God, who rules this world from Eternity, from beyond the starry spheres.

Next the travelers hear one of the souls of the Avaricious invoking three examples of holy poverty: the Virgin Mary, Fabricius and St. Nicholas.

> *Ahead of us by chance I heard someone sigh*
> *"Sweet Mary!"—in profoundest lamentation,*
> *Like a woman in midst of child-birth crying out;*
> *And he continued: "Just how poor you were*
> *Is shown by the sorry nature of that tavern*
> *Where you halted to lay down your holy burden."* [19–24]

The poverty of Mary has to do with her celestial nature. Mary did not come from Heaven as her Son did, but she was so close to God that she was effectively a citizen of Heaven to the degree that she understood the poverty of the world as such. To those who feel the intrinsic poverty of this world, there is little difference between a mansion and a stable. The residents of both shelters are subject to death and to a degree of separation from God, and this is what truly matters, much more so than the quantity of goods or "goodness" that one's terrestrial life has had. This sense of absolute poverty was necessary for the Incarnation because Mary was called to give birth to God Who is greater than the world, in the face of Whom this world is as nothing. The intrinsic poverty of the Virgin, which is a poverty of specific determinations and thus an expression of perfect receptivity, is expressed by the Eastern Orthodox Church in its icon of the Theotokos entitled "She who is More Spacious than the Heavens." It is no surprise that the Son of such a mother would cast the money-changers out of the temple.

Gaius Fabricius was known for refusing to take bribes in his official capacity as Roman consul, and later during his tenure as censor. He made this refusal because he valued qualities of character more than material goods. If this world of *materia* is under "the reign of quantity," conversely it is *quality*, or *forma*, that reigns in the Kingdom of Heaven.

St. Nicholas, Bishop of Myra, was supposed to have anonymously provided three pious virgins with dowries by tossing bags of gold through their window, thus saving them from lives of prostitution; this is both a symbolic dramatization and an actual instance of the truth that holy poverty opens the soul to the generosity of God. This quality of Divine generosity manifesting through St. Nicholas is the true origin of the folk legend of Santa Claus, which has been such a powerful force in the collective psyche of Christendom. Generosity involves the providing of material sustenance, but Nicholas also manifested a spiritual generosity that could actually bring into being a folk character for a people and a time he never knew.[1]

Santa Claus is also a polar or Hyperborean hero, which is why he is pictured as living at the North Pole. The chimney he climbs down to bring his presents to the children on Christmas before he re-ascends and continues on his journey is thus a type of the *Axis Mundi*. Because the three virgins are provided with dowries they can fully incarnate in the corporeal world, otherwise they would have had to remain, as it were, in the psychic world, the world of fantasy, of unrealized potential. Thus the sacrament of matrimony

---

1. The figure of Kris Kringle or Father Christmas was clearly influenced by earlier Pagan ideas, especially those related to the Oak King and the zodiacal sign of Sagittarius—ruled by Jupiter, the planet of kingly largesse—that flanks the Winter Solstice. But the idea of magnificent abundance breaking through from an invisible Source during the cold of winter, at the darkest time of the year, as in the English and German legend of the Christmas Rose, became inevitably associated with the Father's gift of His only-begotten Son at the lowest point of the aeon when the human soul was most congealed, darkened and separated from God.

Canto XX

can be viewed, in Scholastic terms, as a type of the motion from Potency to Act. The generosity of St. Nicholas to the three poor maidens is precisely the generosity of heavenly Form to the impoverished *materia* of this world.

The soul extolling the three examples of holy poverty turns out to be that of Hugh Capet, founder of the Capetian Dynasty, who succeeded the Carolingians:

> *After all the ancient kings had died,*
> *Except one only, a penitent clothed grey*
> *Then within my grip were placed the reins*
> *Of the Empire's rule, and with them such great power....*
> [53–56]

Hugh Capet recounts the worldly triumphs and spiritual defeats of his lineage. In the process of being purged of Avarice, he understands the holiness of a poverty that has the power to receive the Divinity. This poverty, of course, entails detachment both from worldly goods and from worldliness itself; this is the very quality his soul he now seeks. "That hostel where you set down your holy burden" [lines 22–23] is not only the inn where Mary and Joseph rested, but This World itself.

The "monk in gray" of line 54 is the last scion of the Carolingian Dynasty who—according to legend—took monastic vows. When the worldly power of the Carolingian line was vanquished, it entered a spiritual dimension and took on a spiritual work which was invisible to the eyes of this world. And that power may yet exist; perhaps the power to keep France a Catholic country has something to do with unseen streams of influence from Charlemagne and his lineage. René Guénon, in *The Reign of Quantity and the Signs of the Times*, talks about the dangerous psychic residues of dead religions, a danger that may also apply to lost races, lost civilizations, lost causes; and in our own time we have seen the evil that can grow out of such atavism in the form of the revival of Paganism. The ancestral influence spoken of here is positive, however, because it doesn't have to do with the Avaricious attempt to cling, in necromantic mode, to the psychic residues of the dead so as to gain magical

The Ordeal of Mercy

power. Maybe the holy dead sleeping in their tombs can indeed exert a protective influence on the realm because this sort of power is a gift they didn't ask for. It's something separate from whatever personal Avariciousness or desire for power they may have had during life; it is based on their transpersonal function.[2]

Huge Capet mentions three events: the seizure of Ponthieu, Normandy and Gascony by his descendants; the actions of Philip the Fair who suppressed the Order of the Temple that Dante identified with the secret or *pneumatic* Church, the Church of John; and the campaigns of Charles of Anjou who defeated Manfred, King of Sicily, and his nephew Conradin, supporters of the imperial cause against the papacy (Charles was also falsely reputed to have assassinated Thomas Aquinas). He ironically characterizes them as having been done *per ammenda*, "to make amends," because these are acts whose perpetrators must eventually endure the rigors of purgation. What is being described here are the entanglements of worldly history. Avarice tempted these souls to seek political power, thus forcing them into sins that must necessarily invoke the Justice of God.

Hugh Capet now "predicts" the arrival of Charles of Valois, who exiled Dante's White Guelph party from Florence, and Charles of Anjou, who sold his daughter Beatrice to an elderly noble in exchange for a rich dowry. This heartless act reminds us of those fairy tales where a miller sells his daughter to the Devil in return for wealth—the "mill" being a common symbol of this world as ruled by the cycles of nature and subject to astrological fate. Not to care about one's daughter is to have no care for the fate of one's soul, nor for the spiritual inheritance one is preparing for one's descendants. And that Charles of Anjou's daughter is named Beatrice indicates

---

2. The Nazis may have attempted something like this necromancy of psychic residues when they took possession of "the Spear of Destiny" in Vienna which had been part of the regalia of the Lombard kings, and which was used in the coronation ceremonies of more than one Holy Roman Emperor; it was identified (probably falsely) as the spear of Longinus that pierced the side of Christ. Since Judas' betrayal led to Christ's crucifixion, he can be said, in metaphorical terms, to have wielded the spear that pierced the Savior.

that Charles, through his Avarice, has turned against sublimity of soul, the quality capable of guiding other souls to Paradise that Beatrice Portinari exemplifies in the *Divine Comedy*.

Next Hugh "foresees" the kidnapping of Pope Boniface VIII by agents of Philip the Fair in revenge for his excommunication—a violation of papal authority that set the stage for the removal of the Papacy from Rome to Avignon from 1309–1377, and its domination during that period by the kings of France. Here Dante pictures the attempt to set up a Counter-Church through Avarice; and though this church was not ultimately established in the 14th century, nonetheless the possibility of it remains close to history, ready to appear again whenever the opportunity might arise. [See Editorial Commentary Four: *On the Aggiornamento of the Church and the Giant of the World.*]

> *When, O Lord! O when shall I be joyful?*
> *When feast my eyes upon Your hidden vengeance*
> *That sweetens in secret the spectre of your wrath?* [94–96]

Justice comes about in a secret way that doesn't seem like justice to the worldly soul because it doesn't satisfy the ego. Dante loses Florence and all his political hopes, but he gains the *Divine Comedy*; and this is his true vindication.

> *That thing I said regarding the one and only*
> *Bride of the Holy Spirit, which gave You occasion*
> *To turn to me for comment—that will serve*
> *To answer all our prayers while it is day.*
> *But when night falls the opposite is called for;*
> *That's when we must sing a different song.* [97–102]

Here Dante maintains that it was something he said about the Virgin, possibly in his *La Vita Nuova*, that drew God's attention and patronage to his work and thus secured him the Divine commission to produce his *Commedia*. He could well be referring to the episode in Chapter V of *La Vita Nuova* when, while attending church, he so deeply *heard* some words about the Blessed Virgin, perhaps from a

The Ordeal of Mercy

litany, that he had a vision of Beatrice as both a veil and manifestation of Mary, just as another lady of "pleasant flavor" seated near him functioned as both a veil and a manifestation for Beatrice.[3] This seems to foreshadow the advent of the *Divine Comedy*, which arrived through a hierarchy of muses: first the Virgin, then St. Lucy, then Beatrice. For God to request, through the mediumship of these muses, the words of Dante by calling out of him his *Commedia*, is the greatest honor that any poet could wish for, more than enough to last anyone a lifetime. But when night falls, which is the night of Death, then all words return to the One who spoke them originally, and the poet of God is silenced. He no longer receives and transmits the Divine Word, but must murmur his own poor human word—his confession—as best he can.

Now Dante presents seven examples of Avarice from classical antiquity and the Old Testament: Pygmalion, Midas, Achan, Sapphira (and Ananias), Heliodorus, Polymnestor, and Crassus.

According to the *Aeneid*, Pygmalion, Queen Dido's brother, murdered her husband for material gain; Dante may have characterized him as a "parricide" because he also murdered his uncle. To attempt to appropriate, possess and live off of one's heritage without respecting the source of it is like murdering one's father. The ultimate source of all value is God, but if you don't respect the particulars of your heritage, the forms through which it has come down to you, you have cut yourself off from His generosity. Frithjof Schuon pointed out that liberal secular humanism inherited all its "humanistic" values from Christianity, but since it never acknowledged this heritage it has now become morally bankrupt.

In Ovid's *Metamorphoses*, King Midas of Phrygia asked and received from the god Bacchus the power to turn anything he touched into gold; consequently he could no longer eat. Finally he unthinkingly embraced his young daughter, turning her too into gold. Midas, in trying to possess the whole world, is alienated from it. He can assimilate none of the good of the world due to his Avarice, and

---

3. This is an example of the "screen lady" conceit taken from the Courtly Love tradition.

Canto XX

finally can no longer relate in a living way to his own daughter—who is the soul of the world, the *anima mundi*.

Achan, in the Book of Joshua, attempted to appropriate part of the booty collected by the Israelites after the fall of Jericho, a crime for which he was stoned to death. To steal the booty of God is to try, as a mere human, to possess supernatural Grace or claim Divine prerogatives; whoever does so is subject to a Promethean or Luciferian inflation.[4]

In the Acts of the Apostles, Sapphira and her husband Ananias, members of the early Christian community, attempted to secretly hold back some of the proceeds from the sale of their property which they had pledged to the Church; for this crime, and the deception by which they tried to conceal it, both were struck down by God. Such Divine retribution appears at very few places in the New Testament. The property that the couple attempted to hold back represents their souls, which properly belong to God alone, not to the human ego; it's as if Ananias and Sapphira had tried to create value apart from God, out of pure nothingness. Our souls are never our own; to try and possess one's soul is to deaden it to the point where it can no longer choose for life: "Whoever tries to keep his life will lose it" [Luke 7:33; Matthew 16:25]. Their punishment is quick and dreadful in order to demonstrate the grave import of this loss-of-soul. The whole purpose and goal of the Christian revelation is the salvation of souls—and to strive for the salvation of one's soul necessarily entails facing the dread of losing it. As Frithjof Schuon pointed out, "the traditional doctrines that insist most on Mercy have as their point of departure the conviction that we run the risk of hell, or even deserve it, and that we are only saved by the Goodness of Heaven."

According to The Second Book of Maccabees, Heliodorus was sent by the King of Syria to rob the Temple at Jerusalem; God stopped him by sending an angel riding a white horse with a golden

---

4. The parallels in the symbolism of Lucifer and Prometheus show that they represent a similar rebellion against God: Lucifer is the Light-Bearer, and Prometheus stole Fire.

bridle. When Heliodorus approached and seized the bridle, the horse trampled him to death. Heliodorus, unlike Achan, is not of the people of God, consequently his intent to plunder the Temple is not based upon a will to appropriate Divinity, but rather to convert spiritual treasures into material ones. The angel prevents this, demonstrating that these are treasures of the Spirit that are not to be touched, nor are they really capable of being materialized.

Priam was the King of Troy and cousin to Aeneas who, according to Virgil's *Aeneid*, was the direct ancestor of Romulus and Remus, the founders of Rome. Priam sent his son Polydorus with a vast treasure of gold to be deposited for safekeeping with King Polymnestor of Thrace, but Polymnestor possessed himself of the treasure and had Polydorus killed. Priam is the king of the human soul, representative of the spark of the Spirit within man; his son Polydorus comes bringing the gold of the Intellect, the Nous. Material sustenance is one of the legitimate effects or aspects of this gold; Polymnestor, however, can see only material good in the treasure and nothing else, thus imprisoning it in worldliness, in the reign of quantity. Priam, to him, is one of the kings of This World just as he is. This is precisely what we and the world do when we evaluate other people in exclusively worldly terms, when we think of them as worthless unless they can bring us some material advantage. When we deny all human or spiritual value in other people for the sake of some material or quantitative valuation—their jobs, their status, their "net worth," their ability to command attention and sway the masses—it is if we had murdered them.

Marcus Licinius Crassus was the third member of the Roman triumvirate that included Pompey and Julius Caesar; he was notoriously hungry for gold. According to legend, after he was defeated and slain by King Hyrodes of Parthia, the King poured molten gold down the mouth of his severed head. For Crassus to "drink" molten gold suggests a form of counter-Eucharist, given that gold is the metal of the sun and Christ is called "the Sun of Righteousness." Christians receive communion in order to assimilate Heaven, and so become one with it; in the words of St. Athanasius, "God became man so that man might become God." Crassus, on the other hand, tried to devour the material world so completely as to become that world, thus betraying the human function of *pontifex* or "bridge-builder" between Heaven and earth.[5]

> ... [then] I felt, as if it all were falling,
>   The entire Mountain shake—a chill went through me,
>   Like the chill that seizes him who goes to Death.
> Surely not even Delos shook so strongly
>   Before Latona built her nest within it
>   To give birth to her twins—the eyes of Heaven.
> Then on every side there rose a cry,
>   Such that my Master, drawing close to me,
>   Said "Fear not, for I am still your Guide."
> "Gloria in excelsis Deo" *was the cry!* [127–136]

Dante senses something like death in the trembling of the Mountain, but then he immediately feels a joyousness that one doesn't necessarily experience upon earthly death, when he hears the souls shouting "Gloria in excelsis deo!" The cold he feels has to do with the fact that a soul must die to the world it has lived in before it can go on, even if it is dying to Purgatory, or a particular terrace of it. What's striking here is that the coldness of death is instantly coupled with joy, unlike earthly death where, except for the souls of the glorified, sorrow lingers on—sorrow and often uncertainty.

Dante is alluding here to Jupiter's transformation of the Island of Delos from a floating island to an anchored one. The anchoring of Delos bespeaks the kind of openness to the Spirit that was necessary for the titan Latona to become impregnated by Jupiter and give birth to Apollo and Diana who are "the eyes of Heaven"—the Sun and Moon whose spheres make up part of the Paradiso. Purgatory is in perpetual flux; it is related to both worldly time and the transmigration of the soul through higher worlds. But when time ends, Purgatory ends. Paradise, however, is anchored, since it is totally encompassed by the Spirit. The souls in Purgatory can rise from cir-

---

5. The Parthians were likely kin to the Scythians, renowned for crafting superb objects in solid gold; the Scythian gold is one of the most renowned of the ancient treasures unearthed by modern archaeology.

cle to circle, whereas those in Paradise are rooted in their eternal station; though these Paradisical souls can visit each other in different stations, nonetheless, unlike the souls in Purgatory, they never have to place their feet on shifting sands. As Dante and Virgil break with the sin of Avarice, they are actually beginning to transcend the instability of Purgatory and receive intimations of the "solidity and radiance" of Paradise [cf. Plato's *Timaeus*]. Avarice is based on the attempt to establish security and stability through acquisition, but—ironically—nothing is more susceptible to shifts in fortune than the fruits of this passion.

The trembling of the Mountain is an annunciation too, like Gabriel's to the Virgin, and the song of the heavenly host to the shepherds. And the advent of the *Divine Comedy* to Dante must also have been, in a sense, an annunciation like this; at the arrival of it Dante himself must have trembled. Truly inspired art is something like an incarnation of God. Ezra Pound, in the forty-fifth of his *Cantos*, spoke of how Avarice—which he there names *usura* (usury), a notion that includes the production of art for sale, not under traditional patronage—acts to stifle this kind of inspiration:

> *With* usura
> *hath no man a painted Paradise on his Church wall*
> harpes et luz
> *or where Virgin receiveth message*
> *and halo projects from incision.* . . .

Dante can no longer complacently live in ignorance. Knowledge itself is not going to allow him to stay on his former level—the level where ignorance avariciously collects facts through the use of memory—but is leading him inexorably to a greater wholeness and integration of soul.

Canto XXI

The travelers encounter the poet Statius, one of Virgil's great admirers, who is to accompany them on their journey to the Terrestrial Paradise—Statius who, according to Dante, had become a secret Christian. He explains to them the trembling of the Mountain.

> *Natural thirst, which never can be satisfied*
> *Except by the living water and its grace*
> *That the Samaritan woman asked for at the well,*
> *Put me in torment, and driven on by haste*
> *Along the rocky path I followed my Leader.*
> *I felt pity when I saw that righteous vengeance. . . .* [1–6]

The thirst for penance is what creates Purgatory, but the supernatural thirst for grace gives the soul a direct taste of Paradise—"O taste and see that the Lord is good" [Psalm 34:8]. This *natural* taste for penance, this counter-passion, is the appropriate flavor for purgation. Once the soul begins to yearn for the taste of Paradise, however, it has already begun to transcend Purgatory.

The impulse to pity the souls in Hell is a temptation that must be resisted, but it is right to pity those in Purgatory because these souls carry a goodness within themselves despite their suffering. Pity for souls in purgation eases the burden they carry and helps them open to mercy, but pity for the damned is useless. To pity those in Hell only increases frustration because one's feelings and efforts are repelled and driven back to where they began. To pity the souls in Purgatory, however, is to experience an opening in one's own soul because this pity is received as a mercy from God.

Now the soul of Statius appears, and salutes the travelers:

> *. . . "My brothers, may God give you peace!"*
> *Suddenly we turned, and Virgil gave to him*

The Ordeal of Mercy

> *The appropriate response to his salutation.*
> *"May the court of justice establish you in peace*
> *In the blessed congregation" he replied,*
> *"The court that decreed for me eternal exile!"* [13–18]

When Christ appears to the pilgrims on the road to Emmaus [Luke 24:13–35], He shows them His Resurrection, and the universal redemption He brings to all souls able to receive it. Likewise when Statius appears to Dante and Virgil, he is—at least for Dante—a messenger of Christ's redemption. Here Virgil, the good Pagan, extols—with true Stoic virtue—the justice that has assigned him to Hell and destined Statius for Paradise; Mercy is for the Christian, not the Pagan. God's Mercy does not fight against justice, however, but raises it to a higher level. There is an implication in the action of this Canto, never made explicit, that perhaps Virgil can ultimately be saved.

> *"If you be souls deemed unworthy by God to rise*
> *Who has guided you this far up His stairs?"*
> *My teacher answered: "If you note the marks*
> *Which this one bears, placed there by the Angel*
> *You'll clearly see he must reign with the good."* [20–24]

Here Virgil names Dante as *his* guide. The master-disciple relationship is never as cut-and-dried as it would seem to be; sometimes the teacher can learn from the student. It is important to maintain the hierarchy which places Grace above natural wisdom, but sometimes, after having strained to look upward, one may—by God's grace alone—gain insight from something lower than one's own as-yet-unrealized potential; this is the whole meaning of and justification for psychological insight in the context of the spiritual Path.

Statius explains that the trembling of the Mountain in Canto XX, when the soul was released from purgation, has no natural cause, seeing that there is no weather in Purgatory, nor are there earthquakes; it responds only to heavenly causes. Direct celestial influences, those not cycled through natural causality, always have to do

Canto XXI

with the interiority of the soul, even if they sometimes manifest as miraculous occurrences in the outer world.

We are told [lines 52–54] that Purgatory is without weather down to the third and highest step above which sits the Angel with the keys, the Angel who has the power to admit souls to Purgatory or bar their way [cf. Canto IX]. To pass this Angel to enter the Church; if one is a true member of the Church, one is either in Paradise—the Church Triumphant—in Purgatory—the Church Suffering—or on earth, in the Church Militant. And everything one encounters in the Church Suffering, which is secretly present on earth as well, can serve the work of Purgation. The gate to the Church is situated at the threshold of Purgatory because the struggling souls of the Church Militant may also participate in purgation, so much so that some will enter Paradise immediately upon death.

Statius now explains the independent nature of free will:

> "The will alone gives proof of purity.
>> Because it's free to change its company
>> By surprise it takes the soul, and helps it fly.
> Its first will was to climb, but this is blocked
>> By desire to repent, given by God's justice,
>> Where once there was the desire to transgress.
> And I, who have been lying in this pain
>> Five hundred years and more, have just now felt
>> A free choice to cross a better threshold.
> That's why you heard the earthquake, and the pious
>> Spirits along the Mountain giving praise
>> Unto the Lord, that He send them quickly upward."
>
>   [61–72]

The whole purpose of purgation is to "free the free will" from bondage to sin. The will is intrinsically free, but in bondage because of the corruption of the soul. The Intellect can throw light upon the state of the will and tell it what to will, but in and of itself it cannot free the will, any more than the vision of Paradise can give what only Purgatory can accomplish. The Intellect is higher than the will, but it cannot overpower the will, only guide it.

The Ordeal of Mercy

But how exactly is the will saved? This is mysterious because the will cannot save itself through its own efforts, and yet it *must* save itself by choosing the Good and the True. A transcendent Grace calls to the intrinsic freedom of the will and awakens it to the task of making this choice. And when the will is purified—and only then—there is no part of the soul left without openness to God.

Here Penance, which is a good work, is presented as a kind of bondage. Statius' soul is not free until it can cast Penance aside, but this is worlds apart from the attitude of the sinner who wants to deny that Penance is ever needed.[1]

It seems as if the desire for Penance, based upon the love of Divine Justice, could trap the soul forever, but as the soul becomes purified the longing for Paradise overwhelms the desire for purification. The will can will repentance but it cannot will Paradise. The longing for Paradise, in a manner of speaking, brings Paradise itself to the soul. The soul becomes absorbed in its desire for Paradise, and this desire itself is taken up into Paradise.[2]

Statius is freed from the rule of Penance because, in meeting with Virgil, he meets his archetype, his higher self; Statius' encounter with Virgil is like Dante's encounter with Beatrice. Virgil, as archetype not necessarily as individual, is saved through the presence of Dante, a saved Christian—at least for the purpose of this meeting with Statius—as well as through Dante's work on his great *Commedia*, which carries on and completes Virgil's *Aeneid*. The presence of Virgil activates Statius's knowledge of the *Aeneid*; this is what allows his encounter with both Dante and Virgil to symbolize his freedom from Purgatory and the beginning of his ascent to Paradise. In a certain sense, the entire *Divine Comedy* is designed to redeem the

---

1. Likewise the Hindus speak of the "golden chain" of good works which is still under the rule of *karma*, and the Sufis of the need to "repent of repentance." In the words of Omar Khayyam from his *Rubaiyyat*:

> Come, fill the Cup, and in the fire of Spring
> The winter garment of Repentance fling:
> The Bird of Time has but a little way to fly—
> And lo! The Bird is on the wing.

2. As Hafiz sings in the first ode of his *Divan*, "Though we may be far from the field of nearness, /Our desire is not far."

Canto XXI

archetype of Virgil, and with it the whole of that Pagan wisdom capable of being Christianized.[3]

The whole Mountain trembles when one soul is freed from Purgatory because for that soul Purgatory no longer exists—and so Purgatory as a whole is confronted with its own transitory nature. It's as if when one soul is saved all are saved, though this remains a mystery—a mystery possibly alluded to in the parable of the one lost sheep for whom the ninety-nine were abandoned; perhaps if the one sheep is rescued, the ninety-nine are also saved.[4]

Now Statius identifies himself:

> *"Under that name whose honor most endures,*
> *I was highly renowned on earth"* the spirit said,
> *"But I did not yet possess the gift of faith. . . ."* [85–87]

> *"The seeds that lit my fervor were the sparks*
> *Of that celestial flame that kindled me,*
> *By which a thousand or more were set on fire;*
> *I speak of the* Aeneid*. . . ."* [94–97]

> *"And to have lived on earth when Virgil lived*
> *I'd gladly suffer here another year*
> *Beyond the time set down for my release."* [100–102]

Statius is saying that it was due to his poetic fame in this world, which caused his name to be honored over a long period of time,

---

3. William Blake's relationship with his great predecessor, John Milton, is precisely analogous to Dante's with Virgil. Dante intuits that Virgil inhabits Limbo, the antechamber of Hell; Blake sees Milton in vision as "Unhappy tho' in heav'n" because he is estranged from his "Emanation," his feminine soul. Blake consciously composed his great "prophetic books," *The Four Zoas*, *Milton* and *Jerusalem*, in part so as to redeem the spirit of Milton, and we may perhaps discern the same intent in Dante vis-à-vis Virgil in terms of the *Divine Comedy*. And certainly Beatrice may be described, in Blake's terminology, as Dante's Emanation—his *Shakti*.

4. Likewise in Mahayana Buddhism, the Bodhisattva or Buddha-to-be fulfills his vow to "save all sentient beings" by becoming Buddha, at which point the concept of his own Buddhahood and the concept of "numberless sentient beings in need of salvation" both fall away.

that—because he had achieved this fame before finding the faith—his progress through Purgatory was impeded. Christians pray for the dead and so help them to advance, but the Pagans of late antiquity merely enshrined their dead, or the most notable among them, thus binding them to their earthly identities; so much for the late-Pagan ideal of *apotheosis*.

Statius sees what repentance is just as he has passed beyond it. The goal of repentance can only be realized at the moment the soul is released from the necessity of purgation; it is often true that we can view something in its wholeness only after we have transcended it. And Statius is also seeing that the essence of his task in Purgatory was to reach the place where he would be able to meet Virgil—to realize his own archetype.

> *But yet the power of will is not almighty;*
> *For both tears and laughter so closely follow*
> *Those passions in the breast from which they spring*
> *The most sincere have least power to subdue them.* [105–108]

True feeling, and the true love and friendship this feeling manifests, are harbingers of Paradise. The will can and should subdue false feeling, but true feeling partakes of a deeper and higher stratum of the soul, one that the will, while still divorced from feeling, cannot occupy and lacks both the strength and the right to overpower. In union with true feeling, however, which is the "ruling love" of the soul (in Swedenborg's terminology), the will is the very principle of that feeling and that love. Statius, at the moment he is released from Purgatory by his meeting with Virgil, whom he does not yet recognize, lets us know that he would be willing to spend a whole further year in purgation if that would give him the opportunity to meet the poet he so admired. When Statius is told by Dante that he is indeed talking to Virgil, he immediately bows down to kiss his hand; (Dante makes the same gesture toward Pope Adrian V in Canto XIX). Virgil tells Statius to rise since both of them are shades. The transcendence of materiality is worlds apart from the sort of vanity that treats contingent things as if they were permanent. By rising, and by his willingness to stand as an equal to Virgil,

Canto XXI

Statius shows that he is purified of the idolatry that almost always enters into a master-disciple relationship, an idolatry that might have interrupted his journey to Paradise by causing him to mistakenly see his master not as contingent, but rather as eternal as only God is eternal; since Christ is God incarnate, He alone is the real Master. Statius, who is a Christian, has a Christian love for Virgil which is seeded in Paradise; this is why he is able to call him "Brother." Because of this love, both men can, as far as they are capable, participate in the love of Paradise itself.

Statius and Virgil are only able to meet as equals at the point where both of them are dead to corporeal life and its scale of values; yet Statius tells Virgil that his love for him is so great that he has forgotten they are without bodies; it is not materiality that will give them substance, but Love itself. This begins to anticipate a resurrected and glorified body that could live entirely on Love, just as some saints have been able to subsist on nothing but water and the consecrated wafer of the Eucharist.

Canto XXII

The Angel of Justice appears. Dante and Virgil climb to the Sixth Terrace, reserved for the Gluttons. Statius confesses Prodigality as his ruling sin. Virgil speaks of the souls in Limbo. The mysterious tree. Spiritual voices name the Virgin Mary (the perfection of all the virtues), the women of ancient Rome and of the Golden Age, and John the Baptist, as examples of Temperance.

> *Feeling lighter than I did on earlier stairs*
>   *Without undue labor I traveled onward*
>   *Following those swift spirits in their ascent.*
> *Then Virgil began [addressing Statius]: "The love that's*
>   *fired by virtue*
>   *Can awaken answering love within another,*
>   *As long as it outwardly expresses itself.*
> *Thus from the hour that Juvenal [the Roman satiric poet]*
>   *descended*
>   *Among us into our infernal Limbo,*
>   *And made apparent to me your great affection,*
> *The fondness that I felt for you was as great*
>   *As ever linked one to a person to another*
>   *He's never met; that's why these stairs seem short." [7–18]*

Dante feels lighter now, as he approaches the terrace of the Gluttons, because his desires are being sublimated. The reason for fasting is to deny the gross appetite until one knows that any fulfillment that comes cannot come from physical satisfaction, but must derive from a higher Source; blessed are those who hunger for the path of ascent.

Virgil tells Statius that love, when based on virtue and openly manifested, always receives a reply. This is because virtuous love has an objective aspect; it is not simply subjective sentiment attempting

Canto XXII

to awaken a similar sentiment in another. But although this reply is certain, we don't always know how it will come. This is something like the doctrine that prayer is never lost. You may ask "what if I pray for someone thinking they are in Purgatory, while they are really in Hell, and thus unable to receive or profit from my prayer?" But the grace from that prayer is not lost; if the person the prayer is intended for is impervious to it, the prayer itself remains as a vehicle of spiritual help in some way.

When he heard how Statius had praised him in life, Virgil's deepest love for him was awakened because he knew that Statius, a virtuous man, was no flatterer, but spoke out of his love for objective truth. A love for a person one has never seen is mysterious, and partakes of the other world; it is necessarily free from subjective impressions. Traditionally, both Eros and Justice are blindfolded.

Virgil then asks Statius how a man such as he, renowned for wisdom, could have fallen into the sin of Avarice; Statius explains that his sin was not Avarice, but Prodigality.

Avarice has to do with holding on to as much as you can, Prodigality with an expansive tendency to spend that is nonetheless still possessive. It's as if the spendthrift is trying to buy and eat the world, which is why the sin of Prodigality appears at the border between the Fifth Terrace of Avarice and the Sixth of Gluttony.[1]

Statius refers to some lines by Virgil: "Why cannot you, O holy hunger for gold, restrain the appetite of mortals?" [Mandelbaum, lines 40–41], and tells the poet how glad he is that he finally understood their true meaning and did not simply take them as a recommendation for Avarice. The "holy hunger for gold" that can "restrain the appetite of mortals" is the ability to value something for what it is, for its essence, not for its pragmatic usefulness or its ability to

---

1. The sin of Gluttony is traditionally associated with the planet Jupiter, the planet of kingly generosity and largesse; Prodigality here is presented as a kind of negative generosity. One of the things traditionally expected of the rich and powerful is that they hold sumptuous banquets for others of their class; to be generous to those who are in no need of generosity because they are already in a state of surfeit is an important aspect of both Prodigality and Gluttony: see Martin Lings, "The Seven Deadly Sins in Light of the Symbolism of Number" in the anthology *Sword of Gnosis*, ed. Jacob Needleman.

The Ordeal of Mercy

satisfy desire. Here the virtue of *recollection*, the virtue that heals dissipation, is shown as a kind of spiritual thrift. Statius goes on:

> *"Know that when a sin is countered by*
> *Another sin directly opposed to it*
> *Both sins see their foliage wither here."* [49–51]

In Purgatory sins that appear to be opposites are purged together because each is revealed as the hidden principle of the other. At the heart of Prodigality is Greed; at the heart of Avarice is a will to quantify everything which it shares with Prodigality. Both Avarice and Prodigality demand "more!" and thus remain blind to the intrinsic qualities of things, symbolized by "gold" in line 41.

Virgil refers to Statius' treatment of the wars of Eteocles and Polynices, the twin sons born of Jocasta's incestuous relationship with her son Oedipus, taking this to indicate that Statius had not yet become a Christian when he wrote on this subject. This is undoubtedly because his theme was the "impure fruit" of Jocasta's womb rather than the pure offspring of the Blessed Virgin, for whom she is praised in words of the "Hail Mary," "Blessed is the fruit of thy womb, Jesus." Then Virgil asks Statius (in my paraphrase): "If only Christianity has the true light, then by what light—('what sun or what candles,' line 61)—did you find Christianity before you were a Christian?" On the feast of Candlemas, February 2nd, when candles are blessed, the scripture reading tells the story of Simeon, who when he saw the infant Jesus presented in the Temple, said:

> Now, Lord, lettest Thou thy servant depart in peace according to thy word. For mine eyes have seen Thy salvation, which Thou hast prepared before the face of all people, a light to enlighten the gentiles, and to be the glory of thy people Israel.
> [Luke 2:29]

Statius, who was of the gentiles, answers that he was first enlightened by God and then by Virgil; it was God who gave him the light by which he could discern the light emanating from Virgil, though Virgil himself could not see this light. So the original source of the

Canto XXII

light that enlightened Statius is paradoxical. You could say that he was predestined to find Christ, that he was of "the elect from before the foundation of the world"—but what exactly is predestination? It is a mystery, and what Calvin made of it is no help in understanding this mystery. But Statius could not have found that light without the engagement of his will, without being *willing* to find it; so predestination and free will are, mysteriously, one.

> *"I was a secret Christian out of fear,*
> *For a long time appearing outwardly a Pagan;*
> *This half-heartedness destined me to travel*
> *The fourth circle for over four hundred years."* [90–93]

Statius's sin was to make Christianity all esoteric, as if it were something reserved for the few—a characterization which he himself denies in lines 76–78. According to Frithjof Schuon, in line with indications given by Dionysius the Areopagite in *The Ecclesiastical Hierarchy*, Christianity is not an exclusive mystery-cult but (in Frithjof Schuon's phrase) an "eso-exoteric" revelation, an esoterism preached openly to the public.[2] In our time, however, we have seen the opposite problem: an attempt to make Christianity all exoteric, and almost to view any spiritual depth as at least potentially heretical. But to do this is to cut the heart out of the tradition, and to virtually force serious seekers, youthful or otherwise, to look for the dimension of spiritual depth outside Christianity.

The essence of Statius' sin has to do with a split between his inner and outer being; externally he is a Pagan poet, but internally a Christian. This split depletes the very substance of his soul, since he cannot show himself as he truly is; in life he could not manifest his virtuous love by his own living example—which would probably have entailed martyrdom—as he did when praising Virgil in his

---

2. Interestingly enough, the Gnostic sect known as the Mandeans, whose remnant still resides in southern Iraq, name John the Baptist as their founder, but hate Jesus because, they claim, he revealed their esoteric secrets to the masses. Some scholars believe the Mandaeans are descended from the Essenes, a remnant of whom took refuge in what is now Iraq during the Jewish Revolt.

verse. The word "martyr" means "witness." The martyr is perfectly at one with himself, and thus may be compared to a hologram; like the Holy Eucharist, the whole of him exists and is alive in every part. Many Christian martyrs could accept physical dismemberment precisely because their spiritual wholeness remained intact.

> *"Now that we're climbing and have some time to spare,*
> *Tell me, where is Terrence our old friend*
>   *And Caecilius, Plautus and Varro, if you know.*
>   *Are they damned? And if so, what's their station?"*
> *"These and Persius and me, and many others,"*
>   *Replied my Leader, "are quartered with the Greek*
>   *Whom the Muses suckled more than all the others,*
> *Held in the first circle of that blind prison.*
>   *We often speak among us of the mountain*
>   *Where those who nursed us dwell throughout all time."*
>   [96–105]

The circle of Limbo in the "blind prison" of the Inferno is presided over by the blind poet Homer. The poetic vision depends in many cases upon the psychic realm and does not allow enough room for the Spirit as such; this is what makes it blind. On the other hand, Homer was a true sage, whose blindness, like that of the figures of Eros and Justice, could well symbolize not judging by appearances, but seeing into the heart.

The inmates of Limbo think often of Mount Parnassus where the Muses dwell. Parnassus evokes and has some of the quality of Purgatory, but it can't really be Purgatory; it can only suggest it. It seems to be pointing toward spiritual maturation, but it never allows those who scale it to actually arrive—unlike these two, who have indeed arrived at their goal, or at least at the true path which leads to it.[3]

---

3. Many of the figures of classical antiquity mentioned by Virgil and Statius—Antigone, for example, who struggled against King Creon for the burial of her brother's body, or Achilles, who feuded with Agamemnon and the rest of the Greeks before the walls of Troy, or the violent sons of Jocasta, Eteocles. and Polynices—have some relationship to various conflicts within the state or the tribe.

Canto XXII

By now both poets again had fallen silent
   And turned their attention once more to their surroundings,
   From steep stairs and rugged walls set free;
Already the four handmaidens of the day [i.e, the Hours]
   Were left behind; at the chariot-pole the fifth
   Was drawing always higher that burning horn,
When my Guide spoke: "I think the time has come
   To turn our right-hand shoulders to the brink,
   And continue round the Mountain as before." [115–123]

This indicates that Virgil and Statius are becoming more supple; mobility is easier for them. In a way they have already achieved their goal, even though they still have a way to go. Purgation is the elimination of everything in the soul that cannot rest within itself, that cannot realize the soul as its own destination. And for it to rest within itself is for it to have arrived at the Sun of the Intellect; hence this poetic description of the Sun in his chariot rising higher in the sky.

All too soon their delightful talk was halted
   By a tree that grew in the center of the road
   Filled with apples, fragrant and delicious.
And just as a fir-tree will taper upwardly
   From bough to bough, so this one tapered downward;
   It grew like that, I think, to discourage climbers. [130–135]

This mysterious tree, resembling an inverted fir-tree, is the inverse of the Tree of Knowledge with its forbidden fruit; that fruit could easily be plucked, but the fruit of this tree is inaccessible. The poetic knowledge shared by Virgil and Statius has brought them to the point where they can encounter this tree. To desire its fruit is

---

Perhaps this is meant to represent Pagan knowledge as self-contradictory and self-defeating—incestuous, if you will—unless and until, through Christ's redemption, it is raised to the level of Spirit. If objective Spiritual knowledge is reduced to the psychic level, as it was to a large degree in the degenerate Paganism of late antiquity, it turns narcissistically in upon itself, and against itself, as the sexual impulse does in the case of auto-eroticism or incest.

The Ordeal of Mercy

not a false desire—it is an impossible desire. They have now gained the power to desire what truly should be desired, but that desire—at this level, the level of poetic inspiration—cannot be fulfilled. The fruits of this tree—which appears as if rooted in Heaven, not in earth, like many of the inverted trees of world mythology—are spiritual or paradisical. The root is the Logos; the branches, which are nearer to the travelers, are the lesser world of outer manifestation that proceeds from it. The souls at this level of purgation are still trying to reach that paradisical fruit on the basis of carnal desire, which is always involved with worldly manifestation. What is required, however, is for the desire itself to be so transformed that it becomes paradisical like the fruit it is reaching for.

> *On the side where our path was bordered by the cliff*
> *From a high rock fell bright and running water,*
> *And spread itself upon the higher leaves.* [136–138]

Water is a symbol of Mercy and Wisdom; the roots of this tree are closer to both Mercy and Wisdom than the roots of any earthly tree, since they receive it directly from above.

> *When the poets had drawn nearer to the tree*
> *A voice emerged from within the foliage:*
> *"For you this food will be in short supply"*
> *It said; "The Virgin Mary took more thought*
> *To make the marriage feast honorable and complete,*
> *Than of her mouth that now repeats your prayers.*
> *And for their drink the women of ancient Rome*
> *Were content with simple water; likewise Daniel*
> *Rejected food and so acquired wisdom."* [139–147]

Virgil and Statius had been discussing poetry before encountering the tree and the waterfall, whose fruit and water were denied to them. This suggests a symbolic relationship between food and speech, both of which are related to the mouth; here Dante is expressing the ambiguous relationship of Wisdom to words. Words can certainly express and impart Wisdom; without language, the greater part of Wisdom would be lost to the human race. But words can also charm and entice a person to remain on a lower level than the Wisdom they express. As Shakespeare tells us *The Merchant of Venice*, in the words of Portia (partially quoted above) when dismissing a vain and flamboyant suitor—Portia being a symbol of Wisdom:

> *All that glisters is not gold,—*
> *Often have you heard that told:*
> *Many a man his life hath sold*
> *But my outside to behold:*
> *Gilded tombs do worms infold.*
> *Had you been as wise as bold,*
> *Young in limbs, in judgement old,*
> *Your answer had not been inscroll'd:*
> *Fare you well; your suit is cold.*

The *quality* of the Marriage Feast at Cana was more important to the Virgin than either quantity of food and wine or quantity of words—which wine is certainly known to produce. Just as at the feast she spoke sparingly to Jesus, just enough to ensure that the needs of the guests would be met, so now, in the afterlife, she can freely speak as an advocate for those souls who hunger and thirst for justice.

Both speech and eating are *oral*; both can potentially fixate one to the level of oral satisfaction and fulfillment. And the cure for both is *fasting*; the vow of silence often taken by monks is a sort of fasting from words. As St. Athanasius of Alexandria said,

> If you fast, but fail to keep watch over your mouth so as to refrain from evil speaking and angry words, from lying and perjury; if you slander your neighbor, even if your words come from the mouth of one who is fasting, your fast will be of no avail and will be labour lost. [*On Virginity*, 7]

St. John Climacus names, as among the offspring of Gluttony, the vices of Talkativeness, Breezy Familiarity, Jesting, Facetiousness and Boastfulness. As Jesus said, "a man is not defiled by what goes into his mouth, but by what comes out of it" [Matthew 15:11].

In the words of St. Maximos the Confessor:

> Using the mellow thought of pleasure as if it were a sword, the passion of gluttony makes many virtues childless. By means of dissipation it kills the seeds of self-restraint; through greed it corrupts the equity of justice; with self-love it severs the natural bond of compassion. In short, the passion of gluttony ... kills all the divine offspring of the virtues. But that passion itself is killed through the spiritual knowledge acquired by the grace of faith and by obedience to the divine commandments. [*Philokalia*, Volume Two, *Fifth Century on Various Texts*, 57; 58]

True spiritual fasting refines the soul so that it regains the power to appreciate *qualities*—in both food and language—and not hanker after *quantity*. "Not by bread alone doth man live, but by every word that proceedeth forth from the mouth of God" [Matthew 4:4]. In Eastern Orthodox iconography, Christ, the Virgin and the saints are represented with extremely small mouths, symbolizing both the virtue of Temperance and that of discretion with regard to the Mysteries.

> *The primal age was beautiful as gold;*
> *Then hunger made delicious even acorns,*
> *While thirst turned every little stream to nectar.* [148–150]

In the Golden Age—the Pagan analogue of the Garden of Eden—people could feed directly upon the essences of things, upon their intrinsic qualities; this is precisely why they demanded and required less in terms of quantity. Here the sin of Gluttony is being presented as a natural appetite that descends so far into carnality and "the reign of quantity" that it becomes unnatural.

☒

Here for the first time in the *Purgatorio* we see a soul other than that of the two travelers rise from a lower terrace to a higher one.

Canto XXII

Because Statius was a follower of Virgil, he can now allow Virgil to lead him through the upper parts of Purgatory, which Virgil can do because of his relationship to Dante, a saved Christian soul. All souls in purgation are rising, but it's hard to see this on the lower terraces of the Mountain. Here, however, as the end of the long journey is drawing near, the souls are lighter and move more swiftly toward their goal. We all have deep affinities with other souls, many of which we have never met; when we are willing to accept spiritual transformation for ourselves, we are of help to these souls without intending to be or making any special effort. But this influence is usually invisible to both the soul helping and the one being helped.

Canto XXIII

The travelers encounter Forese Donati, who explains how the Gluttons are punished by emaciating hunger and thirst. He praises his widow Nella and rebukes the shameless women of Florence. Speaking to Forese, Dante expresses his gratitude to Virgil for acting as his Guide.

> *While I was peering through the leafy boughs*
> *My attention trapped, as with a constant hunter*
> *Who wastes his life in chasing little birds,*
> *He who was more than a father to me said:*
> *"Come now, son; the time our journey spares us*
> *Should be put to better use than this."*
> *I turned my face and quickly too my steps*
> *Toward those two sages—and the words they spoke*
> *Made the work of climbing no expense.* [1–9]

The real fruit is in the continuation of the journey, not in attachment to the fruit of this tree. At this point true fruitfulness means leaving appearances behind. The birds symbolize spiritual aspiration, but at this point Dante is chasing after such aspiration in the wrong direction, the direction of mental knowledge. Once he turns his eyes away from the tree and toward Virgil and Statius, his vision and his ability to act are coordinated.

> *Then suddenly we heard a song and a lament*
> *"Labia mea, Domine," in such style*
> *That it called up both delight and pain together.*
> *"O sweet Father, what is this I hear?"*
> *"It could be shades who journey on" he answered,*
> *"Hoping to untie their knot of debt."* [10–15]

Canto XXIII

Psalm 51, on which this hymn is based, speaks of the necessity of inward sacrifice. At this point the souls have already passed through great purgation, but they still have more work to do—the work of internalizing and essentializing sacrifices that were once external. Here the Heart is becoming full rather than the stomach: "Out of the fullness of the heart, the mouth speaketh" [Luke 6:45].

The emaciated souls of the Gluttonous now appear. Here Dante mentions two examples of Gluttony from myth and history: Erysichthon, who sold his daughter to buy money for food and ended by devouring his own body, and Mary the daughter of Eleazar, who, during the Roman siege of Jerusalem and the ensuing hunger, roasted and devoured her own infant son. Mary demonstrates how those beset by unnatural hunger end by destroying their own spiritual potential, while Erysichthon—whose daughter had the power to change her shape and so was able to be reclaimed by her father many times, only to be sold again and again—represents an ego-identification with the Divine All-Possibility, the belief that one's potential for "devouring" experience is effectively infinite, leading to dissipation of soul and ultimate self-destruction; with God and God alone are "all things possible" [Matthew 19:26]. Attachment to potentiality is in itself a kind of Gluttony, whether or not this is expressed in terms of food; both Gluttony per se and the identification with potentiality represent a wrong relationship to the Infinite. We learn from Statius, who appeared in the circle of Avarice but was actually being punished for Prodigality, that certain sins have a hidden affinity with others; this implies that the other terraces could represent the purgation of multiple sins that aren't always made explicit.

In life these souls easily satisfied their hunger, but here the basis of this apparent satiety is revealed as an insatiable longing. To the degree that they didn't experience this longing in life, they became unconsciously attached to it; so in the afterlife they are forced to live it out. Their true longing is for fullness of soul, which in life they mistakenly tried to obtain through food. They are hungry for the Bread of Life. According to St. Ambrose of Milan, "fasting is food for the soul and nourishment of the spirit" [*On Elijah and Fasting*, 2, 2] and in the words of St. Jerome:

The Ordeal of Mercy

[One who fasts] feeds like Moses on familiarity with God and his word. He experiences the truth of the text, "Man shall not live by bread alone, but by every word that proceedeth forth from the mouth of God." [*Letter* 130, 10]

Now Dante encounters the soul of his friend Forese, whom he recognizes not by his appearance but by his voice. It's relatively easy for one's outward aspect to become distorted, but the human voice remains closer to one's essence. In life the human form in these souls was distorted through obesity; here it is distorted through emaciation, which forces them to live through every inch of the sin of Gluttony and its effects.

The souls here are beginning to feel that the pain they are going through is also solace; they are intuiting that their suffering is essentially a purification that will finally bring them to the end of the purgatorial road. The inverted tree, which induces longing but does not satisfy this longing until it is transformed into a desire for higher things, is like the tree Christ died upon; it initiates a suffering that leads to salvation. Unexpectedly, Forese characterizes Christ's cry, during His crucifixion, of *Eli, eli, lama sabachthani?*, "My God, my God, why have You forsaken me?" [Mark 15:34] as a *joyous* cry; he is coming to understand that the immense suffering of Christ is really the expression of an inner joy greater even than this suffering, the greatest suffering of all time; if this were not true, Christ's suffering would have no power to save.

Dante asks Forese how he was able to move through Purgatory so much faster than he (Dante) had expected; he answers that he was able to do so by virtue of the prayers of his wife Nella. Nella's prayers for Forese's salvation are not dutiful prayers, but are based on a love that extends beyond the grave. God loves her precisely because she is willing to love in loneliness and isolation—the loneliness both of her widowhood and of her virtuous isolation within a corrupt society.

Forese now rails against the immodesty of the women of Florence, and predicts the disasters that will fall upon the city partly in punishment for it. The bare breasts of the Florentine women are the very image of the sin of Gluttony turning into Lust. St. John Clima-

Canto XXIII

cus says, "A fasting man prays austerely, but the mind of someone intemperate is filled up with unclean imaginings"; and he has the personified sin of Gluttony declare, "My firstborn son is the servant of Fornication."

Forese and the other souls now stare in amazement at Dante because, unlike them, he is opaque to the sunlight. As we have pointed out before, the souls in Purgatory are capable of seeing that Dante is still in his earthly body, which bespeaks a truer consciousness than the souls in Hell, who routinely believed him to be damned just as they were. Dante has more substance than these purgatorial souls, but he still blocks the sun; there is an intrinsic veil in earthly existence that souls in purgation can discern.

Dante now characterizes Purgatory as "this Mountain, which makes straight you whom the world made crooked" [lines 125–126]. It is striking that the spiral path of Purgatory leads to the straightening of souls made crooked by the world. The broad paths of This World seem straight to those who simply "go with the flow," but they actually involve such souls in great inconsistencies and contradictions. In Purgatory, on the other hand, one is moving toward the fixed goal of salvation with all deliberate speed, but in approaching that goal one feels intensely the impurities and distortions that have become part of one's soul, just as they are being overcome.

Forese not only sees that Dante is alive, he can also acknowledge Virgil and see Statius who is about to leave Purgatory; perhaps this implies that his own stay is nearing its end. Here Dante again mentions the name of Beatrice; he is beginning to see beyond the limits of purgatorial suffering to the true goal of the spiritual life.

Canto XXIV

Forese speaks of his sister Piccarda. The travelers see the shades of Ubadin da la Pila, Pope Boniface and Messer Marchese. The poet Bonagiunta da Lucca lectures on the state of poetry. The second tree; a voices from the branches warns the travelers to avoid it. The Centaurs and those Hebrews rejected by Gideon are named as examples of Gluttony. The Angel of Temperance appears.

Dante continues his conversation with the soul of Forese:

> *Speech did not hamper motion nor motion speech;*
> *We bravely advanced, talking the whole time*
> *Like a boat that's driven forward by a fair wind. . . .* [1–3]

> *And I, continuing my discourse without pause,*
> *Said: "Possibly it's for the sake of others*
> *He now ascends more slowly than he might. . . .*
> *But tell me, if you know, where is Piccarda?"* [7–10]

Once again words and actions are coordinated; the will is in line with the intellect, and so progress is swift. The fair wind that drives the boat is the inspiration that Dante speaks of later in terms of the art of poetry. At this point Dante asks about Piccarda, who is already in Paradise; he is near enough to the higher worlds to begin to gain intimations of them.

Dante notes how Statius is delaying his completion of the purgatorial path in order to converse with Virgil. He of course admires Statius' veneration of his respected teacher, yet he may be starting to feel that Statius at this point should be looking toward Paradise and not toward Virgil—what, after all, could he learn from Virgil that Paradise could not teach him many times over? Dante is beginning

Canto XXIV

to transcend his appreciation for great poetry at the very moment it is being fulfilled.

Next Dante interviews the shades of many of the Gluttonous, among whom are a number of poets; here again we see the analogy drawn between food and words. Bonagiunta asks Dante if he is the one who authored "new rhymes" beginning with the line "Ladies who have intelligence of love"—the first words of *La Vita Nuova*. Dante answers with a description of the source and method of the *dolce stil nuovo*, the "sweet new style"[1]:

> *I answered, "I am one who, when Love breathes*
> *Within me, notes the text that he recites*
> *So I may show its meaning outwardly."* [52–54]

Here Dante explains that he writes by dictation, that his verse is inspired by the power of Love. Craft and inspiration can seem outwardly the same, like works and Grace, but inwardly they are poles apart. Inspiration may empower craft, but craft cannot attain to inspiration. Nonetheless, a willingness to put energy into developing one's craft may open the soul to inspiration, in the same way that raising a sail can make use of the power of wind, even though it cannot invoke it. Traditionally the polarity between craft and inspiration, or works and Grace, is represented by Martha and Mary [Luke 10]. In terms of the spiritual Path, Martha stands for contemplative practice, while Mary is the recipient of unasked-for and undeserved spiritual states. Grace and craft appear the same outwardly because "I come not to destroy the law but to fulfill it" [Matthew 5:17], but the *dolce stil nuovo*, born of Grace and Inspiration,

---

1. The line "Ladies who have intelligence of love" reminds us that the consort of Parzival, in the *Parzival* romance of Wolfram von Eschenbach (c. 1170–c. 1220)— the one medieval Christian poet to approach, but certainly not overtake, Dante (1265–1321) in his mythopoetic architectonics—is Condwiramurs, whose name means "Knowledge of Love." It is correspondences such as this which have led certain scholars to discern a stream of esoteric doctrine flowing through the Grail romances, the courtly love tradition, the songs of the troubadours and the works of Dante Aligheri—most specifically *La Vita Nuova*—which some attribute to a semi-secret initiatory order known as the Fedeli d'Amore, the "Faithful to Love."

though certainly not devoid of craft, is the higher art. Only Grace, however, can discern the inner difference between Grace and craft, and Grace can only be given, never acquired.

The union of Love and Knowledge is a characteristic manifestation of the feminine principle, reminding one of the relationship between the poet and his Muse.[2] This higher sort of feeling must be cultivated, both for the sake of the fullness of human life, and because in itself, when conformed to the Intellect and the will, it can be a perfect vehicle for the union with God, not only due to the psychic energy it releases, but also because of the particular perceptions which only developed feeling can give. There are certain avenues to the transcendent Intellect which are opened only through feeling.

Now Dante encounters another tree, heavy with fruit, with the souls of the Gluttonous clustered around it like children begging for a treat; but the fruit of this tree is denied to them. This tree is the direct reflection of the Tree of Knowledge. If Gluttony, traditionally related to the kingly planet Jupiter, is the king of the passions, this indicates that one must *eat* of the passions, incorporate them, in order to be corrupted by them—and every passion is a perverted form of Knowledge. Gluttony is the enemy not only of physical health but of discernment; in the words of Evagrius of Pontus, "spiritual fat is the obtuseness with which evil cloaks the intelligence" [*Centuries*, IV, 36]. Here, however, the souls are taught to hunger for true Knowledge, and to definitively reject the Knowledge of Good and Evil, which is contingent and incomplete. Ironically, it is the very distinction between Good and Evil, though necessary on a certain level, that entangles one in the passions.

Here Dante alludes to two accounts of Gluttony from myth and history. The first is the story of the Centaurs who become drunk at the wedding of Pirithous and Hippodamia, and end by abducting the bride, demonstrating how intemperance can lead to lust—a

---

2. Dante's use of the image of flocking birds in lines 63–69 when describing the souls of poets may be significant. Robert Graves, in *The White Goddess*, informs us that, according to a fable of Hyginus, Mercury, the god of communication, invented the first seven letters of the alphabet after watching a flight of cranes, "which make letters as they fly" [see also Canto XXIII, verse 9].

progression which St. John Climacus makes explicit by placing his chapter on Chastity directly after the one on Gluttony. The second is the episode [Judges 7] where Gideon considers only those thirsty Israelites who remain standing and raise the water of the river to their mouths as worthy of fighting the Midianites, not those who go down on all fours to drink. The "upright" have maintained their connection with the vertical dimension, the dimension of transcendence. Human civilization and human dignity are necessary to contain the water of life, but to drink on all fours as animals do is to use this water to feed the passions. The Centaurs also picture the human form degraded to the animal level.

> *"What's that thought you share, you three apart?"*
>   *Abruptly said a voice—it made me jump*
>   *Like a scared young animal at a sudden sound.* [133–135]

Dante experiences himself as being like a frightened animal because he is in the process of transcending his animal soul; he is sublimating it, and so gaining the power to see it from a higher standpoint. The major elements of the animal soul are aggression and desire. According to St. Maximos the Confessor, "He who believes, fears; he who fears is humble; he who is humble becomes gentle and renders inactive those impulses of incensiveness and desire which are contrary to [human] nature" [*Philokalia*, Volume Two, *First Century on Theology*, 16].

The voice which has startled Dante has come from a glowing red figure, whom some critics have called the Angel of Temperance. Dante is so dazzled by the Angel's presence that he is temporarily blinded; his sight taken away so as to lead him on to greater vision. At this point he can only follow Virgil and Statius by his senses of smell and hearing, reminding us again that Jesus said "those who have ears to hear, let them hear" [Matthew 11:15 et al.] not "those who have eyes to see, let them see." Hearing is related to guidance and obedience, as smell is to intuition; now for the first time Dante smells the breeze from the Earthly Paradise. This breeze is also the Angel, who removes the next-to-last P from Dante's forehead.

The Ordeal of Mercy

And then I heard: "Blessed are they whom Grace
  So illumines that the love of taste
  Excites not too much craving in their breast
Nor makes them hunger beyond the bounds of justice."
                              [151–154]

The grace that illuminates breasts also moderates desire; here Temperance is shown as invoking Justice, which is also Balance. We ultimately overcome the passions not by struggling against them, but by seeing them for what they are.

Canto XXV

Ascent to the Seventh Terrace, that of the Lustful. Dante asks Statius how souls can appear emaciated as if they had physical bodies. Statius replies by giving the doctrine of the generation of physical and subtle bodies. The punishment of the Lustful: fire. The souls of the Lustful cry out the names of examples of chastity: the Virgin Mary, the Goddess Diana.

> *Now we could delay our climb no longer:*
>   *The sun had assigned the meridian to Taurus*
>   *And left to Scorpio the dark of night.*
> *Therefore—like a man who dares not wait*
>   *But presses on, whatever might appear,*
>   *If he's driven forward by the sting of need*
> *This is how we passed into the gap*
>   *One by one, and separately took the stairs,*
>   *Whose narrowness made us walk in single file.* [1–9]

To have no time to pause because one is goaded by necessity is to be absolutely committed to the purgation which leads to the life of the Spirit. In the face of Lust in particular there can be no pause in the journey because this passion, since it is so close to primal generation, can throw one all the way back to the beginning. One aspect of lust is its tendency to drag us back into the maternal realm where life began, and to fall into the maternal is also to fall back into oneself, since the primal design of the psychophysical self is formed within the maternal matrix. The path of purgation, on the other hand, is a continual emergence from both the maternal world and the self that is nurtured and bound by that world. As Jesus said, "Woman, what have I to do with thee? Did you not know that I must be about my Father's business?" [Luke 2:49]

The travelers are now required to proceed single file because, in detaching from lust, they must be willing to be completely alone;

The Ordeal of Mercy

they are not even allowed the simple joys of companionship. This degree of purgation bears a certain similarity to the rigor of being unloved; lust has taken the place of love in the soul, and so the purgation of lust must initially appear as a loss of love. It can be exciting and adventurous to go toward love, but when moving through this narrow pass, one does not have access to such pleasure. This is the point where pleasure itself must be understood as a limitation—an understanding which the "natural man" is in no way capable of.[1]

Dante asks Virgil how the souls of the Gluttonous can become emaciated in Purgatory, where they do not require food; Virgil replies by citing the example of Meleager, and says:

> *Just consider: no matter how fast you move*
> *Your image in the mirror moves as quick;*
> *Grasp this, and what was once hard will be clear.* [25–27]

Meleager's mother, so as to punish him for killing her brothers, throws the log which contains his soul into the fire; as it wastes away, so does Meleager's body, resulting in his death. But if he had known that his attachment to his mother was not necessary, she would not have been able to kill him. An attachment to food always begins with an attachment to the mother's breast; the souls of the Gluttonous, since they are no longer embodied, have no need of external nourishment, but they don't yet fully realize this; they still believe that they are starving, and consequently appear emaciated.

The image of one's body in a mirror is precisely one's *self*-image; to constantly crave food is to visualize oneself as thin and undernourished. The "body" here represents the reality of the soul; the mirror-image, the reflection of the soul's desires.[2]

---

1. Here Dante is presenting us with something like the First Noble Truth of Buddhism: "all life is (or entails) suffering." To not get what you want is suffering; to get what you don't want is suffering; even to get what you want is suffering, because the pleasure derived from it must end.

2. In the mental illness known as anorexia, young girls who are dangerously emaciated due to self-starvation will see their image in the mirror as overweight—the exact reverse of the condition of these souls being purged of Gluttony. Anorexia, then—and the same could certainly be said for bulimia, the practice of over-

Canto XXV

At this point Statius, as requested by Virgil, lectures to Dante on the formation of the body and the soul within the womb and the analogous process by which the subtle body is formed after death. To many this will seem like little more than a kind of primitive biological theory, based in part on Scholastic philosophy and in part on the physiological speculations of the Greeks, that has been disproved by modern experimental science. But since what appears to be a strictly physical theory is in fact based on metaphysical principles, its spiritual validity and use is in no way diminished:

> *"That portion of the perfect blood that's never*
> *Drunk by the thirsty veins, but still remains*
> *Like uneaten food that's taken from the table*
> *Assumes a constructive power within the heart*
> *To form the limbs of another human body*
> *As the circulation of the blood feeds one's own limbs.*
> *Digested again it descends into that part*
> *It's better not to name; from there it drops*
> *In the natural vessel upon another's blood.*
> *There the first blood mixes with the second*
> *The one destined to be receptive, the other active*
> *Because it springs from the perfect place, the heart*
> *Which, once the two are joined, begins its work*
> *Coagulating first, then quickening*
> *The matter it had caused to coalesce.*
> *The active power at first becomes a soul*
> *Like that of a plant—except that for a plant*

---

eating and then vomiting—is a kind of false, inverted purgation, where passion is not overcome by repentance and illumination, but rather struggled against on the basis of passion itself: a hopeless undertaking. Anorexics and bulimics are struggling to overcome a mother-complex while lacking any sense that a source of nourishment outside the mother exists; they have no notion of what it would be to nourish themselves on the Spirit. These girls see themselves as fat because they are fat with self-involvement, with materialistic considerations, with an essential worldliness, which is what an excessive concern with self-image actually is. Matter = *mater*, "mother." First your mother was the world; now the material world is your mother.

The Ordeal of Mercy

This stage is final, while a foetus must still travel.
Next that virtue works till it feels and moves
   More like a sea-sponge, until it undertakes
   To organize all the powers it has seeded.
Now, my son, the power from the heart
   Of the begetter expands and then unfolds
   Till nature's will is realized in all its members.
But how from animal it passes on to man
   You've not yet seen—there's the thorny point
   That once confused a wiser man than you
So badly that he even made the soul
   Separate from the possible intellect
   Since he saw no organ where that mind could sit.
Open your knowing heart to the coming truth
   And see how, just as soon as in the foetus
   The growing brain has reached its final form
The Prime Mover turns to it gladly, and beholds
   So great a work of nature, He breathes into it
   A new spirit, complete with every virtue
Which draws all the active power it encounters
   Into its substance till they become one soul,
   Which lives, and feels, and on itself revolves.
To lessen your amazement at my words
   Consider the heat of the sun, how when it's joined
   To the sap of the vine is transformed into wine.
Whenever the thread of Lachesis has run out
   Then soul divides from flesh, and holds within it
   Potential being both human and divine
But with the human element silent now,
   Leaving intelligence, memory, and will
   Much sharper in their action than before.
Immediately of its own accord it falls—
   Astonishingly—on one shore or the other;
   That's where it learns which road it is to take.
As soon as that soul's proper place surrounds it
   Its formative power begins to radiate
   As much as when it made the living limbs.

Canto XXV

And just as air does when it's filled with rain
  Ornamenting itself with rainbow colors
  By rays from outside reflected now within
So now the surrounding air assumes the shape
  Impressed upon it by that soul's proper form
  In its potential being now established.
From that time onward, like the little flame
  That follows the fire wherever the fire moves
  The new form follows the motions of its spirit.
Since now it takes its appearance from that spirit
  It's called a 'shade', which proceeds to form the organs
  Proper to all the senses—even sight.
It is this by which we speak, by which we laugh
  It is this that forms our tears and breathes our sighs
  As doubtless you have heard upon this Mountain.
According to the stamp of our desires
  And other affections, so the shade is shaped;
  This is the cause of your astonishment." [37–108]

The idea that nourishment is necessary for the sexual generation of bodies appears here as part of the bridge between Gluttony and Lust. The "perfect" blood that generates human bodies gives them substance and density, qualities which are lacking to the souls in Purgatory, since they have lost their earthly bodies but have not yet assumed the glorified bodies that will be theirs after their resurrection. They appear emaciated precisely because they lack human bodies. Here Lust and Gluttony are being presented as a kind of imperfect longing by souls in purgation for the bodies that are proper to them, a longing that cannot be satisfied until that purgation is complete. What the Gluttonous and Lustful really desire is completion, which during life they have pursued in a partial and self-defeating way. Here the highest Pagan explanation of the quality of purgatorial souls, that of Virgil, is superseded and completed by the higher Christian conception provided by Statius.

Christ is the "perfect" blood not originally "drunk" by the veins—i.e., not married to the body—because He is the Transcendent Logos, the origin of all manifestation. He is intimately present in the formation of the soul, which is why the creation of the soul is compared to the action of the Sun on the grape; Christ, the Sun of Righteousness, is the vine, and His blood, the wine. As John the Evangelist tells us, "All things were made by Him, and without Him was not anything made that was made" [John 1:3]. The perfect blood is here compared to leftover food, which usually suggests something less perfect than the original meal. But leftovers were the source of great abundance at Christ's miracle of the multiplication of the loaves and fishes [Matthew 14:13–21]; and at the Marriage Feast of Cana [John 2]—the occasion when God, through Christ, blessed the human act of generation—the best wine, miraculously produced by Jesus, was saved for last.[3]

The Heart is the wholeness of the human being before that being has taken form. Through the Heart the being becomes polarized, and this power of polarity enters the semen and finally the womb—but all of this is pictured as happening within a single soul. The polarization of the generative power into active *forma* and passive *materia* within the Heart, before these powers are corporeally expressed, suggests Plato's doctrine of the primordial Androgyne as the origin of the sexes.

As the foetus grows it first gains the vegetable soul, then the animal soul; and when the brain is sufficiently developed, God breathes into it the rational soul, which becomes the center and principle of the whole being. The brain begins to develop the higher function and consequently the ability to receive the soul itself, or unite with it in a deeper way. The higher development always enfolds the lower, it does not expel it; humans who have been given a rational soul thereby also possess everything that is proper to a vegetable soul and an animal soul.

It seems as if the Heart in this Canto were simply the physical heart of the male parent. Yet Dante presents it as the matrix where

---

3. The idea that the Blood of Christ is the primal principle of generation reminds us of those myths where the primordial Person—the Ymir of the Norse, the Purusha of the Hindus—is sacrificed to create the universe; in Christian terms, in the words of Revelations 13:8, "the Lamb" is "slain from the foundation of the world."

Canto XXV

the generative powers of both sexes appear, and names it a "perfect place." And since all elements of the human person, including the brain, ultimately stem from the spiritual Heart which enthrones the *Imago Dei*, this gives the Heart an implicit superiority; just as the brain represents the rational soul, the Heart, by implication, would symbolize the *Pneuma* or *Nous*. Dante seems to be saying here that the *Nous*, which corresponds to Spirit in the hierarchy of Spirit, Soul and Body, is the first origin of both body and soul. (The rational soul corresponds to the Scholastic *ratio*, the *Nous* to the Scholastic *Intellectus*.)[4]

The "two shores" of line 86 are identified by critics with the shores of the Tiber and the Acheron, based on Canto II, lines 100–105. Those souls who come to rest on the shore of the Tiber are destined for salvation, while those who fall on the shores of Acheron are headed for Hell. The higher faculties—Intellect, Memory and Will—are sharpened after death; unlike the more human faculties they are directly receptive to the Divine, and are thus under the immediate influence of the *Nous*. This traditional Catholic doctrine is in direct opposition to the contemporary Eastern Orthodox heresy of "soul sleep" (which most Orthodox do not accept)—that the souls of the dead have no consciousness until the general resurrection—and the post-Vatican II doctrine, promulgated by Benedict XVI, that the soul cannot exist apart from the body, which implicitly denies the existence of both Purgatory and Hell, and thereby directly contradicts Catholic tradition.[5] One would think that only the saved would be more aware after death, but it turns out that this is true of the damned as well, through for them this is only a misfortune. They didn't nurture the Divine within themselves, and so now their higher faculties must become aware of how they opposed the Divine in life, and how the effects of that opposition continue after death. The saved, on the other hand, now begin to feel a fulfillment of all

---

4. This is in line with the doctrine of Plotinus, who taught that the psychic and material universes emanate from the One via the contemplation of It by the First Intellect, the *Nous*; to see is to conceive, and to conceive is to bring forth.

5. On page 214 of *Introduction to Christianity*, Joseph Cardinal Ratzinger, who was to become Pope Benedict XVI, describes the notion of an immortal soul as "obsolete."

The Ordeal of Mercy

the ways they did nurture the Divine within themselves; neither the saved nor the damned simply fall into oblivion after death.

Corporeal generation is presented in this Canto partly as an analogy to describe the process through which the aetherial body which clothes the soul after death is generated; the soul or formative principle is *forma* and the surrounding "air" (or *aether*) is *materia*.[6]

The travelers now come into the presence of the fire that purifies the soul of lust, which is held back from blocking their path by a wind that blows from the edge of the terrace. Here Dante says "I feared the fire on the left, and on the right the precipice" [116–117]. He has reached the point where his soul must either pass through the fire or suffer a great fall; he is suspended between the fear of purgation and that of damnation. But if the left is traditionally the side of damnation and the right of salvation, as in Matthew 25:31–46, why is the precipice now on the right and the fire of purgation on the left? This is to indicate that purgation requires us to face our limitations and deal with the darkness still clouding our souls, whereas if we attempt to rely upon past spiritual achievements in order to avoid the task at hand, we will fall.

Dante hears the purgatorial souls shouting out two examples of chastity, that of the Virgin Mary, and that of the virgin goddess Diana, who dismissed her nymph Calisto (or Helice) after her dalliance with Jove, and then took refuge in the forest. In reference to Mary they cry out "*Virum non cognosco*," "I don't know man," a reference to Mary's question to Gabriel at the Annunciation in Luke 1:34, "How can this be, since I know not a man?"

The chastity of Diana is physical and worldly, including the negative purity of withdrawal from the world, whereas the chastity of the Virgin Mary reaches into spiritual realms, into realms of knowledge. For Mary not to have known a man, specifically a fleshly man of this world, means that the spiritual Child can be conceived within her, embodying both the Spirit of God and the Perfect Man—or Man as such—Jesus being both the Son of God and the Son of Man. The disembodied angel came to her as the image of the

---

6. According to Aristotle in *De Anima*, "the soul is the form of the body"—a doctrine also accepted by Aquinas.

Perfect Man, but could not of himself incarnate this image. In gnostic terms, Mary's ignorance of "man" opened her to the Spirit which alone can embrace Man in his fullness. This ignorance reminds us of the "Divine Ignorance" spoken of by Scotus Eriugena, which certainly implies no deficiency of Knowledge on the part of God; the Knowledge of the greater already includes the knowledge of the less, thus making this lesser knowledge unnecessary.

After a superficial reading of the *Purgatorio* one might ask why a serious vice such as lust, which has caused the damnation of so many souls, should be put at such a high level, as if it were one of the lesser sins. The purgation from Lust, however, pertains not simply to illicit sexual desire, but to everything we have loved in this world, precisely because we have loved it—at least to a degree—not in God but as part of this world, and loved ourselves by means of it. If we want to become capable of the love of Paradise, all of this worldly love, even the most noble aspects of it, must be burned; each soul, when it comes to the Seventh Terrace, has reached its own "end of the world," the point where the world itself is consumed. In the words of St. Maximos the Confessor:

> It is said that the highest state of prayer is when the spirit leaves the flesh and the world, and in the act of prayer, loses all matter and all form. To maintain oneself unfailingly in this state, is in reality to pray without cease.
>
> Just as the body in dying is separated from all the goods of this life, so does the spirit which dies at the summit of prayer likewise quit all the representations it has of the world. For without dying this death it could never find itself and live with God. [Whitall Perry, *A Treasury of Traditional Wisdom*, 210]

Likewise Meister Eckhart says:

> Verily thou must sojourn and dwell in thy essence, in thy ground, and there God shall mix thee with His simple essence without the admixture of any image. Now seeing that thou hast no image save of what is outside thee, therefore it is impossible for thee to be beatified by any image.... All things

whatsoever must be forsaken. God scorns to work among images....

You must break the outside to let out the inside: to get at the kernel means breaking the shell. Even so to find nature herself all her likenesses have to be shattered. [Whitall Perry, *A Treasury of Traditional Wisdom*, 721–22]

The fire through which the souls of the Lustful must pass is the most severe punishment in Purgatory. Here we are shown in no uncertain terms the seriousness of Lust, which from one point of view is the least of sins because it is the closest to love, but from another standpoint the worst of sins because it is a perversion of Divine Love directly. Yet Virgil describes those within this fire as receiving "care" and "nourishment" through the act of repentance. As St. John Climacus tells us, "A chaste man is someone who has driven out bodily love by Divine love, who has used heavenly fire to quench the fires of the flesh." "Only love," says St. Maximos the Confessor, "overcomes the fragmentation of human nature" [*Centuries on Charity*, quoted in Olivier Clément, *The Roots of Christian Mysticism*].

Canto XXVI

The Lustful express amazement that Dante still has a physical body. A company of souls appear who sinned through unnatural lust, traveling counter to the other souls. Dante dialogues with the poet Guido Guinizzelli and meets one of his major poetic and perhaps initiatory influences, the troubadour Arnaut Daniel, who addresses him in Provençal.

> *My right shoulder was then struck by light of the sun;*
>   *Its rays illuminated all the west,*
>   *Changing its color from azure into white,*
> *While—cast upon the flame—my shadow now*
>   *Made the fire more red; and many passing spirits*
>   *I saw who noted this effect and wondered*
> *At the strange sign that gave them good occasion*
>   *To speak to one another of my appearance.*
>   *"His body is not imaginal!" they exclaimed.* [4–12]

Dante's shadow further reddening the flames in which the Lustful are being purified is a symbol of his own lust; the image of his body projected upon the flames activates them, indicating that lust has something to do with giving energy to the image, the shadow, not the reality.

Dante in the *Purgatorio* is writing for the dead as well as for the living, just as others might pray for the dead. They see that his body is fuller than theirs, not made as it were out of thin air. If Dante can pass through Purgatory in his earthly body this shows him to be a complete pilgrim in the spiritual sense, whereas they are partial pilgrims in the process of completing themselves so they can be one with Paradise. Dante is on a pilgrimage through their realms with his whole self, consequently he can give these souls an image of human wholeness that can facilitate their entry into Paradise and bring them closer to their own resurrection. According to the story of the rich man and Lazarus in the Gospel according to Luke, the rich man, in Hell, cannot receive water from Lazarus, who is "in the bosom of Abraham" [Luke 16:19–231]; but those in Purgatory can receive it from a living soul. In line 18 the knowledge Dante can impart to them is compared to water offered to those dying of thirst; it is an image of *merciful* truth.

> *Straight down the middle of that burning road*
>   *Came walking, in the opposite direction,*
>   *A people who kept me staring with suspense.*
> *I watched that file of quickly passing shades*
>   *Embrace the ones who were moving the other way*
>   *Without pausing, satisfied with a brief salute.* . . . [28–33]

The brief greeting exchanged by the souls moving in opposite directions represents that aspect of themselves that has gone beyond the attachments of lust and can therefore truly salute another soul in its fullness. The encounters are brief because these souls are still in the process of learning what it is to face and accept another soul for what it is, not what they would wish it to be.

One of the two groups is crying "Sodom and Gomorrah"; the other recounts the story of Pasiphaë, who transformed herself into a cow in order to mate with a bull, thus conceiving the Minotaur; these are the homosexuals and those given to the sin of bestiality. Here Dante compares the souls to a flock of cranes who divide into two groups, one flying north as in the summer, the other south as if it were winter [lines 43–46]. In earthly time summer and winter succeed each other, but here they are simultaneous; this is a representation of the *aeonian time* mentioned by the Greek Fathers, where past, present and future coincide.

Lust produces not just heat but cold as well. In neither case have the cranes completely given up their attachment to lust, but are simply attempting to flee its consequences; they do not yet understand that the way to escape both heat and cold is to renounce lust itself. Heat represents the attraction to inappropriate persons and situations, cold the condition of being rejected, the inability to connect with those persons and situations that are right for us, as well

Canto XXVI

as the kind of emotional coldness that allows us to treat another human being as an object. Only True Love can save us from both heat and cold.

St. Maximos the Confessor sees an intrinsic relationship between Lust and Pride:

> When you see Pilate and Herod making friends with each other in order to destroy Jesus [cf. Luke 23:12], you may discern in this a concurrence between the demons of unchastity and self-esteem, who combine together to put to death the Logos of virtue and spiritual knowledge. For the demon of self-esteem, making a pretense of spiritual knowledge, refers to the demon of unchastity, and the demon of unchastity, putting on a hypocritical show of purity, refers back to the demon of self-esteem. Thus it is said, "When Herod had arrayed Jesus in a gorgeous robe, he sent Him again to Pilate" [Luke 23:11].
> [*Philokalia*, Volume Two, First Century on Theology, 72]

The Eastern Orthodox saint, Xenia of St. Petersburg, a clairvoyant and wonderworker, had a mysterious love for her husband Andrei, a soldier, who died as a young man in dissipated circumstances and without the last rites of the church. This love drove her to leave the house they had shared and become a homeless pilgrim throughout Russia; it's as if she were atoning for the lust and drunkenness of her husband by mortifying her own self-esteem. Later she returned to St. Petersburg, where she dressed in her husband's military jacket and continually repeated "I am Andrei." Xenia is known for her ability to guide people who pray for her intercession to the relationships and the homes that are proper to them, and separate them from persons and places that are wrong for them. She was also famous for her miraculous ability to stay warm without fire or shelter in the midst of the St. Petersburg winter; this would represent the right union of heat and cold, something that the souls in this circle lack. She was cold to the world, but on fire with her love for God.

One group of souls is moving in line with nature, the other against it. The cranes who fly north are fleeing excessive heat; these are the heterosexuals who have degraded love to the level of animal

The Ordeal of Mercy

lust, symbolized by Pasiphaë who disguised herself as a cow so as to copulate with a bull. The cranes who fly south are fleeing the cold; these, the souls crying "Sodom and Gomorrah!", are the homosexuals, who have been deprived of the persons and situations that would have been healing for them by some kind of emotional barrenness, which has led them into barren relationships. To fly south is to move toward outer manifestation and ultimately materialism, a shallow external warmth which is cold in essence and deprived of the Spirit. To fly north is to draw closer to Hyperborea, toward the arctic cold that guards the warmth of the Earthly Paradise; but it is also to approach the purifying fire of the Seventh Circle. Each group, in fleeing either cold or heat, ultimately encounters the very thing it has been in flight from. Be that as it may, all who are open to the Holy Spirit will eventually be called to pass through the fire of that Spirit.

The souls within the fire, compared by Dante to gawking rustic mountain-dwellers—"hillbillies" as we would call them—in their astonishment at his possession of a human body in Purgatory [lines 67–70], remind us of those who have lived within the embrace of high spiritual states, but who when they emerge from them look "unhip" to the eyes of the world, due to their inability to transmit the subtleties and the knowledge they have attained. And worldliness also has the power to degrade an exalted state, as love can be degraded to lust, as soon as the grace it springs from has passed, by transforming it into its opposite; this is the fate of any spiritual gift not grounded in established virtue. As Dante indicates [cf. lines 61–63], those whose ruling sin is lust are destined, when purged, to reach the highest circles of Paradise. Lust is, if you will, the crown of the passions, as Pride is the root. It is the highest sin, not because it is of lesser magnitude, but because it gathers into itself all the other sins, and embodies their essence. Lust is closer than any other sin to the fires of Shame, which assist the fires of Purgatory in their final work.

Dante now encounters the soul of Guido Guinezzeli, his poetic mentor, and offers himself to serve the poetic spirit represented by him [lines 103–105], thus preparing himself to compose the Cantos of the Earthly Paradise to come, and the *Paradiso* itself. And Guinezzeli leads Dante's gaze beyond him to the soul of the troubadour Arnaut Daniel, his own mentor, master of the Fedeli d'Amore, whose poetic muse, "Lady Better-than-Good" was the immediate literary ancestor of Beatrice.

Arnaut is on the very edge of the flame; his soul is very close to being freed from Purgatory. Arnaut embodies the *esoterism* of Love; He says "I am Arnaut who, in traveling, both weep and sing"—but who is Arnaut? He is the one who is close to the mysteries that only Love can reveal; he is also close to the sufferings that guard those mysteries, and prevent them from being revealed to the profane. He shows exactly what it means to suffer for the sake of Love. As he says in two of his own songs:

> *I climb up the slope and I don't complain,*
> *since I am moved by this mountain to*
>   *think gentle thoughts....*

> *... and though that fire*
> *burns in my marrow,*
> *I don't want it to be quenched.*

The Ordeal of Mercy

Editorial Commentary Six:
Cor Gentile

Arnaut Daniel's speech in lines 40–47 is given not in Italian but in Provençal, the Langue d'Oc in which he composed; in English the first two lines might be rendered:

> *Your courteous request so pleases me,*
> *I cannot and I will not hide from you.*

This is mysterious, since Dante has voiced no request. Here Arnaut is most likely alluding to, and also expressing, the virtue of *cor gentile* extolled by the Fedeli d'Amore, an important aspect of which is the ability to mute the indiscrete expression of one's own desires, as well as to sense and respond to the unvoiced desires of others—a virtue which is as useful in prayer as in human relations. When Arnaut says "I cannot and I will not," he is expressing what was undoubtedly a central tenet of the Fedeli: the union of the Intellect, the faculty that discerns metaphysical Necessity, with the Will, the faculty that conforms the soul to what the Intellect has revealed, through the medium of Love. *Cor gentile* denotes the "gentle, courteous, and (implicitly) *aristocratic* heart." As Meister Eckhart put it, "the soul is an aristocrat"; the root of courtesy toward man is courtesy toward God. The *gentility* traditionally aspired to by the western *gentleman* ("gentle" originally meant "well-born") was the precise opposite of all crudity and vulgarity; its essence was refinement of feeling, *noblesse oblige* in the realm of the affections. Such refinement however, after descending from the aristocracy to the bourgeoisie, became in its old age a mere arrogant badge of social status. Think of some black-and-white film from the 1930s, 40s or 50s, in which a puffed-up bourgeois character snarls in a haughty tone, "I *beg* your pardon!" Obviously such a figure is not begging pardon from anyone; this is how inverted "courtesy" became degraded to a form of insult, after which it was generally discarded as not worth the trouble of maintaining. It is one of the supreme ironies of "the decline of the West" that those totally devoid of gentility, ignorant even of the concept of it, are still capable of being mortally offended by a lack of gentility in others. This is a sign that gentility or *cor gentile* is more than the behavioral pretension of a particular class, but rather an aspect of our intrinsic humanity, obscured and darkened by the Fall. And the Fall continues.

Canto XXVII

Sunset; the Angel of Chastity appears. Dante, after great resistance and with Virgil's encouragement, consents to pass through the fire that purifies of Lust. The entry into the Earthly Paradise. Dante sleeps and dreams of Leah and Rachel. Virgil's last words to Dante.

> The sun stood at the point of day's departure
>   When the glad Angel of God appeared to us.
> He stood upon the edge, beyond the fire
>   And sang to us "Beati mundo corde"
>   In voice by far more living than our own.
> "None can proceed from here, O holy souls,
>   Unless the fire stings: so enter in
>   And don't be deaf to the song you hear beyond."
> This is what he said when we came beside him;
>   As soon as I heard these words that he had spoken
>   I became like someone placed within his grave. [5–15]

The song of the angel is the direct opposite to the song of the siren; the siren's song, which is the voice of the passions, leads to destruction; the song of the angel leads to immortal life. When the angel directs Dante to concentrate upon it, the implication is that if he can't put all his attention on the song beyond the flames, he won't be able to pass through them, because all his lower desires and instincts will simply balk at the prospect of the coming ordeal.

In passing through the flames his passional self dies, but Dante himself does not die; before he has completed this passage, however, he cannot comprehend how this could be. The passional self will always say: "But if I give my will completely to God, won't I then be no more than a puppet of the Almighty, a plaything of fate?" But the truth is, the passional self is already a puppet to nearly everything it sees and touches. Only when his will has been completely given over to God does Dante's true self come into being in all its fullness.

The Ordeal of Mercy

The poet and priest John Donne speaks of this spiritual death in "Holy Sonnet XIV":

> *Batter my heart, three-personed God; for you*
> *As yet but knock, breathe, shine, and seek to mend;*
> *That I may rise and stand, o'erthrow me, and bend*
> *Your force to break, blow, burn, and make me new.*
> *I, like an usurpéd town, to another due,*
> *Labor to admit you, but O, to no end;*
> *Reason, your viceroy in me, me should defend,*
> *But is captived, and proves weak or untrue.*
> *Yet dearly I love you, and would be lovéd fain,*
> *But am betrothed unto your enemy.*
> *Divorce me, untie or break that knot again;*
> *Take me to you, imprison me, for I,*
> *Except you enthrall me, never shall be free,*
> *Nor ever chaste, except you ravish me.*

☨

> *To fend off the flames I joined my hands together*
>   *Vividly recalling, as I scanned the fire*
>   *The human bodies I had once seen burning.*
> *Then both my faithful escorts turned to me*
>   *And Virgil put to me the following words:*
>   *"Torment may be here, but never death!*
> *Remember now, remember! If I once*
>   *Guided you safe on Geryon's back through Hell*
>   *What shall I do when nearer now to God?*
> *Know and be sure: even if you were to stand*
>   *For a thousand years in the center of this fire*
>   *It could not make you balder by one hair*
> *And if by chance you think I might be wrong*
>   *Approach it now and on your garment's hem*
>   *With your own two hands put it to the test!*
> *Throw off your fear, throw off: the time has come.*
>   *Advance with trust to face the thing you must."*

Canto XXVII

But I still held back, defying my own conscience.
Then, seeing me stand fixed and hard, he said
With some impatience, "Look again, my Son!
Here stands the wall between you and Beatrice!" [16–36]

Dante is more afraid of passing through the fires of Purgatory than he was to travel through Hell. Hell puts everyone half to sleep because it is the kingdom of darkness, but Purgatory is forcing Dante to awake completely, which is why its flames are felt more sharply. Virgil must remind Dante that the Purgatorial fire purifies but does not destroy; in Yeats' words from his poem "Byzantium," which undoubtedly allude to line 30 of this canto, it is "an agony of flame that cannot singe a sleeve." Dante's highest and strongest desire must be invoked or he will not be able to bring himself to enter the fire; to pass through the fires that purify the soul of lust, with love always before one's eyes, is to transform the passions completely.

In front of me he stepped into the fire
Calling on Statius to now bring up the rear
Who had for so long walked that road between us.
When I had entered it, I then would have rather
Thrown myself into molten glass for coolness
So fierce and measureless I found that burning!
So as to bring me comfort, my sweet father
Kept telling me of Beatrice as we went:
"Look there! I seem to see her eyes already!" [46–54]

Here Virgil and Dante are shown for the first time as directly participating in the purifying sufferings of Purgatory; at this point they stop being partial spectators and become full pilgrims. In the normal course of things Virgil would never have entered these flames—his proper destiny being Limbo—but he does so for Dante's sake, in order to complete his guidance of him. And Virgil himself is purified through this guidance, even though, before this point, it was not his destiny to take the purgatorial road, the road to salvation. This is the work of Grace, and Grace is a mystery; it even has the power to change eternal destiny—though of course this change itself is also eternal. The guide who is called to guide by Grace is himself guided. Virgil, as guide, enters the fire first; Dante, as disciple, follows him. Statius comes last because he has no real need to be guided either by Virgil or Dante; his salvation is assured, and so he can graciously allow them to precede him. Here it is Virgil, not Dante, who begins to see the eyes of Beatrice; his insight and wisdom have become so deep that they assure him a place in Purgatory and thereby open to him the road to salvation. This is the point at which Virgil's role as Dante's Guide is completely fulfilled, and also ended.

> *A voice that on the other side was singing,*
>   *Directed us—and, paying strict attention*
>   *Only to that, we emerged where the ascent began.*
> "Venite, benedicti Patris mei,"
>   *Sounded within a Splendor that was there;*
>   *The light was so intense I could not look.*
> *"The sun departs,"* it sang, *"the night approaches;*
>   *Do not delay but hurry on your steps*
>   *Before the darkness falls on the western sky."* [55–63]

The dazzling light is the fulfillment of the flames; Dante's being is so strengthened and purified that what was once experienced as flame is now seen as pure light, though Dante still does not have the power to see *into* that light; this power is reserved for Paradise. The voice of the angel singing *Venite, benedicti Patris mei* ("Come, blessed of my Father") indicates that the travelers can reach the summit of the Mountain through *hearing*, which as we have seen is related to intuition and also to obedience. The Greek Fathers maintained that the soul would first recognize Paradise through its music; here the pilgrims are being led to the Earthly Paradise through a song. Just as the submission of the will must precede the opening of the Intellect, so hearing must come before seeing. As Job exclaimed when his sufferings were nearing their end, "I have heard thee with the hearing of the ear, but now mine eye seeth thee" [Job 42:5]. The travelers enter the intensity of fire but they are never shown as emerging from it; it is as if they have *become* the fire,

Canto XXVII

which now reveals itself as the cool of the evening, the last evening before the Earthly Paradise.

In lines 76–86 Dante compares himself to a goat (not a sheep) and Virgil and Statius to goatherds, because he is still more carnal than they are. He gazes at the stars [lines 88–90] and they appear larger than they normally would; maturity in contemplation brings one closer to heavenly realities.

After the sun sets, Dante falls asleep and dreams he sees the biblical figure Leah picking flowers; she loves the labor of love [lines 94–108]. The patriarch Jacob wooed his beloved Rachel while working for her father Laban for seven years, but on their wedding night Laban secretly sent Leah, Rachel's older sister, in her place, whom Jacob mistook for Rachel. Jacob was required to labor for another seven years before he could finally be united with her. Leah in the dream tells Dante that her sister Rachel loves seeing, and so she looks at herself all day in her mirror; Leah, in traditional scriptural exegesis, symbolizes action, and Rachel, contemplation, like Martha and Mary do in the Gospels: dedication of the will must precede the full flowering of the Intellect. Gazing into a mirror usually suggests narcissism to us, but when Rachel looks into her mirror, she sees not her own image, but only God. She is purified so completely that to the degree that Rachel exists, it is only God who exists. We should remember that, in the *Paradiso*, Dante journeys with Beatrice to her final resting-place, which is at the side of Rachel.

> *Such will and determination came upon me*
>> *To reach the heights, that at each higher step*
>> *I felt wings inside me growing, wings to fly!*
>
> *When all that stairway was at last beneath us*
>> *And our feet were planted on the final step*
>> *Then Virgil fixed his eyes on me and said:*
>
> *"Now you've seen the temporal and eternal fires*
>> *And have finally reached a station beyond which*
>> *I, by my own power, can see no further.*
>
> *Through intellect and art I've brought you here;*
>> *From now on, take your pleasure for your guide. . . ."*
>>> [121–131]

The Ordeal of Mercy

> *"You may sit or walk among them as you will.*
> [i.e., among the shrubs and flowers]
> *No further word nor sign expect from me;*
> *Your will is upright, sound and fully free.*
> *To disobey it now would be a sin;*
> *Above yourself I crown and mitre you."* [138–142]

Now Dante has come entirely into the freedom of his will; his pleasure is all spiritual. The condition in which he was subject to dark pleasures threatening to lead him astray is ended. Therefore Virgil dismisses Dante from his guidance by saying "over yourself I crown and mitre you," indicating that he has now perfected in himself both the power of will (the crown) and that of intellectual contemplation (the mitre). At this point Dante's will is so completely purified that he can follow his senses, the beauty that appears before his eyes, in almost the same way that, on a lower level, a sensualist would follow his own fallen vision of beauty; it is this new ability that prepares him for his encounter with Beatrice. Titus Burckhardt, in "Because Dante is Right," from *Mirror of the Intellect, Essays on Traditional Science and Sacred Art* (94), comments on this development:

> It is significant that here [in Canto XXX, set in the Earthly Paradise] Dante no longer stresses the moral beauty of Beatrice—her goodness, innocence and humility—as he did in his *La Vita Nuova*, but speaks quite simply of her visible beauty; what is most outward has here become the image of what is most inward, sensory observation the expression of spiritual vision.

This quality of being led by a contemplation of visible beauty, however, does not dissipate his soul, but only draws him closer to God. Frithjof Schuon comments on the love of Beauty—in this case, human beauty—as a way to Truth in the following terms: "Beauty in itself ... is a perfect theophany on its own plane ... the theophanic quality of the human body resides uniquely in its form, and not in the sanctity of the soul inhabiting it ..." [*From the Divine to the Human*, 92]. This is a dangerous truth, however. A

Canto XXVII

beautiful body housing a vicious soul will necessary be an occasion not only for sin but also for the deepest form of delusion, given that the soul, which is invisible, has ontological precedence over the visible body; such delusion is represented in Dante's works by the beautiful but stony-hearted woman Pietra. Only in the case of the one who has completed the whole course of purgation, whose will is fully submissive to the Divine Intellect, will outward beauty of form and the pleasure of contemplating it act as an epiphany of spiritual Truth. Furthermore, there is no real Beauty without Virtue; as Schuon puts it: "Virtue is none other than beauty of soul; that is why the Greeks, who were aesthetes as well as thinkers, included virtue within philosophy. Without beauty of soul, all willing is sterile; it is petty and closes itself to grace..." [*Survey of Metaphysics and Esoterism*, 6]. Nor can physical beauty really be isolated from the state of the soul in question, since viciousness of soul will always leave its traces in the physical form, at least in terms of expression and behavior, while a beautiful soul sometimes has the power to transfigure even a body which bears obvious imperfections. As soon as Dante has completed the entire course of purification that the *Purgatorio* represents, to be attracted to a woman with a beautiful form but a stony heart is no longer possible for him.

For all its emphasis on repentance and purgatorial suffering, the Christian tradition also provides intimations of this final purification, where Beauty can be followed with no fear of inflaming the passions; one example of this is the legend of Mary of Egypt. Saint Mary, a reformed prostitute, had the power to walk on water; this symbolizes the soul's triumph over material nature while still in the midst of it, as in Hindu tantric yoga, which calls for the passions to be invoked, then tamed and sublimated. This transformation is alchemical in nature; legend has it that the double boiler, first used by the alchemists, was invented by Mary of Egypt.

The story of Saint Mary can be taken as an illustration of the quality of the purified passions in the Earthly Paradise. Prostitution, for Mary, is an expression of the joy of sensual love rather than greed for material gain. She conceives the desire to go on pilgrimage to Jerusalem, and earns her passage through prostitution, but the pilgrims she meets on the way teach her that pleasure must be mortified, because no-one can love the world as if it were everything; to do so is to forget God. She becomes an anchorite and lives in the desert without clothing, like the Hindu Lalla Yogeshwari, the Shaitive female saint of Kashmir. On one occasion she meets a holy elder who tries to worship her, but she desires more that his attention be turned toward God. She asks him to bring her communion. When he sees her walk on the water he again tries to prostrate to her, but she tells him not to do this since he is a priest who carries the consecrated host. While receiving communion she disappears and is miraculously transported far away. Later the priest finds her corpse; only after her death does he discover that her name is Mary. "Mary" may in fact be an initiatory name, as a nun will be called "Sister Mary (so-and-so)." Her death after receiving communion is the death of the lower self. After her death the old priest finds, written in the sands, her request that he bury her corpse, but since he has no shovel, he has to dig her grave with his hands. Help comes from a lion, who digs with his paws; the passion which on a lower level appeared as lust, which "roams about like a roaring lion, seeking whom to devour" [1 Peter 5:8], has been completely transformed, and becomes a vehicle for the Spirit. Mary of Egypt reminds us of Eve who, according to Eastern Orthodox tradition, is restored to her original beauty through the intercession of the Second Eve, the Virgin Mary.

Entre'acte:
The Ontology of
the Earthly Paradise

The Spiritual Path is traditionally divided into the Greater and Lesser Mysteries. The Lesser Mysteries have to do with the purification and ordering of the soul, the Greater ones with the soul's union with God, its deification. In Eastern Orthodox theology, the Lesser Mysteries are termed *askesis* and the Greater Mysteries, *theosis*. The Earthly Paradise, which pertains to the Lesser Mysteries, is the point where celestial realities and earthly conditions most completely interpenetrate. In cosmological terms it is part of the *mundus imaginalis*, the Imaginal Plane, where bodies are spiritualized and spiritual realities embodied. St. Maximos the Confessor refers to this union of the spiritual and the physical when he tells us that Christ

> unites man and woman ... unites the earth by abolishing the division between the earthly paradise and the rest of the inhabited globe ... unites earth and heaven ... unites sensible and intelligible things ... and ultimately—in an ineffable way— unites created and uncreated nature. [*Quaestiones ad Thalassium* 48: CCG 7, 333, 76–335, 78; PG 90, 436 AB]

It is by the Lesser Mysteries that we regain the primordial or "Adamic" state by which the soul becomes fully human—and the site and seal of the completion of these Mysteries is the Earthly Paradise. This Paradise is so beautiful that one can finally feel the lack of perfection that only the Greater Mysteries, only union with God, can overcome.

Children are closer to the primal innocence of the Adamic state, but not because of their immaturity. "Unless ye become as little

The Ordeal of Mercy

children...."—but childlikeness is poles apart from childishness. To become "as little children" is to come into a spiritual relationship with the Virgin Mary. In the words of Frithjof Schuon: "Specifically Marian spirituality may be summarized in these terms: to become pure prayer, pure receptivity before God" [*Dimensions of Islam*, 98].

The Earthly Paradise is everything that earthly life is leading toward, the fulfillment of it, which—paradoxically—cannot happen on the material plane. Earthly life was created to be more subtle than the crude materiality to which it has finally descended. In our souls we hold a nostalgia for this Paradise, as well as for the celestial one. The Celestial Paradise of the *Paradiso* does not obliterate the Earthly Paradise of the *Purgatorio*, but carries it within itself.

It is harder, however, for many people to believe in the Earthly Paradise than in the higher heavenly realms. Since it is self-evident that our minds in their usual fallen state can't grasp the reality of higher worlds, it is easy to simply allow oneself an abstract belief in them, which is really quite crude. The Earthly Paradise, however, can come almost as close as our dreams. We can't help but feel that the door to it is so near that it would open if only we were to knock upon it. What would happen if that door were to open wide and a new world rush in upon us? Our old world, our old life, would be transfigured; we would find ourselves living in "a new heaven and a new earth" [Apocalypse 21:1]. The world around us would still be the earth, and our lives would still be with us, but we would suddenly find ourselves walking through orchards of golden apples; this new earth would take us to the threshold of Paradise, and beyond. We would discover that we had been wrong to believe that the highest mansions of Heaven exclude the Earthly Paradise, which—unless we are saints who live by grace—is the only world we have ever truly loved. (This vision must be clearly differentiated from the false love of the World which treats this World as self-contained and thus cuts it off from the Earthly Paradise, its archetype. Such profane love only distorts the truth of this World, and in the process reveals itself as barren.) Heaven, however sublime, does not exclude the Earthly Paradise; by the power of this Paradise, even the earth itself becomes part of Heaven. It is only the

Entre'acte: The Ontology of the Earthly Paradise

coarseness of our imaginations that makes us believe this cannot be so.

One reason we reject the idea of an Earthly Paradise is because we have encountered so many parodies of it, based on childishness and self-indulgence. To accept the reality of this Paradise nonetheless requires a childlike faith, but we become childlike in this sense through perfecting the virtues—through purgation. In other words, we achieve this sort of childlikeness precisely by overcoming childishness. In the Primal Innocence moralism is transcended, but such Innocence lies above morality not below it, since all that the moral life has called us to accomplish has now been fulfilled.

In order to gaze upon the Earthly Paradise one needs spiritual eyes; otherwise everything is seen through the veil of the passions. The spiritual Path is not penance alone, but penance united with insight. When Adam fell his *vision* fell, not merely his will.

Virgin Nature per se is not the Earthly Paradise, but it is certainly a reflection of it, and also a door to it. Nature, in its present fallen condition, is a manifestation of Rigor as well as Beauty; this is something we must never forget. But carried—and also protected—by the Rigor of the natural world is a Beauty which stands as a living icon of the Earthly Paradise, and consequently of Paradise as such; this is why Eastern Orthodox Christians consider Nature to be a theophany, a revelation of God. According to Evagrius of Pontus,

> As for those who are far from God . . . God has made it possible to come near to the knowledge of him and his love for them through the medium of his creatures. These he has produced, as the letters of the alphabet, so to speak, by his power and wisdom. . . .

Likewise St. Maximos the Confessor tells us that

> [The Logos], while hiding himself for our benefit in a mysterious way, in the *logoi*, shows himself to our minds to the extent of our ability to understand, through visible objects which act like letters of the alphabet, whole and complete both individually and when related together.

The Ordeal of Mercy

Origen also maintains that

> ... we must necessarily believe that the person who is asking questions of nature and the person who is asking questions of the Scriptures are bound to arrive at the same conclusions.

Likewise, according to St. Paul in Romans 1:20,

> For the invisible things of Him from the creation of the world are clearly seen, being understood by the things that are made, even His eternal power and Godhead. . . .

But to see through the eye of the passions, of fear and desire, distorts everything; this is what destroys our ability to witness the natural world as an icon of the Creator. The words which St. Symeon the New Theologian applies, in the following passage, to the beauties of the human body, apply equally to the body of Virgin Nature:

> One whose bodily eyes are weak cannot at all look on a brightly shining sunbeam; if he stares at it he at once loses such sight as he still has. So he whose spiritual eyes are weak and whose senses are subject to passions cannot contemplate the excellence of beauty of a body without passion or harm to himself. [*The Discourses*, 265]

The Pagan materialist looks on Nature and forgets God. He sees the beauty of Nature, but this leads him only to dissipation. In the words of Portia from Shakespeare's *The Merchant of Venice*,

> *Many a man his life hath sold*
> *But my outside to behold;*
> *Gilded tombs do worms enfold.*

And though the Pagan sees the outward beauty of Nature, he also sees her as terrible, as the realm of the Medusa, the Furies. It is true that the world of Nature in its fallen state is rigorous as well as beautiful, but to regard Nature's Beauty in only an outward way, which is

Entre'acte: The Ontology of the Earthly Paradise

often indulged in as a method of denying her Rigor, is to become fatalistic. It is to separate Rigor from Mercy—whereas in the figure of Beatrice in *The Divine Comedy*, or in the Virgin herself, Rigor leads on to Mercy, then drops away.

The saint, whose soul has become virginal, sees the beauty of Virgin Nature and remembers God. Far from regarding this beauty as something separate from himself that might destroy him, it leads him instead to the Beatific Vision. Since he sees beauty as belonging entirely to God, how could it possibly be an alien thing—like the Furies, the Medusa, the infernal Persephone of the Pagan—something that might destroy his soul? As the saint remembers God through the beauties of Nature, he finds himself in the presence of the Love of God, and witnesses this Love as *natura naturans*, the creative Source of the natural world.

Virgin Nature, when taken as a support for the contemplation of God, makes the Earthly Paradise directly accessible. But sacred art, such as that of the icon—or the *Divine Comedy*—is also a theophany. Such art, even though—or rather, precisely because—it is not naturalistic, trains us to see Nature as a revelation of Divine realities. Sacred art has a deep relationship to Nature; sometimes we are closer to Nature in contemplating such art than it looking upon her directly, because sacred art calls us to set our vision on the *mundus imaginalis*, the subtle embodiment of the world of Ideas, which is the root of Nature.

The Earthly Paradise is that which the ancestors of mankind possessed, then lost. Dante identifies it with the classical Golden Age, when material nature was transparent to celestial realities [Canto XXVIII, lines 39–41]. According to Frithjof Schuon, from *The Feathered Sun*:

> Wild nature is at one with holy poverty and also with spiritual childlikeness; she is an open book containing an inexhaustible teaching of truth and beauty. It is in the midst of his own artifices that man most easily becomes corrupted, it is they that make him covetous and impious; close to virgin Nature, who knows neither agitation nor falsehood, he had the hope of remaining contemplative, like Nature herself. [41]

The Ordeal of Mercy

That the Earthly Paradise can be lost over time, however, distinguishes it from the Celestial Paradise. And even though spiritual beings can visit the Earthly Paradise with ease, the soul needs the Celestial Paradise for true union with God.

The Earthly Paradise is the first stage the soul reaches after it has been purified from sin and contingency. Here is where the soul, having completed its spiritual struggle, waits in receptivity for the coming of the grace of God which will draw it into Paradise itself.

Canto XXVIII

The travelers now find themselves in the Earthly Paradise, walking through a great primeval forest. Dante arrives at the stream of Lethe and encounters a woman named Matilda, who will be his preceptor until the coming of Beatrice.

> *Already eager to thoroughly explore*
> *The heavenly forest, dense and living-green,*
> *Which tempered to my eyes the new-born day,*
> *Without further delay I quit the bank*
> *Taking the level country slowly, slowly*
> *Over the soil that everywhere breathes fragrance.*
> *A softly-breathing air that held no change*
> *Within itself, upon my forehead struck*
> *A blow no heavier than a gentle wind*
> *At which all the branches, lightly trembling*
> *Bowed themselves together toward that side*
> *Where the Holy Mountain casts its morning shadow....*
> [1–12]

That Dante is moved to search (according to Mandelbaum's translation) both "within" and "around" shows how, in the Earthly Paradise, the duality of inner and outer has broken down, not because of chaos but because of a deeper integration; the split between soul and world is being healed by a higher Power.

Dante has now arrived at the dawn of humanity; the wind blowing "in the direction of morning shadows" (Mandelbaum), from east to west, is the Spirit coming into manifestation; the breeze striking Dante upon the forehead acts to transform his consciousness.

The people of the Celestial Paradise can travel straight toward the Sun, whereas in the Earthly Paradise they can't take such a direct route. But they can be permeated by the light of the Sun, the power of which comes to them as a nurturing wind. Dante, since he is now above temporal manifestation, can witness the flow of it, of both wind and water, toward the left, the pole of *materia*. Outer, visible manifestation, since it inclines away from the Sun of the Logos by the very power of that Sun, as shadows do, is revealed to be composed of the shadows of realities that, in the Earthly Paradise, subsist in their substantial forms.

> *Already had my slow steps carried me*
>   *So far into that ancient wood that I*
>   *Could no longer see the place where I'd come in.*
> *And now I found my path blocked by a stream*
>   *Which toward the left hand with its little waves*
>   *Bent down the grass that grew upon its bank.*
> *All the most crystalline waters of the earth*
>   *Would seem impure and turbid when compared*
>   *With this purest of all waters, that hides no thing*
> *Though on it flows with a current brown and brown*
>   *Beneath a perpetual shade that never opens*
>   *To let in ray of either sun or moon.* [22–33]

Dante can no longer see the point where he entered the Terrestrial Paradise because space here possesses a different quality.

No light of sun or moon touches this "purest" water because it is ontologically above the level of the material sun and moon as we see them. The darkness here is a fertile darkness, that of the *materia prima*. In his *Alchemy: Science of the Cosmos, Science of the Soul*, Titus Burckhardt describes the *materia prima* in these terms:

> According to the alchemists, the base metals cannot be transmuted into silver or gold without first being reduced to their *materia prima*. If the base metals are regarded as being analogous to one-sided and imperfectly 'coagulated' states of the soul, then the *materia prima*, to which they must be reduced, is none other than their underlying 'fundamental substance', that is to say, the soul in its original state, as yet unconditioned by impressions and passions, and 'uncongealed' into any definite

Canto XXVIII

form. Only when the soul is freed from all its rigidities and inner contradictions [i.e., after it has completed its *purgation*] does it become that plastic substance on which the Spirit or Intellect, coming from on high, can imprint a new 'form'—a form which does not limit or bind, but on the contrary delivers. Because it comes from the Divine Essence . . . the soul, in its original state of pure receptivity, is fundamentally one with the *materia prima* of the whole world. [97]

In order to demonstrate that the *materia prima* contains in potency all forms of consciousness and thus all forms of the ephemeral world, the ninth-century Arab alchemist Abu'l-Qasim al-Iraqi writes, '. . . *materia prima* is to be found in a mountain [sic] which contains a measureless quantity of uncreated things. In this mountain is every kind of knowledge that can be found in this world.' [100]

This forest is the inverse of the "dark forest" of the *Inferno*; its darkness has an opposite meaning. It exists at the point just before all the qualities of the soul become formed and defined. Its water "hides no thing" because everything here is allowed to return to its own origin; here no thing need be replaced or negated by another, as is the case in outer manifestation, a condition that gives rise to duality and makes this duality seem absolute.

Now Dante sees a woman on the opposite bank, gathering flowers, and speaks to her; this is Matilda.

> *And just as a lady dancing, with feet together*
> *Upon the ground will pivot round a point*
> *And hardly put one foot before the other,*
> *So, on the little vermilion and golden flowers*
> *She turned in my direction, the very image*
> *Of a chaste and modest virgin with downcast eyes.* [52–57]

Dante is fully satisfied by Matilda's approach, and finally her glance, because she is virginity personified—*his own* virginity. This lady in the act of gathering flowers, whom Dante compares to

The Ordeal of Mercy

Persephone, is the *puella aeterna*, the "eternal maiden" in her maturity. She is the finished form of the Persephone archetype, the soul that has completed the lesser mysteries. She is also, of all the characters in the *Divine Comedy*, the closest to being the fulfillment of the figure of the troubadour's Lady—a Persephone before her rape by Hades, one who is inviolable not by negative innocence or naivete, like the Persephone of myth whose virginity could not protect her, but by virtue of her greater maturity. (Beatrice, though she possesses this character as well, is also much more.) Hades' rape of Persephone inaugurated the cycles of nature; Matilda is a Persephone who has gone beyond these cycles, transcended the pull into manifestation and time. She is not simply virgin but *virginal*; she is virginity restored in eternal maidenhood.

> *As soon as she came to where the grasses lay*
> *Bathed by the waters of that lovely stream,*
> *She rewarded me by lifting up her eyes.*
> *I do not think there shone so great a light*
> *Beneath the lids of Venus, when transfixed*
> *Strangely by the shaft of her own son!* [61–66]

As the troubadour's Lady, Matilda is a subtle earthly projection of the circle of Venus in the *Paradiso*. Dante's meeting with her is compared to the sacred marriage between Venus and Adonis, a god of fertility, whom Venus fell in love with when she was pricked by one of her son Cupid's arrows. Persephone, the goddess of the underworld, was also enamoured of Adonis, and so Zeus (or, in some accounts, the muse Calliope) decreed that he would spend half his time with each, thus inaugurating the cycle of the seasons; Adonis is finally killed during a hunt by a wild boar. Dante is here identified with Adonis because, initially, he is fragmentary in relation to Matilda/Venus, who is more complete; as is true in all examples of the son/lover of the Great Goddess, the son passes through the cycle, but the Goddess *is* the cycle. Now, however, through a purified sexual attraction, he has begun to return to his original fullness and integration through his encounter with her; he is being prepared to function not as her servant, but as her consort and equal.

Canto XXVIII

Standing erect on the opposite bank she smiled
  Bearing many colors in her hands,
  Which that high land produces without seed.
The river kept us just three steps apart;
  But even the Hellespont, where Xerxes crossed
  (A warning still to human arrogance,)
Did not feel more hatred from Leander
  For raging between Sestos and Abydos,
  Than that stream from me because it would not open.
"As newcomers here you are possibly perplexed"
  She said, "To see me smiling in this place
  Chosen for human nature to be its nest;
Wonder and uncertainty keep you guessing.
  But the psalm that begins 'Delectasti' shines a light
  Which holds the power to uncloud your mind.
Now you who just stepped forward to beseech me
  Speak if you wish to hear, for I come ready
  To hear your every question, till you're content." [67–84]

These flowers need no seed because they *are* the seed. They are the prototypes, prior in being though not in time, to earthly flowers.

The little stream that separates Dante from Matilda by only three steps seems like too slight a barrier to be compared to the wide and dangerous Hellespont; but Dante must go *through* the stream of manifestation in order to get beyond it, and this is no small task.

Dante admits that before seeing the Earthly Paradise with his own eyes he could not believe in it; only now is his vision purified to the point where he can grasp the reality of this Paradise. It would be easy enough to claim that because the Celestial Paradise is the final goal of the spiritual life there is no need to accept the reality of an intermediary state such as the Earthly Paradise; the Earthly Paradise is a transfiguration of the natural world, and Western (largely Augustinian) Christianity—unlike Eastern Orthodoxy—has tended to see nature more as a sign of the Fall than of the Mercy of God. To reject the Earthly Paradise, however, actually diminishes the vision of the Celestial Paradise itself. If we only have the Celestial Paradise in view, we see only the sublime transcending all form, consequently it

The Ordeal of Mercy

becomes difficult to understand how a person's full humanity could attain the Paradisical state. The denial that our physical and psychic humanity are also destined for Paradise was one of the errors of the sectarian Gnostics.

Because of our fallen nature our vision has become fragmented; immersed in a world of fallen forms, we can only conceive of Paradise as entirely formless and abstract. Christ's incarnation, however, demonstrates that concrete form and Paradisical beauty are not incompatible. The reason that we can no longer enter the Earthly Paradise at will is that our vision is too fragmented to allow us to witness it. Some Eastern Orthodox monks, however, as well as certain monks of the Celtic Church, claimed that they had been able to enter the Earthly Paradise in this life.

The Earthly Paradise is the spiritual center of the Intermediary or Imaginal Plane, which we tend to think of as mere fantasy; yet it is as objectively real as this terrestrial earth. Russian Orthodox priest Pavel Florensky, in his book *Iconostasis*, speaks of the quality of this Plane, which appears in the dream-state, as well as by means of the transition that we call death:

> In the beginning of Genesis "God created the Heavens and the Earth"... [and] when we pray the Apostles Creed we name God as "Maker of all things visible and invisible." These two worlds—the visible and the invisible—are intimately connected, but their reciprocal differences are so immense that the inescapable question arises: what is their boundary? Their boundary separates them; yet, simultaneously, it joins them. How do we understand this boundary?...The life of our own psyche... is the truest basis upon which we may learn about this boundary between the two worlds. For within ourselves, life in the visible world alternates with life in the invisible, and thus we experience moments... when the two worlds grow so near in us that we can see their intimate touching. At such fleeting moments in us, the veil of invisibility is torn apart, and through that tear... we can sense that the invisible world (still unearthly, still invisible) is *breathing*: and that both this and another world are dissolving into each other. [33]

Canto XXVIII

... time in the dream runs ... against the movement of time in waking consciousness [as Florensky has explained earlier, "from future to past, from effects to causes"]. Dream time is *turned inside out*, which means that all its concrete images are also turned inside out with it: and that means we have entered the domain of *imaginary space*. ... [41]

A person I know very well once dreamed (after the death of close relatives) that he was walking along a cemetery, and the other world seemed dark and gloomy. But all at once the deceased in the cemetery ... explained to him how very wrong such a thought was; for, directly beneath the surface of the earth, foliage was growing but with its roots up, not down, so that the same green and succulent foliage and grass were there, just as in the cemetery—but even more green and succulent; and the same trees were there, and their great crowns grew down and their roots reached up, and the same birds sang in the same azure sky where the same sun shone—all of it more radiantly beautiful than in our world on this side.

Don't we recognize in this reverse world, in this ontological mirror reflection of our world, the sphere of the imaginary, an imaginary which is nevertheless actual for one who is [him]self upside down, who reaches into the world's spiritual density—an imaginary truly real in the way one is oneself real? Yes, this realm is real in essence—and not in a way completely different from the reality of our world, for whatever God creates is blessed into unity; rather what the journeyer to the other side sees and what the deceased also contemplates is the same existence as here. The true countenances and spiritual forms of things are seen by the one who has realized his own true, original countenance, that countenance which is the image of God. ... [42]

Compare this passage to Canto XXXIII: 64–68, where Dante speaks of the Tree of Knowledge as growing upside-down. This ontological reversal also appears in the placement of Purgatory as a whole: the base of the Mountain is in the southern hemisphere, but when Dante reaches its summit the constellations of the northern sky appear above it [cf. Canto XXX].

Mankind's true nest is the Earthly Paradise. Here sexual desire is sublimated in favor of Knowledge, reminding us of the biblical sense of "to know," signifying sexual union [cf. Genesis 4:1; cf. also lines 80–81]. The sexual aspect of knowledge is not to be followed out to its literal end; in order to be truly known it must remain a mystery to the created intellect.[1]

This nest is the nest of man as such, but since Christ is true God as well as true man, He also exists beyond this nest. He can enter it when appropriate, but it is not entirely proper to Him, since He also transcends it. Man needs a place to exist in, but God is placeless. When Jesus said "the foxes have holes and the birds of the air have nests, but the Son of Man has nowhere to lay his head" [Luke 9:58], he was alluding to this Divine Placelessness.

> *So that the turmoil made below this place*
>   *By exhalations from the land and water,*
>   *(Which, as far as possible, follow heat)*
> *Might not disturb the peace of humankind*
>   *This Mountain rose up, high and near to Heaven;*
>   *Above the locked gate, all is undisturbed.*
> *Now since the universal atmosphere*

---

1. In the legend of White Buffalo Cow Woman, the mysterious prophetess who brought the Sacred Pipe to the Lakota—equivalent in its degree of numinosity to the Hebrew Ark of the Covenant—she first appears naked to two young braves on the prairie. One wants to rape her, but the other, recognizing her as sacred or *wakan*, refuses. A cloud descends over the first brave, inside of which can be heard the sound of snakes hissing and striking, and when it lifts there is nothing left of him but a naked skeleton. Then the prophetess turns to the second brave and commands him to announce her coming to the people. The first brave wants to "know" her literally and is destroyed; the second, who holds back, respecting the mystery, becomes her emissary: thus "the letter killeth, but the Spirit giveth life" [2 Corinthians 3:6]. The passionate brave sees White Buffalo Cow Woman as *avidya-maya*, the wise brave as *vidya-maya*; in Herself, however, she is precisely *Maya* as a whole, which may be compared to the river of the Terrestrial Paradise before it forks into Lethe and Eunoë.

Canto XXVIII

Wheels in accordance with the primal motion
Unless at a given point the circle is broken
Against this height—where everything is blended
   Into the living air—this motion strikes
   And makes the forest, because it's dense, resound.
And when a plant is struck it breathes such power
   The surrounding air is impregnated with its seed
   Which, in revolving, scatters abroad its virtue.
And the other earth, according to the nature
   Of its soil and climate, conceives and bears
   From different qualities various kinds of trees.
After hearing this, why be amazed
   When you see within the earth a plant take root
   Without the agency of any seed?
Know, then, that this sacred level ground
   You stand upon is full of every seed;
   It bears fruits never harvested on earth.
The water that you see here does not spring
   From channels that clouds, condensed by cold, restore
   Like rivers that sometimes rise and sometimes fall
But issues from a fountain steady, certain,
   Which is replenished from the will of God
   By just so much as it loses on either side. [97–126]

When Matilda, speaking as the "hostess" of the Earthly Paradise, tells Dante that the holy plain at the summit of Mount Purgatory on which he is standing is "full of every seed," she is describing the very same "mountain" which, according to Iraqi, "is full of is every kind of knowledge that can be found in this world," seeing that knowledge is the seed of every created form. In her beautiful depiction of this Paradise, she explains that plants on earth are indirectly nurtured by the plants that grow here; the higher begets the lower. This is the direct opposite of the theory of evolution. Because the Earthly Paradise is really the Imaginal Realm, generation here happens in a way that is the reverse of earthly generation. Instead of water impregnating the earth and bringing forth plants (rain being almost universally regarded in world mythology as the generative power of the Heavenly Father), here plants themselves impregnate the air, which carries the *imprint* of the plants, their vital seed, to earth.² The "universal atmosphere" which "wheels in accordance with the primal motion" (i.e., the *primum mobile*) until it strikes the Mount of Purgatory and the trees of the Earthly Paradise, is the wind of the Spirit invoking manifestation; the seeds it carries to the lower material world are the Platonic Ideas which imprint the *materia* of that world with the *forma* of the Divine creative intent. St. Gregory of Mt. Sinai speaks of the Earthly Paradise in quite similar terms:

> Paradise is twofold—sensible and spiritual; there is the paradise of Eden and the paradise of Grace. The paradise of Eden is so exalted that it is said to extend to the third heaven. It has been planted by God with every kind of sweet-scented plant. It is neither entirely free from corruption nor altogether subject to it. Created between corruption and incorruption, it is always rich in fruits, ripe and unripe, and continually full of flowers. When trees and ripe fruit rot and fall to the ground they turn into sweet-scented soil, free from the smell of decay exuded by the vegetable matter of this world. This is because of the great richness and holiness of the grace ever abounding there. The river Ocean, appointed always to irrigate paradise with its waters, flows through the middle of it. In leaving paradise it divides into four other rivers, and flowing down to the Indians and the Ethiopians brings them soil and fallen leaves. Their fields are flooded by the united rivers of Pison and Gihon until these divide again, the one watering Libya and the other the land of Egypt. [*Philokalia*, vol. 4, 213–214]

---

2. In Islamic terms, according to the Sufi doctrines of Ibn al-'Arabi—whom Miguel Asin i Palacios proved was a major influence upon Dante—the air in this canto would be the *Nafas al-Rahman*, "the Breath of the Merciful," the Holy Spirit in creative mode, which confers concrete existence upon the *ayan al-thabita*, the "permanent archetypes" or Platonic Ideas, the uncreated prototypes of all things within the Mind of God, here symbolized by the various plant species. The Breath of the Merciful, in the language of the first verses of the Book of Genesis, is "the Spirit of God" that "moved upon the face of the waters."

Canto XXVIII

St. Gregory does not teach that the plants of Paradise fertilize our world via the wind of manifestation, but he does describe the rivers of that world as flowing down into earthly existence, carrying fallen leaves from the trees of Eden. In this passage the saint is telling us that all the forms we see in this world find their archetypes in the Terrestrial Paradise. Without this Paradise, which is invisible to our sensorial eyes, we would have nothing—not even the materialistic mindset which tells us that such a realm could not exist. We would certainly not have anything which could truly be described as a *world*.

There is no rise or fall in this river that initially separates Matilda from Dante because it lies above the cycles of time. The seeds of all earthly forms are here, but not every seed descends into the lower levels of manifestation. Higher levels of being are always more complete than the lower because they are more supple and are therefore better able to contain and express the overflow of Divine All-Possibility. At the same time they are more stable and integrated since they are closer to Necessary Being, and thus to Absolute Reality. This "steady, certain" river is another rendition of the *materia prima*. According to Titus Burckhardt in *Alchemy*,

> The mirror of the ground of the soul ... is ... comparable to a pure spring. It is the mythical fountain of youth, from whose depths springs forth the mercury-like water of life. [101–102]

Now Matilda discourses on Lethe and Eunoë, the two streams into which the river of the Earthly Paradise forks:

> *"On this side it [the stream] comes down with the power*
>   *To take away all memory of sin;*
>   *On the other side, the power to recall good deeds.*
> *Here Lethe, and there Eunoë it is named;*
>   *Yet neither one possesses any virtue*
>   *Unless the other one is tasted first.*
> *This is a taste transcending every sweetness;*
>   *And though your thirst might well be satisfied*
>   *Even if I were content to reveal no more*
> *I'll give you the corollary to that taste for free;*

The Ordeal of Mercy

I do not think my words will be less welcome
If I choose to offer more than what I promised:
Those in ancient times who sang the legend
  Of the Golden Age and all its happiness
  In the guise of Parnassus—did they dream this place?
Here innocence was, the root of humankind;
  Here stood eternal Spring and all its fruits;
  Here flowed the nectar that every poet sang." [127–144]

Matilda is apparently pointing downstream to her right—Dante's left—to indicate the point where Lethe and Eunoë fork. From Dante's point of view the stream flows towards the left, toward outer manifestation; from Matilda's it flows right, toward the higher worlds. Lethe, "forgetfulness (of sin)," is the final stage of repentance; Eunoë, "good mind" is the dawning of *gnosis*. In the Earthly Paradise the Intellect has become receptive to the higher levels of *gnosis* which are Paradise per se. It must become as ignorant as it can possibly be of fallen knowledge in order to receive perfect knowledge.

The Golden Age is the material, earthly age closest to the Earthly Paradise, but even it is only a reflection of this Paradise, just as human art is a reflection of the art of God. The vocation of the muses was to invoke a memory of the Earthly Paradise, which is why they were called "the Daughters of Memory," and why their mountain, Parnassus, represents a memory or reflection of the Mountain of Purgatory with the Earthly Paradise at its crest.

That one must drink of *both* rivers "first" is a paradox; it indicates that the action being referred to takes place beyond time. But beyond this, what does it mean that neither Lethe nor Eunoë possesses virtue unless the other one has been tasted? In this world we must try to acknowledge our sins and shortcomings; if we don't do this we enter states of terrible illusion; our spiritual vision is distorted. Eunoë, however—the remembrance of good deeds—comes from the Truth itself, unlike evil which is not only a *privatio boni* but a *privatio veritatis*. And this Truth cannot be approached until one forgets one's sins—which, in their essence, were *truly* illusory. Before one's sins can be forgotten, however, the darkness one has

Canto XXVIII

encountered in both self and life must be acknowledged. But, strangely enough, after one has passed through the deepest part of this darkness, the time when the soul, blind to its shortcomings, foolishly thought it was perfect and pure can suddenly be remembered—and remembered *as if this had been the truth all along*, and as if all the darkness it was required to face on its path had been merely an illusion. At the end of the Path, something that at one point had seemed totally immature turns out to have been the greatest reality all along. St. Paul, in 1 Corinthians 3:1–2, says: "And I, brethren, could not speak unto you as unto [the] spiritual, but unto [the] carnal, as babes in Christ. I have fed you with milk, and not with meat, for hitherto ye were not able to bear it." Christ on the other hand, in Luke 18:16, says: "Suffer little children to come unto me, and forbid them not: for of such is the Kingdom of God."

Canto XXIX

Now Dante, standing on the banks of Lethe preparatory to his crossing, beholds a sacred symbolic procession of seven candlesticks, seven pennants, twenty-four elders, four beasts, a Chariot drawn by a Griffin, seven women (who are the Four Cardinal Virtues and the Three Theological Virtues), and seven more elders.

> *And just as the Nymphs, who wandered all alone*
> *   Took great care, among the forest shadows*
> *   Some to avoid and others to see the sun,*
> *Against the current she then moved onward, walking*
> *   Along the bank, and I keeping pace with her,*
> *   Matching her little footsteps with my own.* [4–9]

Dante is being drawn toward the sun; he sees the nymphs who either seek the sun or flee it—reminding of the Islamic doctrine that some of the Jinn, the elemental spirits, are Muslim and some are unbelievers—because his soul is still in a corresponding state of ambiguity until he is immersed in the waters of Lethe.

Regarding the sun as a symbol of Christ the spiritual Intellect, Maximos the Confessor says the following:

When the sun rises and casts its light on the world, it reveals both itself and the things it illumines. Similarly, when the Sun of Righteousness rises in the pure intellect, He reveals both Himself and the inner principles of all that has been and will be brought into existence by Him. [*Philokalia*, Volume Two, *First Century on Love*, 95]

Now Matilda alerts Dante to a new development: "Brother, look and listen!"

> *I saw a sudden brightness on every side*
> *   That swept across the whole expanse of forest,*

Canto XXIX

So bright I wondered if it might be lightning.
But lightning, after striking, disappears
   While this illumination stayed, and grew;
   I asked within myself "what thing is this?"
And through the shining air a melody ran
   So sweet it made me curse with righteous anger
   The arrogance of Eve within that place.
For there both earth and sky obey their Maker,
   And a newly-created woman, of all His creatures
   Alone refused to sit behind the veil;
If she'd been willing to stay devout beneath it
   Much sooner and for a greater space of time
   I would have tasted these arcane delights. [16–30]

Beneath the verdant boughs the air before us
Was kindled like a fire, incandescent;
   The sweet sound of singing now was heard. [34–36]

The lightning represents a flash of illumination, but this illumination is sustained, because Dante is already outside of earthly time. On earth, such illumination would have only lasted for an instant, but in the Terrestrial Paradise the vision is continuous; consequently he can now see the procession that will bring him Beatrice. The procession is an apparition on a lower ontological level of the Sun of the Intellect, of which Beatrice is the higher manifestation. Dante is now passing beyond Eve in his own soul—beyond *curiosity*, which is the beginning of Promethean pride. He is willing and able to receive illumination because he doesn't inquire after it.

The premature rending of the veil by Eve represents the dawning of spiritual Vision upon one who is not prepared for it. Not being able to endure the veil means being unwilling to accept the real nature of *Maya*. Eve, paradoxically, becomes immersed in illusion (*avidya-maya* or "ignorance-apparition") because she will not *accept* illusion for what it is (*vidya-maya* or "wisdom-apparition," the true nature of God's creation). Had she been able to accept it, she would have immediately known that what the Serpent told her was a lie.

The Ordeal of Mercy

When the air becomes like fire for Dante, he is perceiving light in a different way. Fire is warmth and warmth is love; here the element Air, the mental substance, is infused with the Fire of Love—as with the Apostles on Pentecost—thus opening the way to divine *gnosis*.

> *O holy Virgins! If ever I've endured*
> *Vigils, cold or hunger for your sake*
> *The day has come when I must claim reward.*
> *Now Helicon must release its waters for me*
> *And with her choir Urania must assist me,*
> *To render things that can hardly be conceived.* [37–42]

Mount Helicon had two springs sacred to the Muses, which prefigure the Lethe and Eunoë of the Earthly Paradise. Dante invokes Urania, the Muse of Astronomy—rather than Calliope, the Muse of Epic Poetry—because he is called upon to sing of heavenly things.

Dante now sees in the distance what he believes to be seven trees:

> *But when I had approached so near to them*
> *That things seen falsely through the mingled senses*
> *Did not, by distance, lose their real features*
> *The faculty that provides reason with its matter*
> *Apprehended that they were really candlesticks,*
> *And heard, in the singing voices, the song "Hosanna!"*
> [46–51]

The "mingled senses" are the *ratio* or reason—the *koine aisthesis* or *sensus communis* of Aristotle—that "figures out" or "makes sense" of what the senses offer it by determining the *ratio* or relationship between different sensations so as to produce a synthetic impression, whereas "the power that provides reason with its matter," via the sense of sight, is the immediate, unified knowledge called *Intellectus* by the Latin Scholastics and *Nous* by the Greeks—the power which perceives Truth directly, just as the eye perceives light.[1]

---

1. William Blake, in *The Marriage of Heaven and Hell*, identifies this *Intellectus* (the power he later called the Imagination) with Energy or Desire—conceiving it as

Canto XXIX

Above that beautiful instrument shone a blaze
 Far brighter than the moon on her fifteenth night
 Shining tranquil in the midnight sky.
Filled with astonishment I turned myself
 To my good Virgil—but he answered me
 With visage as full of wonder as my own.
Once more I turned my face to those high things,
 Which moved themselves towards us so sedately;
 Newly-wed brides themselves don't walk so slowly.
The lady chided me: "Why do you burn
 With such affection for the living lights,
 While not regarding what comes after them?"
I then discerned a people following the candles
 As if following their guides, and dressed in white:
 Such a whiteness there was never seen on earth.
The water on my left hand brightly gleamed,
 And back to me my left side it reflected,
 When I gazed into it—precisely like a mirror. [52–69]

Dante's left-hand or feminine side appears reflected in the stream along with the reflected fire because this Terrestrial Paradise is a world of reflection, a realm of archetypal images that mirror higher realities. This is confirmed by the fact that the light of the candelabra is compared to moonlight; the symbolic color of the Moon in alchemical heraldry is white, like the robes of the twenty-four elders.

And I could see the little flames moving forward
 Leaving the air behind them washed with color
 As if by the several strokes of a painter's brush,
Each of a different hue, so the air above them
 Was streaked with seven bands, in all the colors
 Of which the sun-bow is made, and Delia's girdle. [73–78]

---

a kind of suberabundant overflow of the Divine Eros—and defines Reason as "the bound or outward circumference of Energy"; thus "the Messiah ... prays to the Father to send the comforter or Desire that Reason may have Ideas to build on...."

The Ordeal of Mercy

The seven candlesticks are clearly related to the Seven Lamps before the Throne of the Lamb that appear in the description of the Heavenly Jerusalem in the *Apocalypse* of John [4:5].[2]

The "sun-bow" is what we would call a rainbow. "Delia" is an epithet of the moon-goddess Diana; her "girdle" is the rainbow-colored halo that sometimes appears around the moon. The seven bands of light that flow, like unfading after-images, from the moving candlesticks represent a perception of forms as they exist outside time. This level of perception is not yet eternity, but rather what the Greek Fathers call *aeonian time*, which is nonetheless higher than terrestrial time. In aeonian time all the moments of any period of terrestrial duration are perceived simultaneously, as a single form.[3]

> *Under the beautiful sky that I've described*
> *A troop of twenty-four Elders, two by two,*
> *Came forward, each one crowned with a wreath of lilies.*
> [82–84]

The elders, dressed in white and crowned with lilies, who also appear around the Throne of the Lamb in the Heavenly Jerusalem in *Apocalypse* [4:4], represent spiritual virginity and receptivity. Some have interpreted them as emblems of the twenty-four books of the Old Testament; others have seen them as the twelve patriarchs plus the twelve apostles, demonstrating that Christ, the Lamb, is sovereign

---

2. These seven candlesticks or this seven-branched candelabrum, depending upon how we envision them, represent what are called the Seven Eyes of God in the Hebrew Kabbalah. According to Leo Schaya in *The Universal Meaning of the Kabbalah* (67–68), "Insofar as the One is looking at himself alone, he does not go out of his supreme tri-unity, *kether-hokhma-bina*; but when he wishes to contemplate the creative possibilities within himself"—what Frithjof Schuon calls *maya-in-divinis*—"he opens his 'seven eyes' or 'Sefiroth of construction', projecting all the cosmic 'vanities' through their look." Vanity, here, is roughly equivalent to the Hindu *Maya*, denoting the relatively illusory quality of manifestation in the face of the Absolute.

3. The Hindus have a similar concept, known as the "long body." The long body of a terrestrial being is that being's lifespan, from its beginning to its end, perceived *sub specie aeternitatis* as a single form—a kind of four-dimensional "histomap" of the being's total temporal life.

over both Testaments. It may also be significant that the ritual system of the Second Temple comprised twenty-four "courses" of worship.

> *All of them were singing "Blessed thou art*
> *Among the daughters of Adam, and blessed be*
> *Thy loveliness for all eternity." [85–87]*

The elders are apparently singing of the seven candelabra which have preceded them as "blessed daughters of Adam." These candelabra emanate from what the Kabbalah calls the *Adam Kadmon*, Adam as he was before the Fall, who contains all ten *sefiroth* of the Tree of Life, including the seven that project the created universe; they represent the eternal reservoir of soul-substance that animates the human race.

> *Just as star follows star across the sky,*
> *Close after them four animals advanced*
> *Each with a crown of green leaves on its head,*
> *Each beast bearing six wings for its plumage,*
> *And the plumage full of eyes; the eyes of Argus*
> *If they were still alive would be like these.*
> *I'll waste no rhymes describing them, dear reader;*
> *I can't be spendthrift here with my store of art*
> *Since later on I'll have more debts to pay.*
> *Just read the words of Ezekiel, for he describes them*
> *Approaching from the point of the frozen north*
> *Flanked with cloud, with whirlwind, and with fire;*
> *You will find them in his pages, just as I saw them. . . .*
> 　　　　　　　　　　　　　　　　*[91–103]*

> *In the space between the four Beasts I beheld*
> *A triumphal Chariot moving on two wheels*
> *Drawn by a Griffin with a harness around his neck.*
> *Both wings he lifted up near the center one*
> *Of the three encircling bands of the chariot-harness*
> *Such that it was not disturbed in any way;*
> *His wings stretched so far up they were lost to sight.*

The Ordeal of Mercy

His limbs were of gold, so far as he was bird,
The rest of him was of white and blood-red mixed.
                                    [106–114]

The Griffin Chariot is the *sedes sapientiae*, the "seat" or "throne of Wisdom"—an epithet of the Virgin Mary from the Litany of the Blessed Virgin, who is called in Eastern Orthodox Christianity "more spacious than the heavens." That she was able to bear God the Word in her womb demonstrates her power to carry more than meets the eye; this is why the Chariot appears empty. But the Chariot also symbolizes the Church, which is often called a "holy mother" and sometimes identified with the Virgin Mary. St. Joseph, the protecting husband of the Virgin, is also considered to be protector of the Church. The Church carries within herself all those souls who have been saved through Christ; the Chariot is also empty to indicate that we won't be able to see the full company of them until the end of time when Purgatory will be no more. The rainbow aureole surrounding the Chariot is the world in the process of coming into manifestation; as for the Chariot as a whole, Plato's line from the *Timaeus*, "time is the moving image of Eternity," might well be applied to it. The vision of the Chariot represents "the world behind the world" as it were, the Hyperborean world of eternal Spring at the back of the North Wind—the direction from which the theophany of the Four Living Creatures and the Chariot-Throne of God appears in the first chapter of Ezekiel.

On the level of astronomical symbolism, the body of the Griffin Chariot relates to the constellation of Ursa Major, the Big Bear, whose two stars called "the pointers" allow us to locate the Pole Star, "the still point of the turning world" in the tail of Ursa Minor, the Little Bear, also known as the *Septentrion*; the Little Bear is possibly represented by the empty seat of the Chariot itself. The two wheels of the Chariot may in fact be these pointers; in any case, the wheels themselves symbolize the Intellect and the Will, the two primal powers by which we move on the spiritual Path. Commentators on this Canto have often identified the Griffin with Christ, who draws the Chariot of the Church. The colors of the Griffin are gold for his eagle-like head and wings, and white and red for the rest of his body.

Canto XXIX

The color gold, the solar color, is that of the Intellect; in the vertical dimension the Intellect does not stop at any limit, but becomes verticality as such, indicated here by the raised wings of the Griffin which have no upper limit [cf. line 112]. The colors red and white symbolize the will. Red is the will in its active aspect, both protective aggression and dynamic love (Plato's *incensive faculty* and *appetitive faculty* respectively); white is the purity of heart that comes from the mortification of the passions and the submission of the will to God. The reference to the chariot gone astray, via an allusion to the myth of Phaeton, represents the danger of spiritual or intellectual inflation, such as is inevitable when the ego takes the reins.

> *By the right-hand wheel three virgins in a circle*
> *Came forward dancing—the first so very red*
> *That, bathed in flame, you hardly could have seen her;*
> *The second was as if her flesh and bones*
> *Were made entirely out of emerald;*
> *The third looked just like newly-fallen snow.*
> *It now appeared as if the white one led,*
> *Now as if the red one—and from her song*
> *The other two took their tempo, slow or swift.* [121–129]

The three figures dressed in white, green and red represent Faith, Hope and Love respectively, the three theological virtues. Faith and Love can lead because a human being can rely for spiritual guidance either upon Faith (which is virtual *gnosis*) or upon Love—but when the traveler attempts to rely upon Hope alone, this can lead him or her to fall into fate-worship. Hope, to be effective, must be the companion of either Love or Faith. To believe that Hope alone can lead is, finally, a crass attitude—a form of magical thinking like the practice of "affirmations" or "the power of positive thinking" or "creative visualization." Hope must be based either upon the Love that "hopes all things" [1 Corinthians 13:7], or upon the Faith that is "the substance of things hoped for" [Hebrews 11:1].

> *Upon the left appeared four ladies dancing*
> *Dressed in crimson, following the measure*
> *Of one of them who had three eyes in her head.* [130–132]

The Ordeal of Mercy

The three theological virtues appear on the right, the masculine side, because they are active and thus necessarily hierarchicalized on the vertical axis, which is why they form the basis of an "upright" character. (Three is the symbolic number of heaven, in the *I Ching* and many other sources.) The four cardinal virtues, on the other hand—Prudence, Justice, Fortitude and Temperance—appear on the left, the feminine side, because they make up the necessary foundation that allows the theological virtues to be received by the soul. (Four is the symbolic number of earth.) The cardinal virtues are the ones human beings must work at; they appear dressed in red, the color of effort (like the *cardinals* of the Roman Curia) because in the beginning they require human care, human labor and human love in order to be perfected. After reaching perfection, however, they become the passive and stabilizing elements that allow the spiritually active theological virtues to be passively received, through Grace. Once they have completely entered the soul and taken up residence there, however, they come alive and allow all the faculties of the soul to be penetrated by the Holy Spirit, thereby making the soul *eternally* active. Four is the number of substance, or Potency; three is the number of essence, or Act.

The three-eyed lady represents the virtue of Prudence; she has three eyes because thought, feeling and judgment (judgment being the decision of the will based upon the insight that both thought and feeling have provided) are all necessary to build the spiritual strength of the soul. Of the four cardinal virtues, only Prudence, the most intellectual of these virtues, is beginning to have a vision of the theological virtues: through her *thought*, of Faith; through her *feeling*, of Love; and through her *judgment*, of Hope. Hope is related to will and judgment because, of all the theological virtues, it is the one that reveals to us the next concrete step on the spiritual Path.

As if commenting directly on this Canto, Maximos the Confessor says:

> When a man's intellect is pre-eminent in virtue and spiritual knowledge, and he is determined to keep his soul free from evil slavery to the passions, he says, "Women are extremely strong but truth conquers all" [1 Esdras 3:12]. By "women" he means the divinizing virtues... "women" signify the supreme real-

Canto XXIX

ization of the virtues, which is love ... "truth" signifies the fulfillment of all spiritual knowledge.... [*Philokalia*, Volume Two, *Third Century of Various Texts*, 30]

> *Bringing up the rear of the procession*
> *Two old men I saw, unlike in dress*
> *But identical in their grave and dignified manner.*
> *One appeared in the guise of a disciple*
> *Of the great Hippocrates, whom nature formed*
> *For the ones most loved among her many children.*
> *The other seemed dedicated to the contrary duty:*
> *His sword was so sharp and shining that it struck*
> *Terror into me, though I stood on the opposite bank.*
> *Last of all, I saw four humble figures;*
> *And then, behind them all, one lone old man,*
> *As if walking in his sleep—but his look was vigilant.*
> *These seven were dressed just like the twenty-four elders;*
> *But unlike them, it was not wreaths of lilies*
> *They wore as crowns, encircling their heads*
> *But rather roses and other crimson flowers.*
> *From a short distance your vision would have sworn*
> *That red flames rose from just above their eyebrows.*
> [133–150]

The Two Elders—the disciple of Hippocrates and the one carrying the sword—symbolize the mystery of Mercy and Rigor, Life and Death, which are close to the energies of destruction and regeneration that any true healer must understand who does not want to do more harm than good. Here we see pairs of opposites just after they have emerged from their original Unity, still carrying with them the presence of their deep, enigmatic identity. The pairs-of-opposites appear immediately after the virtues because to reach the threshold between duality and non-duality requires that the virtues be perfected.

As the twenty-four elders crowned with lilies are related, via purity of heart, to the Intellect, so the seven last elders relate to Love, which is why they are crowned with roses. This Love is not opposed to the Intellect, however, but is the fulfillment of it. The flames above their eyebrows represent Love in the process of being transformed into Intellect, or as Divine Love intrinsically containing within itself Divine Knowledge.

The "four humble ones" are there to allow the soul to withdraw its attachment to the powerful spiritual images that have preceded them. Only humility allows us to actualize the virtues rather than being dazzled by them. The old man advancing "as if in sleep" recalls the words of The Song of Solomon 5:2, "I sleep, but my heart waketh." When confronting spiritual realities that transcend its capacity, the soul must know without knowing and act without acting.[4]

---

4. In the words of Omar Khayyam,
>Then to the rolling heaven itself I cried
>What lamp had destiny to guide
>Her little children, stumbling in the dark.
>"A blind understanding," heaven replied.

Canto XXIX

Editorial Commentary Seven:
A Kabbalistic Interpretation of the Griffin Chariot

The Griffin Chariot surrounded by the Four Living Creatures, which Dante identifies with the theophany of God's Throne in the Book of Ezekiel, is further elucidated in the Kabbalistic tradition. Leo Schaya, in *The Universal Meaning of the Kabbalah* (84), explains the meaning of this Chariot as follows:

> The 'throne', in its fullness, is the first and spiritual crystallization of all creatural possibilities before they are set in motion in the midst of the cosmos. When the 'throne' assumes its dynamic aspect and cosmic manifestation begins to move, it is called the divine 'chariot' (*merkabah*); then the four *hayoth*, or peripheral axes of creation, spring from the 'throne' become 'chariot', like 'lightning darting in all directions', measuring all the dimensions and all the planes of manifested existence. Under the aspect of 'torches', 'brilliant lights' or spiritual 'flashes' of lightning, the *hayoth* are also called *kerubim*, 'those who are close' to the living God, that is to say those who emanate directly from God in action. While the hayothic axes are traveling in all directions of the cosmos, out of them come 'wheels' (*ofanim*) or angelic powers, which play a part in actualizing the spherical forms and cyclical movements of the created; their spiral vibrations—as it were 'a wheel within another wheel'—are called 'whirlwinds' (*galgalim*).
>
> Aside from these angelological teachings, which go back to the vision of Ezekiel, the prophesy of Isaiah needs to be mentioned, according to which the divine throne is surrounded by the *serafim*, the 'burning ones.' The seraphim are so named because they consume or purify everything they touch with their spiritual fire; by means of their six wings or celestial powers—manifesting the six active 'Sefiroth of (cosmic) construction'—they cooperate in the development of the six cosmogonic phases which evolve from their point of departure in *Araboth*, the 'holy of holies' or celestial 'Sabbath', in the form of the six heavens, the six directions of space and the 'six days' or great phases of time.

Astrologically speaking the *hayoth*—the Lion, the Man, the Ox and the Eagle—are the emblems of the zodiacal signs of Leo, Aquarius, Taurus and Scorpio respectively; over 2000 years ago the solstices and equinoxes occurred while the sun was occupying these signs. Esoterically, the Lion symbolizes the *incensive faculty* or active will (summer solstice); the Man, the *rational faculty* or passive intellect (winter solstice); the Ox the *appetitive faculty* or passive will (vernal equinox); and the Eagle the active intellect, *Nous* or *Intellectus* (autumnal equinox). Together these Four Living Creatures, surrounding the Throne of the Yahweh in Ezekiel and the Throne of the Lamb in the Apocalypse, manifest the totality of the Names of God as incarnate in the human form.

Canto XXX

The disappearance of Virgil and the first appearance of Beatrice; the symbolism of the Pole.

> *When the Septentrion of the highest heaven—*
> *Which star-rise or star-set has never known*
> *Nor any veil nor cloud but that of sin,*
> *The sign that makes every one above aware*
> *Of what his duty is (as the lower Bear*
> *Guides the helmsman home to his destined harbor)—*
> *Stopped its turning, then that company of Truth*
> *That came at first between it and the Griffin,*
> *Now turned themselves to the Chariot, as to their peace.*
> *And one of them, as if by Heaven commanded,*
> *Singing, "Veni, sponsa, de Libano"*
> *Three times shouted, and the others all replied.* [1–12]

The seven stars of Ursa Minor, the *Septentrion*, comprise the cosmic reflection of the *Sedes Sapientiae*, the Throne of Wisdom, which as we have seen is an epithet of the Virgin Mary.

Ursa Minor (the Little Bear, the Septentrion) represents the Intellect as such, the Truth we always have with us, whether or not we are aware of it. The Little Bear symbolizes a higher dimension of Wisdom than the constellation of Ursa Major, the Big Bear, whose two "pointers" allow us to locate the Pole Star in the tail of the Little Bear when seen from earth; the Big Bear represents the sort of wisdom that is directly accessible to the human intellect. The helmsmen who steer by the Pole are the gnostics. The bear is a Hyperborean symbol, and Hyperborea is, precisely, the Earthly Paradise.[1] And when the

---

1. See the citations for 'Hyperborea" in three books by René Guénon: *Symbols of the Sacred Science*, *The King of the World*, and *Traditional Forms and Cosmic Cycles*.

The Ordeal of Mercy

Little Bear/Septentrion stops turning, this indicates the realization of Eternity as such. For the twenty-four elders to begin by standing between the Septentrion and the Chariot, and then turn toward the Chariot at the moment the Septentrion stops—rather than toward the Septentrion itself—is a way of saying that those who attempt to practice "pure esoterism" outside of a particular revealed tradition will end by interrupting the lines of communication between the esoteric Source and its chosen vehicle, as established and willed by God—in this case the Roman Catholic Church. And this will interrupt the communication between that Source and its human vehicle as well. But when Eternity as such is unveiled, then the providential nature of the vehicle chosen for us by God is unveiled along with it; it is no longer experienced as a veil, but as a theophany.

The stars, as with the constellations of the Zodiac, show the archetype of the eternal destiny we are called to embody, and to the degree that we see and understand them, we can follow that destiny in earthly life. If we can do this, then instead of becoming entangled in a fate that tempts us to actualize something other than our true destiny, thus twisting our souls, we are led by our eternal archetype directly to the presence of God.

The venerable elder singing *Veni, sponsa, de Libano* ("Come, my spouse, from Lebanon"), who is not distinguished from the rest of the twenty-four, is not any particular individual—as Virgil was insofar as he was an historical figure—but the pure archetype of the Spiritual Guide, the *staretz*, whom Beatrice fully embodies.

According to Guénon, the Latin name "*Boreas*," the North Wind personified, is related to the English word "bear."

The sacred mountain with seven levels, as Dante pictures the Mount of Purgatory, is a widespread motif in world religion and mythology. The ziggurats of Mesopotamia, symbolic mountains, were often designed with seven terraces, and among the Yakuts of Siberia the shaman climbs a seven-storey mountain with the Pole Star above it, just as Dante does in the *Purgatorio*; Polaris also appears above the Hindu sacred mountain, Meru [cf. Mircea Eliade, *Shamanism: Archaic Techniques of Ecstasy*, Chapter VIII]. These mythical mountains are analogous to the human psycho-physical nervous system with its seven chakras; the purgation of the human soul must ultimately take place within the human form.

Canto XXX

So, upon that celestial Chariot
  A hundred [angels] *rose ad vocem tanti senis*
    ["at the voice of such an Elder']
  Ministers and messengers of eternal life.
"Benedictus qui venis" was their song,
    ["Blessed is He who comes (in the name of the Lord),"
    Matthew 21:9]
  And while scattering flowers above and all around,
    "Manibus," oh *"date lilia plenis."*
      ["With full hands give me lilies,"
      words spoken by Aeneas to his father Anchises in the
      underworld, *Aeneid* VI, 1179.]
I recalled when I had seen, as day began,
  The eastern half of the sky all tinged with rose,
  While the other half was adorned with lovely blue;
And the face of the rising sun so lightly veiled,
  By the tempering mist that the eye was given leave
  To gaze much longer than usual upon that face.
Likewise in the bosom of that cloud of flowers
  Tossed high above by those angelic hands
  To rain down again both in and around the Chariot,
A lady appeared to me, crowned with olive leaves
  With a grass-green mantle and a snow-white veil
  And wearing a dress the color of living flame.
Within that presence—but now so long ago—
  My spirit had often felt what it felt now:
  Fear and trembling, wonder, dissolution.
And though my soul could not see her directly
  Since she was veiled, it nonetheless felt her power,
  The secret and mighty force of ancient love. [16–39]

That the twenty-four "truthful" elders, crowned with lilies [XXIX:84], turn toward the Chariot shows them as representatives of the Intellect, of that which makes possible the vision of the Beloved, who is always and equally Wisdom as well as Love; Intellect is also represented by the hundred angels who rise up from the Chariot, scattering lilies and hurling them into the air until they fall

The Ordeal of Mercy

like rain. The lilies here symbolize the Intellect in its virgin purity. Flowers in the Earthly Paradise are an image of the primordial manifestation of Life. That manifestation is a kind of veil, but it is a veil that allows us to see Beatrice directly, just as the dawn mist makes it possible to gaze directly upon the sun. It is thus a symbol of what Frithjof Schuon calls *maya-in-divinis*. Schuon, in his essay "The Mystery of the Veil," explains that "the saint [is] only a veil whose function is to manifest God, 'as a light cloud makes the sun visible' according to a comparison used by the Moslems," and goes on to describe the veiling-and-revealing function of the Virgin Mary in terms that perfectly apply to Dante's vision of Beatrice in the Earthly Paradise:

> ... the Blessed Virgin ... combines in her person the substance of sanctity and concrete humanity; dazzling and inviolable sanctity and the merciful beauty that communicates it.... Like every heavenly being, Mary manifests the universal Veil in its function of transmission; she is a Veil because she is a form, but she is Essence by her content and consequently by her message.... The Virgin is "clothed in the sun" because, as Veil, she is transparent: the Light, which is at the same time Beauty, is communicated with such a power that it seems to consume the Veil and abolish veiling....
> [*Esoterism as Principle and as Way*, 62]

The hundred angels further symbolize both the resurrection of the body—the glorified flesh of the resurrected being of one substance with the Terrestrial Paradise—and also the hundred cantos of the *Divine Comedy* itself, now appearing, transfigured, in their eternal significance. In their presence, the Chariot—the quintessence of terrestrial life—reveals its spiritual potential.

Beatrice now appears for the first time, crowned with olive leaves, with a white veil, a green cape, and a dress the color of flame—though Dante does not immediately recognize her, since she is veiled. And as soon as she appears and *names* Dante (line 55), Virgil disappears. It is as if he had been an aspect of Dante all along—which means that Virgil is already redeemed. This is the exact

Canto XXX

reverse of Dante's characterization of Virgil in line 51 as the one "to whom I had given myself for salvation." Beatrice in her epiphany appears dressed in the colors of the theological virtues: the White of Faith rising to Gnosis; the Red of Divine Love; and the Green of Hope, the most outward of the virtues, but also the one that is closest to us in our humanity—to the whole world of human fear and desire—and therefore most able to guide us directly.

> *But Virgil had left us plundered of his presence;*
>   *Virgil was gone, the sweetest of all fathers;*
>   *Virgil, to whom I had given myself for salvation.*
> *All that our ancient mother lost—restored—*
>   *Could not keep my cheeks, though washed with dew,*
>   *From darkening again with bitter tears.*
> *"Do not weep yet, Dante, because Virgil's left you;*
>   *Save your tears for what is yet to come,*
>   *To wash the wound another sword must deal."* [49–57]

At last we hear the voice of Beatrice herself. Dante gains the greater—Beatrice and her guidance—but he must first experience the loss of the lesser, his relationship to Virgil. His choice in this is opposite to that of Eve, whose gaze was fixed upon the lesser, the knowledge of good and evil, to such an extent that she lost Paradise itself. Beatrice commands Dante to hold his tears in reserve because his loss of her, in earthly life, was much greater—and the realization about to come to him of the import of this loss will be much greater—than his loss of Virgil.

Now Beatrice reveals herself:

> *Upon the left-hand side of the Chariot,*
>   *When I turned on hearing my own name pronounced,*
>   *(Which of necessity is recorded here),*
> *I saw the Lady who had first appeared*
>   *Beneath the falling screen of angelic flowers;*
>   *She turned to look at me from across the stream.*
> *Although the veil, that flowed down from her head,*
>   *Which was circled with the foliage of Minerva,*

The Ordeal of Mercy

> *Did not permit her to appear distinctly,*
> *Still, her stance was regal and majestic.*
>   *And so she continued, like one who speaks with restraint*
>   *Keeping his hottest words still in reserve:*
> *"Look well at me: I am Beatrice and no other!*
>   *Why did you think yourself worthy to climb this Mountain?*
>   *Didn't you know that man is happy here?"*
> *My gaze dropped down to the surface of the water*
>   *But, seeing my image reflected, it sought the grass,*
>   *So great was the shame that weighed upon my forehead.*
> *As the mother to the little son seems harsh,*
>   *Unyielding, so she appeared to me;*
>   *Bitter is the taste of implacable pity!* [61–81]

Beatrice names herself here because Dante must completely acknowledge her as his other self, his self in Eternity. And, standing before her, he is ashamed for having denied his true happiness; the first appearance of this happiness represents a devastating purgation of his soul. In the words of Rainier Maria Rilke, from the first of his ten *Duino Elegies*,

> ... *Beauty's nothing*
> *but the beginning of a Terror we're still just able to bear,*
> *and why we adore it so is because it serenely*
>   *disdains to destroy us.*

Beatrice appears to Dante on his left, his "sinister" side, because she is now reflecting back to him the hidden or shadow aspects of his soul; she must therefore manifest as Rigor. (We must not forget, however, that the Heart too is on the left.)

Now that he sees his alter-ego, Beatrice, in the other world, Dante sees himself more clearly in this world [lines 76–77].[2] No longer immersed in his own subjectivity, he has become objectified. As

---

2. In Zoroastrian terms, Beatrice would correspond to Dante's *fravashi*, the eternal aspect of his soul that never descended into time, the celestial *anima* encountered by the earthly pilgrim after his departure from this world.

Canto XXX

long as Beatrice was alive and he saw her as sharing his terrestrial existence, that objectification could not be actual. But as surely as the archetype of humanity did not originate in this fallen terrestrial existence, neither do our own archetypes have their origin here.

Happiness, and the aspiration to the Terrestrial Paradise, are not some form of self indulgence as we might be tempted to believe, but rather an intrinsic duty of man. It is a higher duty than necessary labor, which is an inescapable element of earthly life; this is why Christ gave Mary precedence over Martha. Remorse over sin is necessary for purgation, but here Dante is called to repent of that repentance, to experience remorse not for his transgressions but for not having been happier earlier in life, as if the whole of earthly life were being subsumed into its final end. Dante is ashamed to see his sorrowful countenance reflected in the stream, because all his reflected self-knowledge reveals only shame and sorrow now. However, when he hears the hymns sung by the angels and feels them as mercy, his heart melts:

> *Even as snow among the living timbers*
> *Along the spine of Italy will freeze,*
> *Blown and drifted by Slavonian winds,* [from the North]
> *And then, in melting, will trickle through itself*
> *Whenever the wind breathes north from the shadowless lands*
> [from the South]
> *Just as a candle melts beneath the flame,*
> *So I remained without a sigh or tear*
> *Until I'd heard the songs of those whose notes*
> *Sound in accord with the notes of the eternal spheres.*
> *And when I heard in their sweet melodies*
> *Compassion for me, even more than if they'd said,*
> *"Why, O Lady, must you shame him so?",*
> *The ice that lay congealed around my heart*
> *Was changed to air and water, and in my anguish*
> *Came gushing from my breast through my mouth and eyes.*
>
> [85–99]

The Ordeal of Mercy

In the words of Frithjof Schuon, "Instead of reposing in the immutable purity of Existence, fallen man is drawn into the dance of things that exist, and they, being accidents, are delusive and perishable. In the Christian cosmos, the Blessed Virgin is the incarnation of this snow-like purity; she is inviolable and merciful Existence or Substance...." [*Light on the Ancient Worlds* 43–49]. The soul must freeze and be crystallized under the influence of the North Wind so that it may be purified; simultaneously the heart must melt under the influence of the South Wind so that it may absorb Love in all its warmth. This is indicative of a profound annihilation; the very places the snow disappears into as it "trickles through itself" are themselves annihilated.

It is only after Dante feels the mercy of the angels that his sorrow, expressed through tears and sobs, becomes manifest. Animals can be sad, but they cannot weep. This is because they do not intuit the potential presence of God's Mercy that would allow their sorrow, through anguish, to be transformed into relief and gratitude.

Canto XXXI ends with Beatrice's great speech of instruction to the angels:

> *"You keep your constant watch in eternal day;*
> > *Neither night nor sleep can steal away from you*
> > *One step the ages take upon their way;*
> *I have therefore greater care to form my answer*
> > *To well instruct that one who's weeping yonder*
> > *Till transgression and repentance make one measure.*
> *Not only by the work of those great wheels,*
> > *That destine every seed unto its end,*
> > *According as the stars are in conjunction,*
> *But by the bounty and largesse of heavenly graces,*
> > *Raining down upon us from clouds so high*
> > *That even our farthest sight cannot approach them.*
> *Such had this man become in his new life*
> > *On earth, that every virtuous potential*
> > *If acted upon, would have come to great fruition.*
> *But the more of earthly vigor a soil possesses*
> > *The more savage and malignant it becomes*

Canto XXX

> *When left untilled, or sown with evil seed.*
> *My countenance sustained him for a while;*
>   *Showing him my youthful eyes I led him*
>   *Along with me in paths of righteousness.*
> *But as soon as I reached the door of my second age*
>   *And upon the threshold of it changed my life,*
>   *He removed himself from me and sought out others.*
> *When from flesh to spirit I had ascended*
>   *And beauty and virtue were in me expanded,*
>   *Less dear to him I was, and less delightful.*
> *He set his steps upon a deceitful path*
>   *Chasing fantastic images of the good,*
>   *That were never known to keep a single promise.*
> *Neither prayer nor its inspirations were sufficient*
>   *Though I put them to work, through dreams and other methods*
>   *Trying to call him back—but he didn't heed them.*
> *He fell so low that every means of salvation*
>   *Was already exhausted—except this one:*
>   *To unveil to him the legions of the damned.*
> *To perform this task I visited the gates of death*
>   *And to the one who has guided him thus far*
>   *My intercessions were carried with many tears.*
> *The Almighty's deep design would be frustrated*
>   *If he were to cross over Lethe and drink its waters*
>   *Before the price of transgression had been paid*
> *With tears of his own, gushing forth in floods."* [103–145]

It's as if the angels had asked Beatrice why, if Dante is destined by the stars for salvation, she must manifest as rigor. The answer is that Mercy cannot manifest to mortal eyes except through rigor. As Frithjof Schuon says of the Virgin Mary in his chapter "The Wisdom of Sayyidatna Maryam" from *Dimensions of Islam*, 89:

> The connection between fear and Mercy—enunciated in the *Magnificat*—is of cardinal importance: contrary to prejudices current in the world of lukewarmness and psychologism, the

The Ordeal of Mercy

traditional doctrines which insist most on Mercy have as their point of departure the conviction that we run the risk of hell, or even deserve it, and that we are only saved by the Goodness of Heaven; the way then consists, not in wishing to save oneself by one's own merits, since this is considered quite impossible, but in conforming to the requirements of a Mercy which seeks to save us while demanding of us *a priori* the fear of being lost. Mary's hymn is impregnated with elements of Mercy and Rigour, and it thus reflects an aspect of the Virgin herself: the mildness of the Virgin is accompanied by an adamantine purity and also by a strength of soul which evokes such biblical figures as Miriam and Deborah, and which represents a dimension inseparable from the greatness of her who was called *o clemens, o pia, o dulcis Virgo Maria*.

Beatrice, like Mary, can instruct the angels because she is manifesting from a plane higher than the one they occupy. In the Orthodox prayer to the Theotokos—the title given to Mary as "Mother of God"—she is called "more honorable than the cherubim and more glorious beyond compare than the seraphim"; Beatrice, here, is acting as a reflection of the Virgin Mary.

Here Dante stands in for mankind as a whole, whose fallen nature is redeemed by being made to realize its limitations, thus mortifying its Promethean pride in its own unique, divine capacities. Man is not an angel, and so must be addressed as man; it is for this reason that Christ incarnated, died, and rose again from the dead.

Grace, here, is shown as being higher than spiritual destiny—the explanation being that Dante is now being offered something higher than personal salvation: in Hindu terms, *moksha*: perfect and final Liberation.

I would say more than that Beatrice speaks for Divine Knowledge; I would say that she embodies it. Divine Knowledge comes as a spouse.

As St. Augustine showed us in his *Confessions*, the greater the spiritual capacity of the soul, the greater its capacity for sin; *corruptio optima pessima*. When Beatrice died Dante was separated from her. Her death was a call for him to understand higher spiritual realities in a subtler way, but though she had become even more beautiful through her death, his attention to her wavered; he became distracted by "another woman"—by all that appears to be Wisdom but actually leads the soul further into delusion—and so fell into a deep spiritual lethargy. He abandoned *Pietà*, piety, in favor of *Pietra*, the hard, stony heart of This World. Only through Beatrice's inspiration to him, which she had received from God, to compose his *Divine Comedy*, could this lethargy be overcome—an inspiration which had to reach to the depths of Hell. The oblivion of Lethe is not a failure of consciousness but a forgetfulness of all that is worth forgetting because it is without intrinsic substance. If Dante had not been able, through the composition of his *Commedia*, to become conscious of all his sins, Lethe for him would not have been a liberating oblivion affecting his whole nature, but would have destroyed those parts of his soul he had not yet become conscious of. This could never really have happened, however—because the truth is, God's deep design is never frustrated.

The Ordeal of Mercy

Editorial Commentary Eight:
The Hyperborean Mary

In his essay "Sedes Sapentiae" from *In the Face of Absolute*, Frithjof Schuon presents the symbology and metaphysical exegesis of the Throne of Wisdom, including its reflection in the throne of Solomon, identifying the *Sedes Sapentiae* with the Virgin Mary. The six steps up and down this throne are clearly related to Schuon's Six Stations of Wisdom as presented in his book *Stations of Wisdom*: Purity and Spiritual Combat (the passive and active aspects of the *will*); Peace and Fervor (the passive and active aspects of the *affections*); and finally Discrimination between the Real and the Illusory, and Concentration upon the Real (the negative and positive aspects of the *Intellect*). And given that the Franciscan monk St. Bernardine takes the Pole Star in the tail of the *Septentrion* or Little Bear to be the *stella maris*, "the Star of the Sea," and thus an emblem of the Virgin—who is called "Star of the Sea" in the medieval Litany of the Blessed Virgin—it is natural to envision the remaining six stars as the steps of the Throne [see Rama Coomaraswamy, "Saint Bernardine on the Holy Name of Mary," *Sophia: The Journal of Traditional Studies*, Volume 12, Number 1]. This six-fold hierophany resonates with the Six Grandfathers of the Lakota as seen by Black Elk in his great vision, with the "six men who came forth from the higher gate, which lieth toward the north" in Ezekiel's vision of the imaginal Temple [Ezekiel 9:2], and possibly with the six *lokas* in the cosmology of the Buddhist Kalachakra Tantra. The prime cosmic symbol of this level of being is the six directions of space, with the transcendent seventh point as their common center. Furthermore, the seat of the Polar Mary in the *Septentrion* corresponds to the *Caer Sidi* of the ancient Welsh, a name that means "Revolving Castle." It is considered to be the seat of the goddess and/or enchantress Cerridwen, who—since she possesses the Cauldron of Inspiration—would appear to be kind of a Celtic Sarasvati, a Goddess of Wisdom. The identification of the Throne of the Virgin with a cup or cauldron appears in the Eastern Orthodox icon known as the "Theotokos of the Fountain," whose correspondences with the Holy Grail of the Arthurian cycle should be obvious. In Christianity, however, the Virgin Mary is not a goddess but rather the perfection of womanhood—and thus a fit symbol of the human soul perfectly receptive to the will of God: "Let it be done unto me according to Thy Word." [Luke 1:38] This is the *esoteric* truth of which the goddesses of antiquity were the *exoteric* projections. In the words of William Blake, "all gods reside in the human breast."

Canto XXXI

Dante confesses to Beatrice and is chastised by her. Matilda immerses him in the waters of Lethe. The role of the Seven Virtues. The theophany of the Griffin. Beatrice unveiled; her eyes; her lips.

So long as we are manfully engaged in the holy warfare of ascetic or practical philosophy we retain with us the Logos, who in the form of the commandments came from the Father into this world. But when we are released from our ascetic struggle with the passions and are declared victor over both them and the demons, we pass, by means of contemplation, to gnostic philosophy; and in this way we allow the Logos to mystically leave the world again and make His way to the Father. Hence it is the Lord says to His disciples: "You have loved me and believed that I come from God. I came from the Father and have come into the world; again I leave the world and make my way to the Father" [John 16:27–28]. [St. Maximos the Confessor, from the *Philokalia*, Volume Two, *Second Century on Theology*, 94]

Beatrice now demands a confession from Dante, one based on *informed self-accusation*, not on blind submission. And though he loses the power of speech, he still succeeds in making himself understood:

> *A mixture of fear and confusion forced from my mouth*
>   *A Yes, but such a Yes that the sense of sight*
>   *Was needed if I hoped to be understood.*
> *Just as a cross-bow will sometimes break when shot*
>   *If the bowstring and the bow are too tightly drawn*
>   *And with less force the arrow hits its mark,*

The Ordeal of Mercy

So I too broke beneath that heavy burden
Pouring out a torrent of sighs and tears;
My voice on its outward course was stripped of strength.
                                                        [13–21]

Needing eyes to see Dante's "yes" is a reference to *gnosis*. A voiced "yes" would have to had do with the will alone, but this seen "yes" is symbolically related to the Intellect. Dante repents of ignorance here, of taking appearances as reality—a repentance that requires Wisdom.

Beatrice asks Dante what brief, delusive worldly beauty had the power to replace her in his heart after she had passed from this world; he is cut to his root by remorse. This sounds terrible, but in fact this remorse initiates an ontological change that brings with it a greater capacity for gnosis, which he will need if he is to see Beatrice unveiled.

"What allurements or what benefits appeared
Upon the foreheads of those substitutes
That you should turn your steps in their direction?" [28–30]

she says. Because Dante, in composing his *Commedia*, has absolutely fulfilled the function of a poet, he finds himself in a place where his "promenading" poet-self [Mandelbaum, line 30] can no longer help him. He has passed from Wisdom reflected in the mirror of the psyche, which always has to do with some form of narcissism, to the direct vision of Wisdom Unveiled that Beatrice represents.

Weeping, I said: "It was the present things
And their false delight that turned my steps aside
As soon as I could no longer see your face." [34–36]

As long as she was in earthly existence, Dante had no way of knowing the difference between Beatrice as she appeared and other kinds of appearances. But at the very time he was going after false objects of desire, he was also developing the deep intuition that they

Canto XXXI

were indeed false. It was these very false objects that drove him to the Dark Wood at the beginning of the *Inferno* and to the path that would eventually lead him to Beatrice herself—but not without repentance.

> *"If you'd maintained your silence or else denied*
> *What you've confessed, your guilt would still be known*
> *Before the bench of the Judge of perfect Justice!"* [37–39]

The sinner must believe that he can do things in secret, "behind God's back"—but Dante's confession before the Divine Court is not the revelation of a secret. By confessing what is already known, he comes into the objective knowledge that the Just Judge is always present; consequently he can now also see *himself* objectively.

Beatrice continues to shame Dante for following lesser beauties; she tells him that he should have died when she did instead of becoming involved with the world; he should have died to the carnal self and allowed the wings of the Spirit to expand—but he became distracted. Here the discourse is already beginning to partake of the simplicity of Paradise.

Now Beatrice commands him to elevate his gaze and look at her:

> *And hardly yet reassured, my uncertain eyes*
> *Saw Beatrice turn round to face the creature*
> *That holds two natures within a single person.* [79–81]

The Griffin here is clearly Christ; what on one level is the union of intellect and will, on a higher one is the hypostatic union of Christ's Divinity with his humanity. Beatrice herself reflects this union; through her, Dante is able to see the hypostatic union of Christ's two natures in a unique manner. Beatrice here reveals her link to the Virgin, the Theotokos herself, who is the mother not only of Christ's human nature (the Nestorian heresy limited her to this role) but is precisely the "mother of God." Likewise Beatrice, as Holy Wisdom, is the mother of the union between the Intellect and the Will.

Dante faints with remorse—and when he returns to himself, Matilda immerses him in the waters of Lethe. For Dante to be bathed in

The Ordeal of Mercy

Lethe is for him to forget his evil deeds. When he loses consciousness, his *being* forgets these deeds all the way up to the point of his waking consciousness. Paradoxically, however, he must regain consciousness before he can truly forget. Lethe is not repression: he must forget *consciously*, and know what he is forgetting. This sort of forgetting is the direct opposite of the Platonic *amnesia*, man's forgetfulness of God, which must be struggled against in the spiritual life. It is more akin to the Divine Ignorance of Scotus Eriugena, who taught that God has no knowledge of anything less than Himself—not in the sense that He is less than Omniscient, but rather that He sees all things *as* Himself: consequently the forgetfulness of sin represents no loss. In Shakespeare's *Julius Caesar* the character of Mark Antony says: "The evil that men do lives after them; the good is oft interred with their bones." Our goodness often seems external to us, so much so as to appear hypocritical. But it is really our evil that is external, while the good has its place in the marrow of our bones. The truth of this, however, can only be revealed through death in the Spirit.

After he emerges from Lethe, Dante enters the dance of the Four Cardinal Virtues, who tell him:

> *"Here we are nymphs; in heaven we are stars.*
>   *Before Beatrice came down into the world*
>   *We were assigned to serve as her handmaidens.*
> *We'll guide you to her eyes—but the Three beyond*
>   *Who see more deeply, in the light that shines*
>   *So blissfully within her, will increase your light."*
> *So, singing, they began—and then they led me*
>   *Unto Griffin's breast, where, placed before it,*
>   *Beatrice stood facing us. They said:*
> *"Do not be slow to spend your vision here;*
>   *We have stationed you before those emeralds*
>   *From which, in former days, Love aimed his shafts."*
> *A thousand yearnings, hotter than fire itself*
>   *Locked my eyes upon those radiant eyes*
>   *That, motionless, were fixed upon the Griffin.*
> *Exactly like the sun within a mirror*
>   *The double-natured creature shone within them,*

Canto XXXI

Revealing now one aspect, now the other.
Imagine my astonishment, dear Reader,
To see an object completely devoid of motion
Even as its reflected image kept on changing! [106–126]

The Cardinal Virtues appear as nymphs in the Earthly Paradise, but in the Celestial Paradise as stars, because they contain their own realm within themselves; their being both nymphs and stars reminds us of the Pleiades, daughters of the earth-titan Atlas, who were transformed into stars by Zeus to save them from pursuit by Orion. The four Cardinal Virtues are of the earth, of the natural psyche, whereas the three Theological Virtues are of the spiritual world.

Beatrice's two "emerald" eyes reflect the two natures of Christ; she is the emblem of the Hypostatic Union. That her eyes are green—the color of Venus, the planet of Love—shows that Love is the mysterious agent of that Union. Her humanity, by the power of Love, becomes such that it can unite with the Divinity, thus making her the very presence of Wisdom. The light of the Griffin reflected in her eyes—in which motion and stillness are mysteriously united, as humanity and Divinity are united in Christ—changes but does not pass; in this it is a prefiguration of the Eternity that is fulfilled in Paradise.

... my soul was feasting on that nourishment
Which, even as it satisfies, makes hungry.
The other Three, whose exalted stance revealed them
As occupants of a higher rank, came forward,
With heavenly Harmony dancing to the measure.
"Beatrice! Turn your eyes of holy power
Unto your faithful servant" they implored
"Who, only to behold you, has come so far;
By your grace, now do us the grace to unveil
Your mouth to him, so that he may witness
The second beauty that you've kept concealed." [128–138]

"... that nourishment which, even as it satisfies, makes hungry" is Love eternally expanding into Wisdom. Because Beatrice is Dante's

The Ordeal of Mercy

alter-ego, the revelation of her mouth, mediated by the Three Theological Virtues, is deeper than that of her eyes, while the reverse is true of Dante [13–21]: his seen "yes" is deeper than his spoken "yes," which cannot be heard. Beatrice is Dante's mirror-image. In her presence, being *heard*—self-expression—gives way, for Dante, to being *seen*—the end of all subjectivity in pure objectification. But with Beatrice, though her eyes are a symbol of pure seeing, and thus of Being itself—"Knowledge is the foundation and basic principle of all being" says Meister Eckhart—the kiss of her lips is the actual taste of it. The Cardinal Virtues, Beatrice's handmaidens, reveal her eyes, but the Theological Virtues reveal her deeper essence, her lips—the full actualization of Knowledge in the spiritual life, its incarnation as pure Being. In the words of Psalm 34:8, "O taste and see that the Lord is good."

In Chapter Ten of *The Church's Mystagogy*, St. Maximos the Confessor says:

> The spiritual kiss, which [in the Divine Liturgy] is extended to all, prefigures and portrays the concord, unanimity and identity of views which we shall all have among ourselves in faith and love at the time of the revelation of the ineffable blessings to come. In this situation those who are worthy will receive intimate familiarity with the Word of God. For the mouth is a symbol of the Word, precisely through Whom all those who share in reason as reasonable beings are united with the first and unique Word who is the cause of every word and meaning.

Likewise St. Bernard says, in his "Second Sermon on the Song of Songs," commenting on the first verse of that book ("let him kiss me with the kiss of his mouth"):

> [The Father's] living and effective Word is a kiss . . . a full infusion of joys, a revelation of secrets, a wonderful and inseparable mingling of the light from above and the mind on which it is shed, which, when it is joined with God, is one spirit with Him [1 Corinthians 6:17].

Canto XXXII

The procession turns to the East. The Tree of Adam appears. At first it is stripped of leaves, but it bursts into flower when the pole of the Griffin Chariot is tied to it. Dante falls into a supernatural sleep, during which the Griffin disappears. Beatrice steps down from the Chariot; she gives Dante his mission. Then the Chariot is attacked by an Eagle, a Fox and a Dragon, after which it grows feathers, is occupied by a whore, and is dragged off into the forest by a giant.

> *Upon this side and that my eyes were blocked*
> *By walls of indifference; thus her holy smile*
> *Drew them to itself with its same old net*
> *Until my sight was forced to turn away*
> *Towards those goddesses standing on my left*
> *Who warned me: "You are staring too intently."*
> *I found my sight affected by the condition*
> *Of eyes just recently dazzled by the sun;*
> *What I saw had momentarily blinded me.*
> *But when my vision returned to lesser sights—*
> *Lesser, that is, in comparison with the greater*
> *Splendor which had forced me to withdraw—*
> *I saw that the glorious army had wheeled to the right;*
> *They'd turned themselves toward the east again*
> *To face the sun, and the seven holy flames.* [4–18]

Focus is important, but it should not lead to exclusivity; one-pointedness of attention can become an obsession. To go blind through staring too insistently at the "holy smile" is to be enamoured of the intensity of the Divine without allowing that intensity to illuminate the other aspects of one's life, as if God were jealous of his Divinity rather than generously giving of it. Thus returning to "lesser sights" is actually coming into a vision that is more whole, and richer. Here Dante must adjust his spiritual vision to the

The Ordeal of Mercy

increased spiritual light of his environment. To stare too fixedly at something is to attempt to possess what you see, and therefore to risk being petrified by it. In spiritual vision, however, we are called upon not to *possess* what we see, but to *become* it. The theological virtues are gifts to be received, not goods to be possessed.

The procession, in turning east, is now returning to its source in the celestial realm, preparing the way for Dante's ascent into Paradise. This return leaves a space, a vacuum, in which the vision of what is about to befall the church, and earthly life as a whole, can be seen. In Christian doctrine the "latter days" are always at the door. The motionless features of the Griffin [line 27] express a serenity which indicates that the home to which he is about to return is on a higher level of being, beyond even the Earthly Paradise. The essence of the Terrestrial Paradise leads on to Paradise as such.

> *As, underneath its shields, to save itself,*
>   *A squadron of troops will wheel to follow its banner*
>   *Before the whole body of men can change direction,*
> *So the soldiers of the heavenly kingdom*
>   *Who marched in the van completely passed us by*
>   *Before the chariot-pole had made its turn.* [19–24]

For the procession to have come from the East, and for it now to turn back in the direction it came from, means that its linear and even cyclical movement has now come to an end; the next phase will be direct vertical motion, ascension. This vertical motion is represented by the pole-shaft of the Chariot, now upright like the flagstaff of an army. The East the Source, the Origin; the upright chariot-pole once again echoes the polar, Hyperborean symbolism of the Earthly Paradise as a whole. Turning to the right—that is, clockwise—the chariot-pole points first to the West, then to the North, then to the East; here the polar symbolism appears again, as if teaching us that an orientation toward timeless Eternity (the polar North) is the very thing that will allow progress in the Spirit (sunrise in the East). Here we can discern the second great *enantiodromia* of the *Divine Comedy*. As the descent into the Inferno (clockwise) becomes, below Cocytus and without changing direc-

Canto XXXII

tion, the ascent of the Mountain of Purgatory (ultimately counter-clockwise)—while the Mountain itself is transferred from the Southern Hemisphere to the Northern—so the direction of motion here changes for a moment from counter-clockwise to clockwise, before becoming *pure ascent*. Counter-clockwise is the direction of laborious spiritual aspiration; clockwise is the direction of the descent of Divine Grace, like that which carried Christ into Hell on His mission of punishment and liberation. Such a descent is necessary if Purgatory is to give way to Paradise—the Celestial Paradise—where the travelers no longer walk, but fly.

> *The lovely lady who'd helped me cross the Lethe*
> *With myself and Statius following the wheel*
> *That turned right about the inner, smaller arc*
> *Slowly passed through the vacant, towering forest....*
> [28–31]

This turn is like a conversion within the soul that has both an outer and an inner movement. The outer movement, represented by the left-hand wheel that turns through the greater arc, is the whole of the psyche conforming itself to the Spirit; the inner movement of the right-hand wheel is the human spirit itself becoming more vertical, and hence more receptive to Grace. The arc of the left-hand wheel reminds us of the Great Bear, and that of the right-hand wheel, of the Little Bear. These constellations turn counter-clockwise; the motion pictured here, however, is clockwise, as if the two Bears were being viewed from above. This is a movement outside nature—not opposed to nature, but entirely in response to a spiritual influence coming from beyond the natural domain.

> *I heard them all together murmuring, "Adam!"*
>   *As they circled around a tree that had been stripped*
>   *Of all its leaves and flowers on every bough.*
> *The higher it grew the wider spread its branches*
>   *Till it reached so high that even the Indians*
>   *In their own mighty forests would've been amazed.*
> [37–42]

The Ordeal of Mercy

Adam contains within himself the potentialities of the human race as such, which is why the characters in this Canto breathe his name with awe. This is precisely why the fall of Adam was so tragic—and yet, according to St. Augustine, also a *felix culpa*, a "fortunate fault," in making Redemption, by God Himself through Christ, possible. In traditional iconography, the buried skull of Adam appears beneath Christ's cross in Calvary. Had there been no Fall, Adam would have remained in the Earthly Paradise as Sovereign over God's creation [cf. René Guénon, *Le Roi de Monde*, as well as the symbolic novel *Perelandra* by C.S. Lewis]. But the Fall changed everything; consequently Adam, who for a period of time had to suffer in Hades, is now in the Celestial Paradise, higher than the earthly one.

> "Blesséd are you, O Griffin, who refuses
>   To pluck from this one tree the forbidden fruit
>   Sweet to the taste, but on the stomach bitter."
> This is how, around that mighty tree
>   All shouted—and the beast that had two natures:
>   "Thus is the seed of all righteous men preserved."
> Then, turning to the shaft which he had dragged,
>   He drew it to the foot of that widowed tree
>   And tied it side by side to a waiting branch.
> Just as our own trees, when the great light falls
>   Downward, mingled with that second light
>   That shines out from behind the celestial Fishes
> Begin to swell, and then re-clothe themselves,
>   Each in its own color, before the sun
>   Yokes its horses in another constellation:
> Likewise with a color less than rose
>   But more than violet the present tree reflowered
>   Whose boughs had been so desolate before
>
> [43–60]

The fruit here is the world of generation and corruption, but the seed of the righteous is beyond corruption; it is the immortal soul. To attempt to eat the fruit of the Spirit outside the will of God is to

Canto XXXII

swallow perdition; to refrain from eating it until it is given by God Himself is to feast on immortality.

The tree first appears "stripped of leaves and flowers"; it is a Winter tree. Next the assembly praises the Griffin, symbol of Christ, for not eating the ripe fruit as Adam did, so now we are in Autumn. Finally, when the pole of the Chariot, symbol of Christ's Church, is tied to a branch of the tree, it bursts into flower, as in Spring. Once again, the motion is counter to that of the natural world. Christ is resurrected in the Spring, and yet St. Paul calls Him "the first *fruit* of those who sleep," indicating that the Resurrection happens beyond the cycles of natural duration. The liturgical year of the Eastern Orthodox Church has twelve major feasts—but Pascha (Easter) is not one of them, because it is outside of time. The twelve feasts are like the spokes of a wheel, but Pascha is the hub. Christ (the Griffin) did not eat of the fruit because He is called on to embody the fruit, to become it—a motion that happens in Eternity and is only then manifested, progressively, in time [cf. Luke 2:52: "And He grew in wisdom and age and grace before God and men."]. The fruit He became, as is suggested some verses later, was the apple, but of course it was also the grape —"I am the Vine and you are the branches" [John 15:5]; "this [the wine of the Last Supper] is My Blood" [Mark 14:24 et al.], etc.—which may be why the color of the rejuvenated tree is a purplish red. When Christ resisted Satan's temptation in the desert that He turn the stones to bread to relieve His hunger, He redressed Adam's sinful eating of the fruit of the Tree of the Knowledge of Good and Evil.

The Chariot, a common symbol of the human body or psychophysical entity [cf. Canto XXXIII, below] is now revealed as the Church, the mystical body of Christ on earth. It is an aspect of the doctrine of the Incarnation that the Church is deeply called upon to *embody* Christ; a visible Church and a visible sacramental order are necessarily a part of that doctrine. Since Christ incarnated on earth, the mystical body of Christ must also appear in earthly flesh. But since it is indeed a body inhabiting this world, that it should become corrupted in space and time, as all mortal bodies must, is also inevitable. But no matter how degenerate the earthly church may become, the Eternal Church, the Church Triumphant, remains inviolable. The Church carries within it the grace of Christ, whatever its outer corruption; Wisdom is still hidden within it. Therefore when the Chariot is tied to the tree, the tree blossoms.

> *I never heard, because it's never sung on earth*
>   *The hymn which afterwards that people sang,*
>   *Nor could I follow its melody to the end.*
> *If I could describe just how those merciless eyes*
>   *Fell asleep listening to the tale of Syrinx*
>   *Eyes that by long wakefulness lost so much*
> *As if I were a painter working from a model*
>   *Then I could portray how I was lulled to sleep;*
>   *Let whoever can paint lost consciousness try his hand.*
> *So I pass on to the moment when I awoke*
>   *To say how a radiance rent the veil of sleep*
>   *And a voice addressed me, "What are you doing?*
>   *Wake up!"*
> *As, to behold the Apple Tree in blossom*
>   *Which makes the angels greedy for its fruit,*
>   *And keeps perpetual wedding-feasts in Heaven,*
> *Peter and John and James were overwhelmed*
>   *At first, till they recovered at the word*
>   *By which much deeper sleep has been dispelled*
> *To see their conclave poorer by the loss*
>   *Not of Elias only, but also Moses,*
>   *And the clothing of their Master greatly changed;*
> *So I awoke to see that merciful one*
>   *Standing above me, who had been my guide*
>   *Before, when I had walked beside the river. . . .*
>   [61–84]

Dante is put to sleep by the celestial hymn because a higher dimension than he can comprehend now approaches; it makes him sleep—but on the other hand, because it exudes an unearthly radiance, it also wakes him up. Dante's sleep is compared to the apostles' witnessing of Christ's Transfiguration, and during his trance-like sleep the Griffin disappears. This is likened to Moses and Elijah in the

Canto XXXII

Transfiguration, who disappear after Christ again assumes his everyday human form; the Griffin, who is Christ, has ascended to Paradise. At this point Beatrice takes the place of Christ, in that she is revealed as the medium through whom Dante—as a *pneumatic*, an esoteric—can relate to Christ. As Holy Wisdom, she has become the human face which Christ can turn toward Dante, and also the embodiment of the Inner or Spiritual Church, the Church of John. After awakening, however, Dante still needs the guidance of Matilda because he is not yet entirely at one with the radiance of Paradise; his faculties are still being trained and purified so as to be able to apprehend it.

The Christ of the Transfiguration is compared by Dante to an apple tree. Mandelbaum, in his note to line 60, quotes Ruskin as comparing the reddish-purple leaves or blossoms of the revived tree to apple blossoms. But apple blossoms can also be white, like the garments of the Transfigured Christ; and this is probably what Dante is suggesting here. The "heraldic" colors of Christ, we should remember, are primarily red and white (sacrifice and innocence), particularly in the Western Church.

"Jesus Christ the Apple Tree," an American hymn based on an anonymous English poem, begins with the following stanza:

> *The tree of life my soul hath seen,*
> *Laden with fruit and always green.*
> *The trees of nature fruitless be*
> *Compared with Christ the apple tree.*

It is likely that this hymn was inspired by the third verse of the second chapter of the Song of Solomon, which also suggests the image of Beatrice sitting beneath the tree in lines 87ff:

> *As an apple tree among the trees of the wood,*
> *So is my beloved among the young men.*
> *With great delight I sat in his shadow,*
> *And his fruit was sweet to my taste.*

The Ordeal of Mercy

According to the Jewish *midrash*, the apple tree is a symbol of the Messiah. All this recalls the practice in the Eastern Orthodox Church of blessing fruit on the Feast of the Transfiguration.[1]

> *Then I asked, in bewilderment, "Where is Beatrice?"*
>   *And she [Matilda] said: "See her sitting underneath*
>   *The newly-sprouted foliage, at the root of the tree;*
> *See as well her encircling company.*
>   *The rest are gone; they rose behind the Griffin,*
>   *Took to the sky with a deeper, sweeter song."*
> *I don't know if she said any more than that. . . .* [85–91]
>
> *Alone she sat upon the simple earth,*
>   *Left behind as guardian of the Chariot*
>   *Which I had seen two-formed beast secure.*
> *The encircling nymphs around her made a cloister*
>   *Each one holding in her hand a lamp*
>   *That wind could not snuff out, neither North nor South.*
> *"For a little while you'll dwell here as a forester,*
>   *But with me you'll be a city-man forever*
>   *A citizen of Rome, where Christ is Roman!*
> *And so, for the good of the world that lives so badly*
>   *Fix your eyes on the Chariot, and what you see*
>   *Write down truly when you've returned to earth."*
> *Thus Beatrice spoke. . . .* [94–106]

Beatrice now steps down from the Chariot; this represents the spirit of Wisdom deserting the visible Church just before its final corruption, though she still remains the guardian of it from the outside. She grieves beneath the Tree just as Mary did beneath the Cross, sitting on the "simple ground," surrounded by the seven nymphs bearing lamps, who as we have seen represent the Four Cardinal and the Three Theological Virtues. These lamps cannot be

---

1. Interestingly enough, the apple tree is also central to the Gaelic Otherworld, *Tir Nan Óg*, the Land of the Ever-Young—which is pictured, precisely, as an Earthly Paradise.

Canto XXXII

extinguished by either the North Wind or the South. The South Wind represents being overcome by outer manifestation and worldliness so that the Virtues are smothered; the North Wind symbolizes being overwhelmed by false or excessive ideas of Transcendence that obliterate all particularity, leaving no room, no human soul, in which the Virtues could live. Beatrice, as guardian of the Chariot, symbolizes the Church of John, the inner understanding of the Christian mysteries; she does not, however, represent some sect of esoteric Christians distinct from the Church as such. Beatrice makes it clear that she is talking about the *Roman* Catholic Church and no other—remembering, of course, that Byzantium is the Second Rome according to the Eastern Orthodox, just as Moscow is the Third.

As a "forester," a rustic, Dante will dwell in the Earthly Paradise; but as a city man he will be a "citizen of Heaven" as the early Christians called themselves. The rude rustic has, in a sense, a complete possession of his soul, but that soul needs to be refined and transformed, and so raised to another level. The Heavenly City is ultimately Jerusalem, which is also the city of the communion of the saints. Rome is the sensorial manifestation of Jerusalem, which is heavenly and thus in essence beyond the senses. The lesser "forest" mysteries are Adamic, but the greater, "urban" mysteries are Christic; according to them, Rome is the earthly Jerusalem; Jerusalem is the heavenly Rome.

> *With so swift a motion there never fell*
> *Lightning from a heavy cloud, when rain*
> *Cascades down from the highest point of the sky,*
> *As then I saw the bird of Jove descend*
> *Down through the tree, tearing away the bark,*
> *Scattering the new foliage and the blossoms,*
> *Till he struck that Chariot with all his might.*
> *Like a ship in a violent storm it pitched and reeled,*
> *Tossed by waves, now port-side and now starboard.*
> *Then I saw, as it leaped into the body*
> *Of that triumphal vehicle, a Fox,*
> *Who looked like he'd never eaten wholesome food.*

The Ordeal of Mercy

But denouncing him for all his ugly sins,
　My Lady quickly put that Fox to flight—
　At least as fast as fleshless bones could run.
Then by the same path it had used before
　The Eagle dove again into that Ark
　Leaving it feathered with an Eagle's plumes;
And like the moan that rises from a mournful heart
　A voice came down from Heaven; I heard it say:
　"My little ship, what evil freight you carry!"
Then it seemed to me the earth split open
　Between the Chariot's wheels; a Dragon rose
　Who drove his tail straight up through the wagon's floor.
And just as a wasp at last withdraws its sting
　He drew back to himself his vicious tail—
　Ripping out part of the floor—then slithered away.
The part that was left behind re-clothed itself—
　Just as grass will cover a fertile field—
　Not with grass but feathers, offered perhaps
With sound and kind intent—and then more feathers
　covered both wheels, and the pole as well
　In less time than lips must part to pass a sigh. [109–141]

 The Eagle here is not, as some critics have suggested, primarily the imperial eagle, symbol of the Holy Roman Empire, but rather the Eagle of the Spiritual Intellect, emblem of John the Evangelist. The Chariot is wracked and twisted by the Eagle because, when the Spirit descends upon a corrupt Church, that Church will experience it as Wrath.
 The Fox is the spirit of deceit, which tries to occupy the center of the Church—the Papacy, that is—but Beatrice goes to war with it, just as the Virgin Mary crushed the Serpent's head under her heel [Genesis 3:15]. But why does the Fox occupy the Chariot immediately after the descent of the Eagle? The Fox here is a false response to the Spiritual Intellect, one that degrades *gnosis* to the level of intellectual cunning, which is the mere skeleton of true Intellection.
 And why does the Chariot grow feathers after the second descent of the Eagle, causing the voice from Heaven to declare that "your

Canto XXXII

freight is wickedness"—even though Dante allows that the Eagle might have offered the Chariot its feathers "with sound and kind intent"? This indicates that the Spiritual Intellect is to be reborn within the Church in the Latter Days, but in an incomplete and imbalanced fashion. The Church no longer possesses the moral strength, the sacramental grace, or the doctrinal stability to keep that Spiritual Intellect whole; consequently, under the influence of this unveiling, it wanders away into degeneration and corruption.[2]

The Chariot is now transformed [lines 142–147] into a grotesque object with seven heads and ten horns, like the Beast which appears in the 17th chapter of Revelations. This is the Church finally acquiescing to the power of the Antichrist.[3]

A Whore appears next, seated upon the grotesquely transformed Chariot, and attended by a Giant; the pair repeatedly embrace [lines 148–153]. The Giant is the tyrannical power of the World and also the World's Prince; the Whore is the collective psychic substance drawn from the corruption of many souls, which is precisely the

---

2. The works of such modern Catholic metaphysical writers as Hans Urs von Balthasar, who in better times might have been a Doctor of the Church, as well as the apparent interest of the Papacy in certain non-Catholic and non-traditional esoteric writers like Rudolf Steiner and Valentin Tomberg, author of *Meditations on the Tarot*—both of whom have much to recommend them in other contexts—may be indications of this development. Metaphysics is the crown of the spiritual life, but to place one's hope in a metaphysical Renaissance of the Latter Days partly in an attempt to compensate for, as well as to deny, the destruction of the moral, doctrinal and sacramental foundations of the Church, is to turn metaphysics itself over to the Devil.

3. That the four heads on the corners of the Chariot each have one horn, and the three heads on the chariot-pole, two, is puzzling. The four heads represent the corrupt forms of the Cardinal Virtues; the three heads, inversions of the Theological Virtues. Consequently one would expect the three heads to manifest the Divine Unity, being reflections of the Persons of the Trinity, whereas the four heads, representing the more earthly virtues, ought to partake of the polarity upon which all manifestation is based. That this is not the case demonstrates just how complete an inversion of virtue the monstrous Chariot represents. Duality and ambiguity have invaded the image of the Transcendent, whereas the Unity that is proper only to the Transcendent now shows itself on the earthly plane, indicating that the pre-eminence of the Spirit has been usurped by the World. This inversion is precisely descriptive of the direction and intent of the Western Church since the Second Vatican Council.

The Ordeal of Mercy

guise assumed by the earthly Church of the Latter Days. The Whore is obviously suggested by the Whore of Babylon of the Book of Revelations, and the Giant—who first attends her and then devastates her [cf. Apocalypse 17:16–18]—is another form of the Beast, that is, the Antichrist:

> ... and I saw a woman sitting on a scarlet beast which was full of blasphemous names, and it had seven heads and ten horns ... and [the angel] said to me ... the ten horns that you saw, they and the beast will hate the harlot, and they will make her desolate and naked, and they will burn her up with fire. ... [Revelations 17:3, 12]

The corrupt Church believes that she is only building up her power by her *aggiornamento* with the World; too late she learns that the World is not her ally, but her dominator and destroyer.

The Whore is just about to gaze upon the soul of Dante—which, as a newly-innocent soul, is destined for Paradise—and thus engulf it in her own corruption. But at this very moment the conflict between the Whore and the Giant erupts, saving Dante from that fate; the Giant drags the Chariot occupied by the Whore away into the forest, and it is seen no more [lines 154–160]. This is the providential aspect of the corruption of the earthly Church, which causes it to have less and less power to engulf and destroy the true Remnant. Instead, *it* must flee from *them* into the wilderness.

When the Whore turns for a moment and looks at Dante, it is as if she is attracted by his very innocence; however—like a pedophile, and like many serial killers—she cannot possess herself of this innocence without destroying it.

Dante can witness the affliction of the worldly Church, which amounts to a second crucifixion of Christ, because he himself is now beyond affliction. In the words of St. Maximos the Confessor:

> He whose practice of the virtues has succeeded in mortifying whatever is earthly in him [Colossians 3:5], and who by fulfilling the commandments has triumphed over the passions within him, will experience no more affliction, for he will have

Canto XXXII

already left the world and come to be in Christ, the conqueror of the world of the passions and the source of all peace. He who has not severed his attachment to material things will always experience affliction, since his state of mind depends upon things that are naturally changeable, and so it alters as they do. But he who has come to be in Christ will be totally impervious such to material change. That is why the Lord says, "I have said these things to you, so that in Me you may have peace. In the world you will experience affliction; but have courage, for I have overcome the world" [John 16:33].

[*Philokalia*, Volume Two, *Second Century on Theology*, 95]

The Ordeal of Mercy

Editorial Commentary Nine: *The Exile of Holy Wisdom from the Post-Conciliar Church*

In our own time we can clearly see the image of Holy Wisdom deserting the visible Church. When Pope Francis said, in one of his many "unofficial" pronouncements, delivered on July 21, 2013 in St. Peter's Square, "A prayer that does not lead you to practical action for your brother—the poor, the sick, those in need of help, a brother in difficulty—is a sterile and incomplete prayer," he came near to invalidating the entire contemplative tradition of Christianity—it being abundantly clear that he does not regard prayer as any kind of "practical action" in itself—as well as directly contradicting the teaching of Jesus Christ in Luke 10:41–42: "Martha, Martha, thou art careful, and art troubled about many things: But one thing is necessary. Mary hath chosen the best part, which shall not be taken away from her." To enjoin corporal works of mercy is in line with Christ's commandments, but to deny the validity and perfection of spiritual works of mercy, as well as (by implication) of apophatic contemplation as exemplified by St. John of the Cross, by reducing prayer to a sort of "motivational exercise" rather than a petition offered to One with the real power to grant it, is to draw dangerously close to blasphemy. How could Wisdom possibly remain seated in a chariot with such a reckless driver? In the same address Francis also warned that the Church must not become eaten up by activism, presenting Jesus' admonition of Martha quoted above as the basis of this warning. But when he invalidated the role of the pure contemplative by asserting that contemplation and action must always be united, rather than differentiated under certain circumstances according to the spiritual call of the particular believer—when he put contemplation and action on the same level—he in effect made action the informing context for contemplation, not contemplation for action. In doing so he contradicted St. Thomas Aquinas who, following the scriptural passage above, taught that contemplation is intrinsically higher than action.

But Francis truly surpassed himself when, on Vatican Radio [10/10/2014] he opined: "'What do you believe in?'; 'In God!'; 'But what is God for you?'; 'God, God.' But God does not exist: Do not be shocked! So God does not exist! There is the Father, the Son and the Holy Spirit, they are persons, they are not some vague idea in the clouds.... This God spray does not exist!"[4]

---

4. http://www.news.va/en/news/pope-at-santa-marta-what-we-dare-not-hope-for

So it would seem that Francis has finally embraced the *tri-theism* that Muslims have been accusing Trinitarian Christianity of—wrongly so—for centuries. This shocking papal pronouncement was explained to me both by an Archbishop and a Cistercian monk as being based on the doctrine that God, since He is Pure Being, does not occupy the category of the various things that "exist" in the sense of concrete particularization, which—leaving aside, of course, the Incarnation of the Second Person of the Trinity in the person of Jesus Christ—is metaphysically correct. But how many Catholics are capable of understanding such subtleties? Here we can see the use of metaphysical casuistry to conceal and/or justify theological heresy, as predicted by Dante Alighieri in Canto XXXII of the *Purgatorio* by the allegory of the Eagle attacking the Chariot. Furthermore, is not "Pure Being" the very kind of "vague idea in the clouds" that Pope Francis has declared invalid?

Editorial Commentary Ten:
Beyond the Transcendent Unity of Religions

It was Frithjof Schuon's belief that esoterism, traditionally kept secret so as to protect both it and those who might be tempted, inflamed or bewildered by it due to their lack of spiritual capacity, is now the only thing that can save religious faith from the assaults of scientific rationalism and the inevitable religious pluralism of the modern world, as well as from the militant exclusivism that religious exoterists feel it necessary to adopt in order to protect their faith against this very rationalism and pluralism. As he points out in *Esoterism as Principle and as Way*, [World Wisdom Books, 1981, 7–8],

> We live in an age of confusion and thirst in which the advantages of communication are greater than those of secrecy; moreover, only esoteric theses can satisfy the imperious logical needs created by the philosophic and scientific positions of the modern world.... Religious theses are certainly not errors, but they are cut to the measure of some mental or moral opportuneness; men come in the end to see through the adaptation as such, but meantime the truth, for them, is lost. Only esoterism can explain the particular "cut" or adaptation and restore the lost truth by referring to the total truth ... just as rationalism can remove faith, so esoterism can restore it.

The Ordeal of Mercy

Agreed. However, if a particular religion is relativized by being seen merely as an "opportune" doctrine or a particular "cut" made into the pie of universal truth, faith is lost in any case; this, to take only one example, is the inevitable effect of the relatively exoteric, if not heretical, interfaith promiscuity of the post-conciliar Church—as when Pope Francis prayed from the Holy Qur'an as a gesture of "solidarity" with Muslims, without necessarily actually believing in the Book or in any way accepting Muhammad as God's Prophet. It is necessary to go further, to pass beyond even the best sort of "comparative religion"—*esoteric ecumenism* as Schuon called it—to the understanding that one's chosen religion, if it is indeed among those revealed and authorized by God, is itself host to that "total truth" he refers to; in Schuon's words, "A given religion in reality sums up all religions... all religion is to be found in a given religion, because Truth is one" [*From the Divine to the Human*, 137–138]. In terms of the present book, doctrines from non-Christian religions are mentioned precisely to demonstrate this fact. One might in this context paraphrase a well-known passage from William Blake to the effect that "I question not the doctrines or practices of my religion any more than I would question a window concerning sight; I look through them, not with them." Schuon spoke of "the metaphysical transparency of phenomena," but (as he often implied) we must also come to a vision of the metaphysical transparency of *dogma*. To view the religions as truthfully as possible from the *outside* is to understand their moral and philosophical "opportuneness," but to actually avail oneself of the opportunity offered by one's own religion is to see it as a window opening, at its higher reaches, directly upon the total Truth, which is the Presence of God. In the face of this Divine Presence the need to make "ecumenical comparisons" between the faiths, no matter how ingenious these comparisons might be, and how useful and even necessary on their own level, becomes irrelevant—and it is only the faithfulness of both the intellect and the will to a single Divine revelation that has the power to conduct us to this Presence.

Canto XXXII

Editorial Commentary Eleven:
The Virgin Mary's Predictions of the Fall of the Post-Conciliar Church

This development was predicted by the Blessed Virgin in her apparition at La Salette in 1846: "Rome will lose the Faith ... and become the seat of antichrist" [quoted in Rama Coomaraswamy, *The Destruction of the Christian Tradition*, World Wisdom, 2006, xiv]. The Third Secret of Fatima also apparently alluded to the apostasy of the Western Church. Father Joaquin Alonso, the official expert on the Fatima Message and author of the 24-volume *Fatima Texts and Critical Studies* (who had many interviews with Sister Lucia, the longest-surviving of the recipients of the Message from the Blessed Virgin), said this in 1981:

> It is therefore completely probable that the text [of the Third Secret] makes concrete references to the crisis of faith within the Church and to the negligence of the pastors themselves [and the] internal struggles in the very bosom of the Church and of grave pastoral negligence by the upper hierarchy.... If "in Portugal the dogma of the Faith will always be preserved" ... *it can be clearly deduced from this that in other parts of the Church these dogmas are going to become obscure or even lost altogether* [Quoted in Frère Michel de la Sainte Trinité, *The Whole Truth About Fatima*, Volume III: *The Third Secret* (Buffalo, NY: Immaculate Heart Publications, 1990), 704].

In the year 2000 the Third Secret was apparently published by Pope John Paul II, 40 years after the date set for its revelation by the Blessed Virgin; it predicts the persecution of the Papacy and many new martyrs. Some, however, believe this Secret to be spurious (though the prophesy of "many new martyrs" is certainly being fulfilled), or at least incomplete—particularly in view of the fact that, after 1960, a woman was presented to the faithful as Sister Lucia who, unless the photographs of her available on the web have been doctored (which is not impossible), bore only a passing resemblance to the real Lucia; a comparison of photographs (note particularly the line of the jaw) certainly suggests that the later Lucia was a different woman. This is an example of the work of the Fox. And in view of the pre-eminent place held by St. Lucy in the *Divine Comedy*—St. Lucy whose name means "light," whose intercession cures blindness, and on whose feast day, December 13, I was born—we can

The Ordeal of Mercy

almost see in this counterfeit "Lucy" an intent in some quarters to suppress the degree and quality of Wisdom expressed in Dante's great work (even as the Roman Catholic Church shows signs of renewed interest in Dante), and to veil the light it throws upon the dark destiny of the greater part of the Church Militant—or, as we must perhaps now call it, the Church Compliant.

Canto XXXIII

The Seven Virtues beseech Beatrice to have mercy on Dante, and she relents. She prophesies the descent of the vengeance of God upon the Whore, the Giant and the Dragon, and the coming of a mysterious figure called "Five-hundred, Ten and Five." She discourses on the sacrosanct mystery of the Tree of Adam. Dante is shown the further mystery that Lethe and Eunoë, forgetfulness and gnosis, flow from the same source. Finally he is immersed in Eunoë, and made ready for Paradise.

The man who has struggled bravely with the passions of the body, has fought ably against unclean spirits, and has expelled from his soul the conceptual images they provoke, should pray for a pure heart to be given him and for a spirit of integrity to be renewed within him [cf. Psalms 51:10]. In other words, he should pray that by grace he may be completely emptied of evil thoughts and filled with divine thoughts, so that he may become a spiritual world of God, splendid and vast, wrought from moral, natural and theological forms of contemplation.
    [St. Maximos the Confessor, from the *Philokalia*, Volume Two, *Second Century on Theology*, 79]

"Deus venerunt gentes" *sweetly sang*
  The seven weeping maidens, first the Three
  And then the Four in alternating chorus
While Beatrice, breathing sighs and filled with pity,
  Listened to them with such a countenance
  Mary at the Cross was hardly more affected.
When they were done they yielded place to her
  To let her speak; she rose to her full height
  The color of ardent fire, and answered them:

The Ordeal of Mercy

"Modicum, et non videbitis me;
Et iterum, *my delightful sisters,*
Modicum, et vos videbitis me." [1–12]

The psalm the maidens sing is psalm 79: "O God, the heathen are come into thine inheritance; Thy holy temple they have defiled; they have laid Jerusalem on heaps." On the surface this refers to the corruption of the Church, but in a deeper sense it has to do with the manifestation of *avidya-maya*; Beatrice weeping to hear that the gentiles have inherited the kingdom is like the sorrow hidden behind universal manifestation, behind *Maya* as such; as Frithjof Schuon says, "*Maya* . . . weeps behind her veil" [*In the Face of the Absolute*, 61]. But that the maiden virtues sing this song is actually the highest manifestation of *vidya-maya*; when ignorance is unmasked for what it is, then Wisdom is complete. After gazing upon these maidens, and in a sense seeing through them, more of Beatrice's true nature, which is the essence of Wisdom, can be revealed to Dante; this is why she now appears to him as both ardent and pitying.

Beatrice will disappear due to the influence of *avidya-maya*, but she will reappear in Paradise, because Dante has seen in her the fullness of Wisdom, and that vision will never completely leave his soul. Lines 10–12, which translate as "In a little while you will not see me, and again in a little while you will see me," are taken from John 16:16 in which Christ is speaking to his disciples, after which He ascends into a cloud [Acts 1:9]. The cloud is *avidya-maya*. Manifestation could not hold the full form of True Man and True God for long; this is what causes Him to disappear; but He appears again, as Wisdom Perfected, to St. Paul on the road to Damascus. Christ said, "I will be with you all days, even until the end of the world" [Matthew 28:20]. He is always with at least some souls; if He were not, this world could not continue. These souls are stronger than *avidya-maya*, consequently they must draw the manifestation of Christ back into the world in the fullness of His glory at the Second Coming; this is why, after His resurrection, He tells Peter, speaking of John, "If I will that he tarry till I come, what is that to thee?" [John 21:22]. And as the saints are stronger than *avidya-maya*, so Christ is stronger than the world—since, according to his words in John 16:33, He has already overcome it.

> Then she placed before her all the Seven
>   And after her, signaling us to follow,
>   Myself, the Lady, and the one remaining Sage. [13–15]
>
> "Why do you hesitate, brother" she said to me
> "To ask me questions, now that we walk together?"
> Like someone who is much too deferential
>   When trying to speak to persons who outrank him
>   And can drag no vigorous word up to his teeth
> It happened that, with less than perfect voice
>   I answered her: "My need you know, my Lady,
>   Just as you know the good that will fulfill it."
> "Now it is my wish for you," she answered
>   "That you fully strip yourself of fear and shame
>   And no longer speak like one immersed in dreams." [23–33]

Here the hierarchy of Wisdom appears: Beatrice, Wisdom as such; Matilda, the perfectly purified soul open to Wisdom; Statius, the human vehicle who can articulate and express that Wisdom. That Dante now walks beside Beatrice and is addressed by her as "brother" indicates that his soul is becoming purified, and consequently increasing in its readiness to accept and be conformed to Paradise.

It's wise for Dante defer to Beatrice at this point—because what exactly is the *need* for Wisdom? Curiosity is an indulgence in knowledge that inflates the soul, like the pursuit of knowledge and information for worldly gain: the vice of corrupt academia. What's called for here is the Wisdom that fulfills not the soul's shallow desire, but its true need—the need for salvation. When Dante asks Beatrice to impart what she knows, he's asking not just for celestial Wisdom, but for the *desire* for Wisdom that comes not from his own fallen nature, but from Heaven itself.

Dante's fear and shame have come to the surface; he is now called to see how these qualities, which are often associated with humility,

The Ordeal of Mercy

can also be a veil to spiritual vision. Fear narrows one's sympathies and makes one afraid to see, which is appropriate when withdrawing the attention from the passions, but inappropriate in the presence of Grace and enlightenment; fear may be the beginning of Wisdom [Psalm 111:10; Proverbs 9:10], but it is not the end. Likewise shame can result in a false belittling of one's own perceptions; one feels intrinsically unworthy of Wisdom and hence repudiates it. It is now high time, however, for Dante to awaken from the dream of shame and fear.

> *Know that this vessel that the Serpent broke*
> *Was, and is not; but let him who bears the guilt*
> *Know that the vengeance of God cannot be stopped.*
> *The Eagle who left his plumes upon the Chariot*
> *That made it first a monster, they a prey*
> *Won't remain without an heir forever;*
> *What I see is true, therefore I say it:*
> *The stars are already drawing near the hour*
> *Which no created thing can block or hinder*
> *In which will come a Five-hundred, Ten, and Five,*
> *Sent from God, who will kill the Robber Woman*
> *And that same Giant who's whoring with her now.* [34–45]
> [See *Editorial Commentary Seven*, p. 253]

The vessel broken by the serpent is the soul with the power to contain the vision of God, which was lost when Adam sinned. However, the soul never entirely lost that power; the vestiges of it—the Eagle's plumes—still remain within the Chariot, which is a universal symbol of the human psychophysical vehicle.[1]

When the human form becomes closed to the Spirit, that form becomes a monster; it fantasizes that it has powers and potentialities it does not in fact possess, or that at least cannot be lived out without the Spirit's power and guidance. It has become *titanic*. (*Compassion might rein in the titanic soul; unfortunately, such a soul usually*

---

1. Both the Hindus and the Platonists employ the symbol of the Chariot in this sense; see Ananda K. Coomaraswamy, *Selected Papers, Vol. 2: Metaphysics*, 128.

Canto XXXIII

belittles compassion, and so exiles it.) In modern times we have seen the full drama of the titanic soul, culminating in World War II. But now, in the "postmodern" 21st century, the human soul has been transformed from a triumphant monster into a prey, without however losing any of its monstrousness. It has become a prey and a victim to infrapsychic forces because it is drained of all life, even the residual psychic vitality it subsisted upon after the Spirit largely deserted it. Without the Eagle, the Spirit which is its real Life, the soul must eat, and be eaten by, everything in existence.[2]

The human form in which the *Nous* is veiled—the Eagle of St. John being, precisely, a symbol of this *Nous*, the spiritual Intellect—is like an empire whose Emperor is dead or in exile. But Beatrice predicts that the true heir will some day regain his throne. Critics have identified this heir with a number of different figures, including Emperor Henry VII of Luxembourg, whom Dante apparently hoped might restore the Holy Roman Empire to its true function as protector of the Roman Catholic Church, thus purifying the Church of its worldly corruption. But in the highest sense, the Heir to the Kingdom is Jesus Christ, both the Christ of the Second Coming and the Christ who is to be born anew in the purified and virgin soul. Thus the Chariot is a symbol both of the body to be resurrected and of manifestation as such, of which the Human Form is the quintessence. But for all that it still remains a symbol of the Church, which is Christ's *mystical* body.[3]

If the Holy Roman Empire had remained intact, Europe could have preserved Christendom as such; it could have been a kind of Byzantium of the West, perhaps strong enough to heal the schism

---

2. Friederich Nietzche, in *The Will to Power*, saw this exactly: "... there will be wars the like of which have never yet been seen on earth ... [but] in the 21st century will occur something worse than the great wars: namely, the total eclipse of all values."

3. Plato, in the *Republic*, compares the human form to a political entity, a *polis*, a "body politic"; and his ideal *polis* is to be constructed according to the pattern of the cosmos. In many traditions Man is pictured as a little cosmos, and the cosmos as a Great Man. Our English word "world," for example, comes from the Anglo Saxon *wer-eld* meaning "Old Man."

between the Eastern and the Western Church—which, if it were healed now, would only accelerate the destruction of both parties. The crusades united the Western Church temporarily, but the crusades couldn't last.

But now we see the Western Church moving ever closer to full membership in, and full submersion beneath, the New World Order, losing whatever independence it once had, and progressively becoming a tool and a plaything of the globalist elites. If this fatal drift is not stopped and rolled back, whatever remains to be called "The Roman Catholic Church" after the spirit of that church has departed may well become, as some have predicted, the seat of Antichrist.

> *But possibly my mysterious way of speaking,*
>   *As with Themis and the Sphinx, will not convince you*
>   *Since such expressions can cloud the intellect.*
> *But soon events themselves will be the Naiads*
>   *With power to solve this difficult enigma*
>   *With no destruction of the crops and herds.*
> *Note well: These words, exactly as I've said them,*
>   *Word for word you must repeat to those*
>   *Who live the life that is a race to death.*
> *And also bear in mind, when you write them down*
>   *Not to hide what you've seen regarding this tree*
>   *That's already been plundered two times over.*
> *Whoever robs or damages this tree*
>   *With that blaspheming action has offended God,*
>   *Who made it holy, for His exclusive use.*
> *For tasting of that tree the first soul waited*
>   *Five-thousand years and more in grief and yearning*
>   *For Him who avenged that taste upon Himself.*
> *Your intellect is asleep if it cannot grasp*
>   *The singular cause that makes this tree so tall*
>   *And makes it grow in an upside-down position.* [46–66]

That the destined savior "Five-Hundred and Ten and Five" will do his work "without injury to grain or herds" [see Apocalypse 9:4]

Canto XXXIII

means that the Apocalypse he brings will be primarily internal, operating not first and foremost on the field of history, but within the human heart. According to Nicholas Constas, in his article "To Sleep Perchance to Dream: The Middle State of Souls in Patristic and Byzantine Literature" [*Dumbarton Oaks Papers*, No. 55],

> Byzantine apocalyptic and eschatology was not the type that was expected to break into the world violently from without. The exteriorized apocalyptic of John's Revelation was sealed within the only book of the Bible that was never publicly read in the Byzantine church. Instead, the Kingdom of God was a reality that promised to break through, not from a point outside the cosmos, but from within the depths of the self.

As William Blake said, "Whenever a man rejects Error and embraces Truth, a Final Judgement passes on that man." Whatever form the consummation of history may take, it will simply be an outer reflection of this inner Apocalypse. Nonetheless, history *will* reach its consummation; this is a truth that the Eastern Church sometimes forgets. If the literal meaning of scripture is not kept intact, the moral, allegorical and anagogical meanings collapse.

Be that as it may, the riddle of Five-Hundred, Ten, and Five will be solved through simplicity of soul, not through complicated mental gymnastics; simplicity is closer than ingeniousness to true Intellection.

There is a deep feminine intuition—sometimes symbolized by subtle elemental beings such as Fairies or Naiads, like the *dakinis* of Tibetan yoga—that in certain instances can be called on to help rightly orient one's soul toward spiritual potentials that still lie hidden in the future. The future will come when it will—but when it does come, will the soul be aligned with its true destiny, and so able to cooperate with the potentials that the future will then actualize, or will one still be at odds with that destiny? If so, one will simply be crushed by events. The riddle of the Sphinx went as follows: "What animal walks on four legs in the morning, on two legs at noon, and on three legs in the evening?" The solution given by Oedipus was, "man, who as an infant crawls on all fours, as an adult walks upright, and as an old man uses a cane." The destiny of man that Oedipus himself encountered was dark, since it was enclosed within the cycles of nature—symbolized by his blinding intercourse with his mother—consequently that destiny was blind to the Spirit; but in the Christian view man's destiny is bright, because he is destined for Paradise.[4]

Those who value life only for its own sake, as separate from spiritual realities that transcend earthly existence, are creating death and deadness all around them; for them, life is all too short. Yet the "race to death" also has an inner meaning. As Fr. Rama Coomaraswamy once said to me shortly before his own passing, "it is not life that is important, but death"; in other words, how we face our death is of more ultimate significance than what we have done in life—though of course the way we have lived has everything to do with the way we die. And all this, however true on its own level, is merely a reflection of the state of the soul, which must "die before it dies" so as to consummate the spiritual life. Viewed in this way, "those who live the life that is a race to death" are those traveling the spiritual Path, and longing for its end; in the words of St. Paul [Timothy 4:7], "I have fought the good fight, I have finished the race, I have kept the faith."

This Tree is the Tree of Knowledge, but it is also the Tree of Life. The Tree of Life is pure Being; it is not only the tree of manifestation but the source of Life itself, as well as the channel through which the Life prior to manifestation comes into existence—that is, the Logos. And Life is inseparable from Consciousness. How, then, is it sinful to eat of the Tree of Knowledge? Is not Knowledge the same as Con-

---

4. Themis, mentioned in line 47, was a Titaness who founded the Delphic Oracle; she was considered to represent the Divine Order as expressed through the social order. Hera, the wife of Zeus, was sometimes called "Lady Themis." When Oedipus solved the riddle of the Sphinx—who is believed by some to have represented an oracular priestess dedicated to Themis—the Titaness sent a beast to devastate the crops and herds of the Thebans. This indicates that Oedipus, though he was clever enough to come up with the "right" answer, did not grasp the deeper import of the Sphinx' riddle: the vision of the whole cycle of human life on earth as seen from the standpoint of Eternity. Oedipus' type of knowledge was *impious*, like that of Adam after he ate the fruit of the Tree of Knowledge of Good and Evil. Only after you've stopped betting on the horses will you be able to pick the winner of every race.

Canto XXXIII

sciousness? Certainly it is. But the Knowledge of Good and Evil is secondary to the Divine Life because it involves the duality of the Knower and the Known. To eat of the Tree of the Knowledge of Good and Evil is to see knowledge and consciousness as separate from Pure Being, as if they were capable of creating their own world without reference to it.

First this Tree is despoiled by the separation between Knowledge and Being; secondarily, it is despoiled by the split within Knowledge itself that produces the Knowledge of Good and Evil; in admitting the existence of evil, which is pure negation, Knowledge becomes intermingled with it. In this it resembles "carnal knowledge," intrinsic to which is an intermingling with the object, such that the knower becomes identified with the thing known.[5]

Life belongs to God, which is why the soul chooses neither when it is born nor when it dies. That this tree is holy and for God's sole use indicates that human beings can only be destructive to life insofar as they try to control it. It was a Fall when Knowledge no longer directly adhered to Life, but within that Fall was a mercy, seeing that it prevented human beings from going too far in violating the Divine Life itself.

We are not called on to be ignorant of spiritual realities, but we must realize that the Divine *gnosis* puts the one receiving it outside of the human realm and within the Divine one, which means that it is incumbent upon him to obey Divine authority alone and let go even of the legitimate human privileges that are his by right. It is as if he were in a foreign country where his knowledge of his own native tongue no longer applies. (This foreshadows the point in *Paradiso* I: 70–71 where Dante says: "Passing beyond the human cannot be worded," indicating that the soul is now completely at home

---

5. Cf. the terrified and despairing lament in William Blake's *Jerusalem*: "They became what they beheld!" When Aquinas said "the knower becomes the thing known," he was describing the transcendence of subject and object on a level higher than the ego. Blake's lament, however, has to do with the ego's identification with this or that object on the basis of a partial and distorted knowledge, in such a way that its perception of a particular object is transformed into a subjective impression, thus adding to the ego's store of unconscious entanglements and further veiling the true Self.

in the Divine.) To "rob" the Tree of Knowledge and Life is to try to put the Divine *gnosis* on the human level rather than letting one's humanity transcend itself until it becomes one with the Divine.

The inverted tree, as we have already seen in Canto XXII, has its roots in heaven. Our perception of spiritual realities tends to be inverted, because we see the reflection of them in the mirror of manifestation, not the realities themselves. Adam's trespass was to place the Divine on the wrong level, as if the root of the tree were more accessible than its branches, leaves and fruit.

God, in Genesis, did not prohibit Adam and Eve from eating the fruit of the Tree of Life, or only did so after they had eaten of the Tree of Knowledge. Thus we may speculate that, if they had eaten of the Tree of Life first, the Tree of Knowledge would not have been forbidden to them; this is another way of talking about the difference between mental greed and Divine Gnosis. We are allowed to contemplate the Names of God [cf. Dionysius the Areopagite], also known as His Uncreated Energies [cf. St. Gregory Palamas], but—as St. Maximos the Confessor teaches—we are prohibited from contemplating His Essence because this is impossible. Adam attempted the impossible, and so fell from Paradise.

> *If useless fantasy did not encrust your mind*
>   *Like waters of the Elsa, and your pleasure in it*
>   *Make you like Pyramus when he stained the mulberry,*
> *Then you would have been able to recognize*
>   *It its form and height the moral sense*
>   *That led the Almighty to declare this tree forbidden.* [67–72]

(The water of the Elsa, a tributary of the Arno, has a high mineral content, causing it to form a stony crust around objects that fall into it.) In Ovid's tragic legend of the Babylonian lovers Pyramus and Thisbe—enacted as a farce in Shakespeare's *A Midsummer Night's Dream*—their union is opposed by their parents, so they agree to meet in secret at the tomb of Ninus, legendary founder of Niniveh. Thisbe arrives first and encounters a lioness, drops her veil and flees. Then Pyramus arrives and sees the shredded veil in the lioness' claws; believing Thisbe to be dead, he stabs himself at the foot

Canto XXXIII

of a mulberry bush; his blood stains the white berries red. Thisbe returns, sees Pyramus about to breathe his last, and stabs herself as well; it is her dying prayer that the fruit of the mulberry be blood-red from then on in memory of her lover.

The legend of Pyramus and Thisbe has unexpected depths. Pyramus believing Thisbe to be dead, and despairingly committing suicide, is a type of Knowledge separated from Life; Thisbe, in contemplating the death of her lover, is viewing the tragedy of life, as surely as a Christian mystic does when meditating on the Passion of Christ. But if one's vision merely stops at the image of pain and loss, there is a danger of spiritual death, for which suicide is an apt symbol. However, when seen from a more esoteric perspective, Pyramus' death is something different; he is dying to that vision of loss for the sake of the eternal life symbolized by the white fruit of the mulberry tree. When Pyramus' blood stains the mulberries (here Christ's two symbolic colors, white and red, appear again), it indicates that life (the red blood) has entered into eternity itself (the white berries), and thus no longer depends upon time. Now all life is contained in eternity and does not depart from it. Thisbe's falsely imagined death was spiritual death in despair; her real death is an entry into eternity through her love for Pyramus. The same thing can be said for the deaths of the lovers in Shakespeare's *Romeo and Juliet*. This in no way a defense of suicide, as some of the Romantic poets undoubtedly believed, but rather an affirmation of death to the world.

> "*Just as the design engraved on a signet ring*
>   *Is in no way altered by the wax it stamps*
>   *Just so you're now imprinted on my brain*" *I said.*
> "*But why does your speech, that I have so long wished for*
>   *Rise so high above my understanding*
>   *That the more I strive to grasp, the more I lose?*"
> "*This is in order to demonstrate to you*
>   *The nature of the school of thought you've followed*
>   *And learn to what degree it conforms itself*
> *To my discourse, so that you may discern*
>   *Just how far mere earthly thought diverges*

The Ordeal of Mercy

From thought that the highest heavenly sphere impells."
In response to her I answered: "I don't remember
   Ever having estranged myself from you,
   Nor is my conscience troubled on that score."
"If you can't remember now" she answered, smiling
   "Remember instead how, on this very day,
   You've deeply drunk the waters of the Lethe;
If the existence of fire can be deduced from the sight of smoke,
   So your present forgetfulness logically demonstrates
   That your will has been intent on other things." [79–99]

Here it is revealed that Dante, in turning away from *gnosis*, did not only forget, but forgot his very act of forgetting. If you remember that you've forgotten, then you have become aware of the machinations and transgressions of the will—but if you forget that you've forgotten, you have buried the will and veiled it from your consciousness because you don't want its transgresssions to be revealed; consequently repentance is impossible for you. Having drunk of Lethe, Dante has become forgetful, which is why conscience does not gnaw at him for his forgetfulness. But Beatrice, in reminding him that he has drunk, is trying to awake him to that forgetfulness. To remember *that* you have forgotten is to begin to remember *what* you have forgotten—a remembrance or *anamnesis* that is only perfected when the soul has drunk from the river of Eunoë: divine *gnosis*. Here purgation is becoming so complete that even forgetfulness can act as a support for remembrance.

Augustine conceived of the Fall of Man as arising primarily from a misuse of the will; the Eastern Orthodox theologians, on the other hand, tend to see the initial movement of the Fall as a darkening of the Intellect: there is no sin that is not first announced as a temptation, and every temptation must include an element of deception. The misuse of the will does indeed darken the intellect; in this sense Augustine is right. And Dante is right that the will is entirely free to choose. But only an Intellect that is already darkened can present the will with a choice other than the True and the Good; consequently it is only Eunoë, the source of *anamnesis*, the Remembrance of God, which completely reverses the effects of the Fall.

Canto XXXIII

More brilliant now, and with slower steps
   The sun was pacing the line of the meridian
   Which changes according to the observer's point-of-view
When the Seven Ladies reached a shadow's edge
   And halted, as a squadron and its escort will
   If they encounter something new upon their path—
A shadow such as those, beneath green leaves
   And black branches, that the Alps will wear
   Upon its frigid borders. In front of them
I thought I saw the Tigris and Euphrates
   Springing from a single mighty fountain
   Then, like friends, slowly and fondly parting.
"O light and glory of the human race!
   What stream is this which here unfolds itself
   From a single source, then from itself withdraws?"
Responding to this prayer of mine I heard
   "Ask Matilda for the answer, she'll inform you";
   And sounding like one who frees herself from blame
The lovely lady said: "I already told him
   This and other things; I'm confident
   That Lethe did not wipe them from his memory."
                       [103–123]

    Purgatory, since it is a world of transmigration, is not one of the "last things"; along with time, it finally passes away, which means that it is ultimately illusory in nature. This is why, at the summit of the Mountain, the Mountain itself appears as a shadow. The "halting" of the seven maidens at the border of this shadow means that time ends, which implies that our whole conception of motion and duration is transformed. The Seven Lady Virtues are vehicles who help us arrive at this end; consequently, when we do in fact arrive, their action is at an end as well; they are absorbed into the Divine as such.

    Within the shadow the Seven Ladies see the Tigris and Euphrates arising from a single spring, and then slowly separating, "like friends." These rivers come from beyond manifestation, from the Essence, but they retain the bond of their essential unity, though this bond may be invisible even to them. But how can Tigris and Euphrates, Lethe and Eunoë, Ignorance and Knowledge spring from the same Source? Simply because there is no other Reality for them to spring from; *avidya-maya* and *vidya-maya* are both modes of *Maya* herself, the universal manifestation of the Unknowable. And, as we have already seen, the time may come when even Ignorance serves Knowledge; as William Blake put it, "If the Fool were to persist in his folly he would become wise." Sometimes things which appear foolish on one level are revealed as wise from the standpoint of a higher one, as in case of the "foolish brother" motif which is to be found in so many fairy tales.

The "blame" of Matilda is removed from her now because Dante has finally understood her. Here Matilda is unveiled as *Maya* herself, the universal manifestation of Reality which, in revealing this Reality, also obscures it. But now that obscurity is at an end; this reminds us of the tradition that Eve—*avidya-maya*—having lost her beauty through sin, had this beauty restored to her through *vidya-maya*—the Virgin Mary.

The Source of Truth is greater than the manifestation of ignorance, which has nothing but Truth to base itself on in any case; therefore even ignorance, in its deepest essence, at its original Source, has no power to veil the identity of ignorance and Truth. This is a dangerous principle, however, which has been revealed only to the detriment of many spiritual lives in these latter days. Nonetheless the quality of our age seems to demand the full manifestation of *Maya* as an eschatological sign and an instrument of judgment.

> "Perhaps a greater care" said Beatrice
> "Which is often known to weaken memory
> Has brought darkness to the vision of his mind.
> But there the stream called Eunoë springs up;
> Lead him to it and, as you're used to doing
> Bring his half-dead virtue back to life." [124–129]

This "greater care" is Dante's love of Truth, both manifest and unmanifest; this love has itself made him susceptible to the dark-

Canto XXXIII

ness of ignorance, precisely because it has opened him—as a poet—to reception of *images* of the Truth he loves, and he gives himself unreservedly to these images, which ultimately enwrap him in the veils of ignorance. Truth is always involved with ignorance because it possesses an aspect that is beyond conception. However, since the source of his susceptibility to ignorance and illusion is this very love, it will eventually cause the darkness of ignorance to evaporate, thereby unveiling the full light of the midday sun.

If one were to stop here, however, this very freedom from the veils of imagery would make one an iconoclast, which is something no true Christian can be. Thus even after coming to a full understanding of the treachery and limitation of giving oneself over to images, Dante relates to us how Matilda invites Statius too to drink of the waters of Eunoë. As a poet it is the profession and call of Statius to bring forth images, along with all the truth and illusion they both express and imply. Here, in the person of Statius, the poetic art itself is fully purged of the ignorance of *Maya*, thus allowing the final movement of the *Commedia*, the *Paradiso*, to be born.

Dante joins Beatrice now; both of them are like trees who have brought forth new leaves. They are ready to ascend to the stars.

The Ordeal of Mercy

Editorial Commentary Twelve:
The Riddle of Five-Hundred, Ten and Five

Though Dante rightly says that this riddle will be solved only through simplicity, not mental gymnastics, the editor of this volume has not yet purified himself of the desire to engage in such gymnastics. And only if the soul is receptive in its simplicity to the total Truth as a single, complete, yet inarticulate intuition, will such speculations bear any fruit; only someone who has eaten of the Tree of Life can deflect the curse of Themis. To solve the riddle of Five-Hundred, Ten and Five by mere human ingenuity is impious, like attempting to date the *parousia*. It is enough for us to know that Christ *will* come—and as we shall see, the riddle itself has everything to do with the second coming of Christ and the consummation of the age.

Some have solved the riddle of "500, 10 and 5" by representing this number as the Roman numerals D, X and V, and then transposing them as DVX so as to spell *dux*, the Latin word for "leader." This appears a bit labored, but certainly not more so than my own conjecture, which is as follows: The Arabic numerals first appeared in the West in the 980s when Gerbert of Aurillac, later Pope Sylvester II, began to diffuse the knowledge of them in Europe, and were later promoted by Leonardo Fibonacci in 1202 in his book *Liber Abaci*; they did not come into general use, however, until the 1400's with the advent of printing. So in Dante's time they were undoubtedly known among the elite of the intelligentsia but not necessarily to every literate reader; consequently they could have been used by some as a vehicle for expressing arcane knowledge. If 500 + 10 + 5 is first written in Arabic numerals as 515, and if these numerals (though not the number they designate) are then transliterated into Roman numerals, the result is VIV, the root of the Latin word for "life." Returning to Arabic, the number 5 is represented by the letter *ha*, and the number 1 by *alif*. In Sufi symbolism, *ha* signifies "Guide," which in Arabic is *al-Hadi*, one of the 99 Most Beautiful Names of Allah in the enumeration of al-Ghazali; likewise *alif* is seen as a symbol or representation of *al-Kalam*, the "Pen"—the creative Logos. So the number 515, expressed in Arabic letters, indicates the Word of God flanked by and radiating the power of Guidance or Truth—just as, transposed into Roman numerals, and in view of the fact that both the Roman numeral "I" and the Arabic letter *alif*, which are similar in form, stand for the number "One" (*alif* being the origin of our own numeral), the same number indicates the Logos as radiating the power of Life. In

Canto XXXIII

John 14:6 Jesus describes Himself as "the Way, the Truth and the Life." He is the Guide to wayfarers on the spiritual Path; the Word or Logos containing all Truth, which is *with* God and simultaneously *is* God [John 1:1–2]; and the Divine Life within the human soul, and the souls of all things. So the One who is to come so as to slay both the Whore and the Giant who sins with her (the Giant, as we have seen, being substantially identical to the Beast, the Antichrist, in the 17th Chapter of the Apocalypse), is Christ—the Christ of the *parousia*. In Apocalypse 19:11–16 Christ appears as the Rider on the White Horse, called Faithful and True, who will smite the nations and rule them with a rod of iron; Islamic tradition, however, explicitly predicts that, upon his Second Coming, Jesus the Messiah will slay *al-Dajjal*, the Antichrist.

Editorial Commentary Thirteen:
On Romance, Alchemy, Scholastic Philosophy, Sufism and the Fedeli d'Amore

In addition to the motif of *ascent*, the other keynote of the *Purgatorio* is *polarity*, the play of opposites; the purgatorial ascent is dialectical in nature. This quality of polarity gives it its affinity both with alchemy, based as it is on *solve et coagula*, the dissolution of false unions and the consummation of true ones, as well as with the tradition of romantic love, an affinity which in Dante's case undoubtedly derived in part from the Fedeli d'Amore or Fede Santa, the esoteric spiritual order with which he is reputed to have been associated, along with Guido Cavalcanti, Cino da Pistoia, Moroello Malaspina, Pedro de Pisa, Boccaccio, Petrarch, Andreas Cappelanus, Cardinal Francesco Barberino, Dino Compagni and Brunetto Latini; the Fedeli d'Amore are often characterized as a third (lay) order of the Knights Templars. René Guénon, Julius Evola, Dante Gabriel Rosetti, Luigi Valli, Eugene Aroux, Mircea Eliade, Alfonso Ricolfi, Arthur Schult, Henry Corbin, William Anderson and others have published researches on this order.

There are indications that the Fedeli d'Amore may have had certain affinities with *tasawwuf* or Islamic Sufism, perhaps deriving from esoteric contacts made by the Templars in the Holy Land. In the words of one follower of René Guénon (who wishes to remain anonymous),

> It is said that the three secrets of the Fedeli d'Amore were: Love, Beauty and the Heart. Suhrawardi [the Persian Sufi and *Ishraqi* or

The Ordeal of Mercy

"Illuminist"] speaks of Beauty, Love and Nostalgia [which perhaps refers to "remembrance" in its spiritual sense—the Sufi *dhikr*, the Hesychast *mnimi Theou*, also known as the Prayer of the Heart]. This is the visible, communicable secret. The second secret, reserved for the initiates, is that one must learn how to read the rule of divine Love in the book of human love. The third secret belongs to adepts. It is the Faith of the Faithful, which is the direct vision of God in a human form, beautiful to contemplate, but without the agitation of the carnal nature.... The Fedeli d'Amore appeared to the later Sufis as an unexpected variant of the Shadhiliyya; their particular way of symbolically mixing love and poetry is common to both systems.

Mircea Eliade, in *Rites and Symbols of Initiation*, writes as follows of the symbolism employed by the order:

> "Woman" symbolizes the transcendent intellect, Wisdom. Love of a woman awakens the adept from the lethargy into which the Christian world had fallen because of the spiritual unworthiness of the pope. In the writings of the Fedeli d'Amore we find allusions to a "widow who is no widow"; this is Madonna Intelligenza, who was left a widow because her husband, the pope, died to spiritual life by devoting himself entirely to things temporal.

The redemptive polarity between the Knight and his Lady in the Courtly Love tradition can be considered as the outer (though no less esoteric) aspect of the alchemical union of Sulfur and Quicksilver; Sulfur is identified by Titus Burckhardt, in his *Alchemy: Science of the Cosmos, Science of the Soul*, with the Aristotelian/Scholastic *forma*, as Quicksilver is with *materia*. According to Jacques Thomas in *Aperçus sur l'Operation Intellectuelle et la Connaissance Initiatique* [1998],

> In the same way as, in the formation of an individual being, the *forma* is united with the *materia*, the act of the intellect is marked by the conjunction, the *copulatio*, of the possible intellect with the active intellect that is part of the transcendent Intellect or Intelligence (itself emanating from Wisdom). The passive intellectual principle receives by reflection the universal ideas of the omniform Light of the active Intellect that, in a certain way, brings to real existence the colours that are potential [within it]....

Canto XXXIII

Dante's laborious ascent of the Mountain of Purgatory, at whose summit Beatrice appears, reminds us of the difficult tasks often imposed upon the Knight by his Lady. Just as the personality of the Knight must be purged of subhuman lust and vanity in order to become worthy of union with his Beloved, so the soul in Purgatory must be purified of the seven deadly sins so as to fit itself for union with God. And the rhythm of this purgation proceeds by alternations, contraries. The successive "terraces" of the Mountain of Purgatory correspond in many ways to the various *maqamat* or "stations" in the spiritual Path according to Sufism, stations that often manifest as contrary states such as Fear and Hope, Contraction and Expansion, Gathering and Dispersion, Intoxication and Sobriety, Fluctuation and Stability, Presence and Absence, and Annihilation and Subsistence [see *Sufism II* and *Sufism III* by Javad Nurbakhsh, Khaniqahi-Nimatullahi Publications, 1982 and 1985]. A similar schema of spiritual development is found in *The Ladder of Divine Ascent* by St. John Climacus, which has been copiously quoted in this book. These polarities also appear in the Grail material—especially in the *Parzival* of Wolfram Von Eschenbach, the most alchemical of the Arthurian romances—in the guise of love unions and knightly jousts.

According to the esoteric dimension of the Courtly Love tradition, the Lady is *forma*, a manifestation of the Active Intellect or Necessary Being, while the Knight represents *materia*, the Receptive Intellect—or the intellect that must become receptive through struggle and sacrifice—and thus of Possible Being. This, of course, reverses the traditional gender attributions of *forma* and *materia*—just as the lovers Krishna and Radha, in the *Sahaja* poetry of India, are sometimes pictured dressed in each other's clothes; in the words of the Qur'an [2:187], *They* [the wives] *are raiment for you and ye* [the husbands] *are raiment for them*. The Knight has needs, goals, agendas; the Lady is complete in herself. Her "severity," her intrinsic inaccessibility, simply indicates her lack of needs, as opposed to the unfulfilled needs of the Knight, who is the human soul as yet to become self-actualized through its union with Holy Wisdom; he is the Seeker, she the Sought. In the spiritually immature soul, "potency" can only be transformed into "act" by meeting the challenges and completing the tasks She imposes upon it. Dante's Beatrice is thus the highest and most complete incarnation of the Lady of Courtly Love, a tradition which found its undeniable culmination in the *Divine Comedy*. In the "esoteric Aristotelianism" of the Fedeli d'Amore, whose outer expression was romance and whose inner one, alchemy, the split in the psyche of Christendom between the orthodox

The Ordeal of Mercy

Scholastic Philosophy that culminated in Thomas Aquinas and the counter-ethos of Romance, filled as it was with heterodox tendencies—a split that was in some ways expressed in the Albigensian Crusade—was triumphantly overcome. It was only the few, however—those perceptive enough to discern the form of Holy Wisdom through the veils of psychic concupiscence and social corruption, and courageous enough to brave the rigors of the path to Her chamber—who could avail themselves of that triumph. What remained incomplete and wounded in the body of society, nonetheless came to final completion in the *athenor*, the alchemical vessel of the Heart. In addition, there is some evidence that Aquinas himself could have been among that triumphant few. It was the overpowering vision he experienced shortly before his death at a Cistercian monastery that apparently inspired him to dictate his last work, a commentary on the Song of Songs; this is what led Jungian analyst Marie-Louise Von Franz to speculate that his final ecstasy, in relation to which all his written works seemed to him "like straw," might have been a vision of Holy Wisdom herself.

Epilogue:
The Meeting with God[1]

I, who do not know my own soul's name
have already seen her,
disguised as the shadow of a river,
saying to me:

"Cry as much as you can
for you cannot live another day
without meeting God.
Your heart cannot be broken more."

When I came back into the world
all those of the world made me forget you,
saying that I'd loved you more
than anyone could love God;
God would punish me, they all said,
by making me love even more.
How can I pretend not to know you
when I have loved you since
before the day I was born?
You are among a new people.
And my soul has come here
to help me find you.

"Give up the last thing you could own,"
   she says,
"Take the last bite of food out of
   your mouth.
Give up this life."

---

1. Jennifer D. Upton, *Black Sun Poems: 1965–1985* (Finishing Line Press, 2013).

www.ingramcontent.com/pod-product-compliance
Lightning Source LLC
Chambersburg PA
CBHW030102170426
43198CB00009B/462